James DeKoven

James DeKoven

Biography of a Famous Yet Forgotten Man

John E. Magerus

Foreword by Sheryl A. Kujawa-Holbrook

WIPF & STOCK · Eugene, Oregon

JAMES DEKOVEN
Biography of a Famous Yet Forgotten Man

Wipf & Stock
An Imprint of Wipf and Stock Publishers
199 W. 8th Ave., Suite 3
Eugene, OR 97401

www.wipfandstock.com

PAPERBACK ISBN: 979-8-3852-2908-6
HARDCOVER ISBN: 979-8-3852-2909-3
EBOOK ISBN: 979-8-3852-2910-9

VERSION NUMBER 02/20/25

"First Page of the Journal of James DeKoven," Used with permission from Nashotah House Theological Seminary.

"Panoramic of the East Building DeKoven Center, Racine, WI," Photography by Denise Zingg.

Quotation from Bishop Jeffrey Lee used with his permission.

"St. James DeKoven Stained Glass Window at Nashotah Theological Seminary," Used with permission from Nashotah House Theological Seminary.

In respectful memory of the
Rev. Travis T. DuPriest
and the Rev. James R. Braun.

Contents

Foreword

Even though I was raised in Wisconsin, my theological education taught me comparatively little about the beauty and richness of the history of the Episcopal Church in the state, including blessed ancestors like James DeKoven, who shaped the tradition and institutions there. Instead, the Spirit had her reasons for sending me east for seminary and graduate school, where narratives of the blossoming of the catholic revival on the frontier occupied a few paragraphs, or at best several pages, of standard Episcopal histories, marginal to dominant accounts of the institutional church. Three years ago, I returned to Wisconsin to begin research on a group biography of the Sisterhood of the Holy Nativity when I was fortunate enough to visit the DeKoven Center in Racine for the first time. Once there, I was introduced to another retired dean and biographer, Dr. John Magerus, who was already hard at work on this biography of James DeKoven. His insights and commitment to sharing James DeKoven's life and ministry informed my research. His work inspired me to learn more about the history of the Episcopal Church in Wisconsin and the indefatigable and committed Anglo-Catholics who deeply inform the ministry there today.

This book is a significant milestone, marking the first comprehensive biography of James DeKoven in 125 years. It is a rare and privileged opportunity for all of us to delve into the life and legacy of a figure who played a pivotal role in shaping the Episcopal Church in Wisconsin and beyond.

Writing a historical biography is a consuming task, one that requires dedication and commitment. The hunt for primary source material and the long hours in archives are preliminary to an even longer stage, which is the deep discernment of the mind, heart, and spirit of the subject studied.

Across time and space, we biographers study our subjects empathetically to better understand their inner lives and, through this encounter, evoke how they interpreted their social context. There is a spiritual element in compelling biographies. Yes, a person's life is told within a narrative arc, and assertions must be supported through rigorous research. At the same time, biographers strive to recognize our subject's interior and emotional lives, including their struggles and vulnerabilities.

When James DeKoven was alive, biographies of church leaders emphasized their piety, good works, and contributions to important institutions, often at the expense of revealing their complexities as living human beings. History teaches us that even the holiest of saints were complicated people, imperfect as we are, and yet inspirational because of their utter devotion to the gospel. Complex people are also more interesting, believable, and accessible to those who struggle to live lives of purpose today.

This biography is a testament to the dedication and commitment of John Magerus to provide readers with a fuller portrait of James DeKoven as a man. It is successful because the author reconciles the widely known church leader with his inner life, struggles, failures, and legacy. This biography is the first to study the records of the DeKoven family in depth. Notably, the author is among the first to significantly include insights and reflections from DeKoven's journal (1862–79). DeKoven was at the center of the controversies surrounding the nineteenth-century catholic revival in the Episcopal Church. His influence extended far beyond Wisconsin. Known for his intellectual gifts and commitment to catholic liturgy, DeKoven was considered the "American Keble" and was an acclaimed orator in the House of Deputies of the General Convention of the Episcopal Church. However, despite his visibility, DeKoven never achieved ecclesiastical success in public life on the level of some of his contemporaries. He was offered some of the most prestigious pulpits in Boston, New York, and Philadelphia but chose to remain in Wisconsin. Though twice nominated and once elected, he was never consecrated as a bishop. His widely known theological and liturgical positions caused some to criticize and mistrust him. Though DeKoven was thoroughly dedicated to his students and his role as an educator, the schools he founded did not survive very long.

In this book, John Magerus interprets James DeKoven's dedicated but often stressful public and private lives with keen insight and notable sensitivity. Beyond the external markers of James Dekoven's institutional successes and failures, the book provides a deeper picture of his private life as a devoted pastor, teacher, family member, and friend. He was a man of generosity and humor who worked tirelessly for the children and families in his care. This long overdue and highly readable book invites academic and general readers to explore the life and legacy of one of the central figures of the nineteenth-century Episcopal Church.

(The Rev.) Sheryl A. Kujawa-Holbrook, EdD, PhD
Editor-in-Chief, *Anglican and Episcopal History*
Historiographer of the Episcopal Church
The Feast of St. Mary the Virgin, August 15, 2024

Preface

My decision to write a biography of James DeKoven was one that evolved slowly as I worked on organizing the archival collections at the DeKoven Center. When I began this task in 2014, my knowledge of James DeKoven and the institution named for him was minimal. What I did know had come from conversations with the then executive director of the center, Max Dershem, and his predecessor, the Rev. Travis DuPriest. As I worked with the material that would form the basis of the archives, I was amazed at the importance of the documents that had been saved. At the same time, I was saddened to discover what had disappeared over the years. I was also surprised at what I did not find: a solid biographical study of this important man.

Due to a well-developed historical curiosity, I wanted to learn more about the DeKoven Center. Why and when was this historical campus on the shores of Lake Michigan named after him? Sorting through the boxes and files, I found the results of various efforts at writing the history of Racine College and its successor institutions. As I pursued additional knowledge, I learned a great deal about what had and had not been written about James DeKoven. I also learned about the Community of Saint Mary and the efforts these dedicated sisters put into preserving the site that had been Racine College. For more than fifty years they worked at honoring the memory of the priest who brought them to Wisconsin. As part of this work, their community had tried unsuccessfully to honor him with a biography. I discovered that other efforts were also made, and I have chronicled the details of these attempts in the introduction which follows. It wasn't until 1899 that the only book-length biography was published by William Cox Pope.[1]

With the support provided by grants, I have been able to conduct research at several locations. The DeKoven Foundation of Racine, Wisconsin, funded a visit to the Archives of the Episcopal Church in Austin, Texas. A research visit to Connecticut, where DeKoven was born, was made possible by a grant from the Historical Society of the Episcopal Church. In Connecticut, I learned a great deal about the DeKoven family at the Middlesex County Historical Society, the Archives of the Episcopal Diocese of Connecticut, the Connecticut State Archives, and the Connecticut Historical Society. Closer to home, the Western Province of the Community of Saint Mary provided funding for visits to the Archives of the Episcopal Diocese of Chicago and the Frances Donaldson Library of the Nashotah House Theological Seminary.

In working on the DeKoven biography, I've studied in detail what has been written about him, and I've attempted to add what is missing from the historical record. No author has studied the importance of his family, both to James as well as in the society of the day. Little has been written about his education, other than the fact that he studied at Columbia College and the General Theological Seminary in New York City. Who were the teachers and leaders of these institutions who influenced him? What was his life like as a college administrator and Episcopal priest in mid-nineteenth century Wisconsin? What role did he play in his newfound society?

One important source that I have used repeatedly is the personal journal[2] that DeKoven kept rather irregularly from 1862 through 1879. Although other writers have mentioned it, no one has studied it in detail. He entitled this memoir *The Story of a College*, but it is much more than that. It provides insight into his thinking about education, religion, and leadership. Because of this journal and other research discoveries, I am comfortable claiming a certain completeness for this work that I've entitled *James DeKoven: Biography of a Famous Yet Forgotten Man.*

1. Pope, *Life of the Reverend James De Koven.*

2. The manuscript of this diary is currently housed in the Frances Donaldson Library of the Nashotah House Theological Seminary. Two typescript copies were made in the early 1930s. I used both the original manuscript and a typescript for my research.

Acknowledgements

As a result of working with the DeKoven Center Archives, I had the good fortune to meet and develop friendships with two wonderful Episcopalian priests. Travis DuPriest had served as executive director of the DeKoven Foundation and encouraged my earliest efforts at researching the life of James DeKoven. James Braun, a native son of Racine, joined me in the day-to-day task of organizing the archives soon after his retirement from St. Matthew's Church in Kenosha. Both men were inspiring examples of the calling to the priesthood and embodied the essence of Christian goodness. They both had a great sense of humor that James DeKoven would have appreciated. I am honored to dedicate this life story of another priest to these two departed friends.

An unexpected benefit of writing a biography and dealing with the past has been meeting and benefiting from the help of many people in the present. In addition to my work in Wisconsin and Illinois, I have been able to travel to new places and profit from the efforts of other researchers and historians.

I extend special thanks to the staff and volunteers of the DeKoven Center of Racine, who have helped and encouraged me for several years, especially Susan Shore, Lindsay Smith, Lynn Kancian, Nicole Miller, and Matt Hilbert. The current executive director, Lynn Biese-Carroll, has provided important moral and financial support that has made my work possible and enjoyable.

Rory Graves joined the staff in September 2023 and has proven to be an invaluable player in the DeKoven biography project since then. Rory's varied skills and talents seem to be endless, and without them this work could never have been completed.

There are many people whose dedication to the memory of James DeKoven has made the current biographical project possible. First and foremost is the Community of Saint Mary whose efforts to preserve the campus and reimagine the mission of the DeKoven Center created the positive atmosphere that still exists. I extend a special note of appreciation to Mr. James Huismann, whose careful attention to the heritage of the sisters has resulted in continuing benefits of their work.

Earlier researchers led the way for my efforts. These individuals include the Rev. Sydney Hugh Croft, who as chaplain at DeKoven in the 1930s collected material about James DeKoven, and the Rev. Richard Crist, who as a student at the General Theological Seminary in 1959, undertook extensive historical research in New York City archives.

My first efforts as a community volunteer were at the Racine County Heritage Museum, where Chris Paulson encouraged my interests in history and provided guidance toward several very rewarding projects. There I also benefitted from the experience and expertise of Mary Kay Nelson, archivist.

I received several grants that provided general funds and travel support. These included financial awards from the Western Province of the Community of Saint Mary; the General Society of Colonial Wars and the Society of Colonial Wars of the State of Wisconsin; the DeKoven Foundation for Church Work, Inc. (Max Dershem, executive director); and the Historical Society of the Episcopal Church, Grants and Projects Committee (HSEC).

It was the HSEC grant that enabled me to go to Middletown and Hartford, Connecticut. In Middletown, I was most warmly welcomed and aided by Diane D. Reid, archivist and historian of the Church of the Holy Trinity. At the Middlesex County Historical Society, Interim Director Maria Weinberger and its current executive director, Jesse Nasta, enabled my research of the DeKoven family. I also visited the Archives of the Episcopal Church in Connecticut (Gregory Farr, archivist); Godfrey Memorial Library and Russell Library; Olin Library Archives at Wesleyan University; and the Connecticut Historical Society. In all these efforts I was helped by Bryna O'Sullivan, a professional historian in Middletown.

A week-long research trip to the Archives of the Episcopal Church in Austin, Texas, enabled me to consult the largest collections of James DeKoven-related letters. I made several visits to the Richard R. Seidel Archives in Chicago, where I was welcomed and guided in my research work by the wise Newland Smith, archivist and historiographer of the

Episcopal Diocese of Chicago. Members of the staff of the Frances Donaldson Library at Nashotah House Seminary, including Director David Sherwood, were incredibly helpful with the records relating to DeKoven's early years in Wisconsin and the rich collection of historical church publications. I am especially grateful to Diana Grosso, Amy Cunningham, and Bramwell Richards.

Over the course of writing this book I have been blessed with the good counsel and professional advice of many individuals, including the following: Laura Gellott, Randy Miller, Chris Paulson, Susanne Sklar, Cindy Percak, and Hollace Graves. Their willingness to read many drafts and provide feedback is deeply appreciated.

Unending thanks to the special person in my life, Everett McKinney. Living with someone researching and writing a biography requires a special kind of patience and understanding. Everett has those qualities. He encouraged me when I was down and was able to explain to others why the only topic I seemed to discuss was James DeKoven. I know that at times it seemed like there were three of us living in the house. He made this book possible.

Introduction

This biography of James DeKoven is essentially my response to what has been written and what has not been written about his life. My reaction to what has been written centers on the fact that most of the material published about him over the years relates to his religious and theological ideas. There have been few writers who have tried to go beyond the very public person that he had become over his brief lifetime. What has not been written is anything in depth about James DeKoven the man. No one has ever studied in any detail the importance of his family, the influence of his educational experiences, the nature of his personality, or the depth of his spiritual life. His reaction to the challenges he faced, and the impact of several very public controversies on his health have never been addressed fully.

Another important factor that has guided me is the almost total lack of source references or factual data in most earlier writing about James DeKoven. There are, in general, few dates given or actual references recorded. My attempt to situate the events of his life within a context has resulted in a detailed timeline (See Appendix).

Calls for a biographical study of James DeKoven began almost immediately after his death in 1879. In his preface to the collected sermons of DeKoven, published in 1880, Morgan Dix, friend and colleague, recognized the importance such a biography would have for the American church.[1] Another DeKoven colleague, John Henry Hopkins, began collecting personal letters and documents from family and friends soon after DeKoven's death, with the ultimate goal of writing his life story. Hopkins

1. Dix, "Preface," In *Sermons Preached on Various Occasions by James DeKoven*. iv.

never brought such a biography to completion, although he did write a series of articles based on his personal recollections.[2]

In 1892, Frederic Cook Morehouse published a very well-researched work entitled *Some American Churchmen.*[3] The final and longest chapter is devoted to "James DeKoven, Warden of Racine College." This chapter is an excellent summary of his public life from 1868 through 1879. Great detail is given to the theological and religious debates surrounding DeKoven and his speeches and writings. Although thorough, it is not a complete biography of the Warden.

The search for a qualified author to undertake the biographical task continued for many years. In 1896, the Board of Trustees of Racine College, acknowledging the lack of a suitable biography, voted to authorize the Rev. Clinton Locke of Chicago to author such a work. The minutes of the Trustees' meeting of June 9, 1896, provide this entry:

> The Bishop of Nebraska moved that Dr. Clinton Locke, the DeKoven family concurring, write for publication, the life of the Rev. Dr. DeKoven and that the profits from its sale go to the DeKoven Endowment Association to aid them in their work for the College.[4]

Clinton Locke never did write this biography, and it was only in 1986 with the posthumous publication of Locke's personal reminiscences that an explanation was given:

> The Church very much needs a good life of Dr. DeKoven, for the existing one is a small work, not even touching the fringe of his garment. The Trustees of Racine College wished me to undertake the task, and I would gladly have done it, but John DeKoven, the Doctor's brother, disliked me and objected to it. John DeKoven disliked most things and most people.[5]

The first and only book-length biography of James DeKoven was written and published in 1899 by the Rev. William Cox Pope, an early graduate of Racine College. When Pope began work on the biography

2. Seven personal recollections were published in the *Nashotah Scholiast*. Hopkins, "A Few Recollections," *Nashotah Scholiast,* Vol. II, No. 6 through Vol. III, No. 1.

3. Morehouse, *Some American Churchmen,* Milwaukee, The Young Churchman Co., 1892.

4. *Minutes of the Board of Trustees of Racine College, March 10, 1852–June 9, 1896,* Vol. I, 475. DeKoven Center Archives.

5. Locke, *Personal Reminiscences of the Diocese of Illinois, 1856–1892.*

of DeKoven, he wrote to friends, former students, and surviving family members asking for their reminiscences and suggestions for this life story. Their replies and Pope's other papers are housed in the Episcopal National Archives.

The Pope biography is a relatively modest publication containing eight chapters. The interesting insights given into DeKoven's personality are very limited and leave the reader essentially unsatisfied about the nature of the man. Facts about his life are minimal and long quotations from other sources dominate the text. A lingering question remains: did Pope wait twenty years to write this life story until after the death of DeKoven's brother John on April 30, 1898?

A renewed interest in publishing a more complete biography of Father DeKoven came with the creation of the DeKoven Foundation by the Community of Saint Mary. The retreats the Sisters organized starting in 1938 brought many people to the Racine campus who were curious to learn more about the namesake of this institution. The Sisters were diligent in seeking possible authors and locating source documents for what they called an "up-to-date" and "full scale" biography. Their efforts, however, did not result in a published work. Due to a decrease in numbers, the Community was forced to withdraw from the administration of the DeKoven Center in 1989.

The biography I have written presents DeKoven's life story using a combination of techniques: some of the chapters are chronological while others deal with information thematically. The first chapter starts the life story with an event that was literally the beginning of the end. A fall on an icy sidewalk in Milwaukee caused DeKoven to be confined to his rooms at Racine College. This accident happened as he celebrated twenty years of leadership of the school and twenty-five years of work in Wisconsin. I used this period of relative calm to begin the biography as a reflection on his past and the significant events in his life.

Chapter 2 provides information about DeKoven's ancestors and his parents, Henry Louis and Margaret Sebor DeKoven. The second part of chapter 2 is devoted to James DeKoven's eight surviving siblings and their equally fascinating lives. The increased availability of family history records has been a great help in providing facts for these two chapters. James DeKoven's family represented the change from a New England centered economic culture to the financial and manufacturing importance of the Midwest.

Chapters 3 and 4 further develop the idea of the two important loci of DeKoven's life. Although his early studies occurred in Connecticut, his formal education took place primarily in New York City, where he studied at Columbia College and the General Theological Seminary. In 1854, upon completion of his seminary work he moved to Wisconsin in response to the missionary zeal that was becoming more important in the Episcopal Church. His first assignment was a dual one: instructor in Church History at Nashotah House Seminary and Rector of the Church of St. John Chrysostom in Delafield, Wisconsin.

In 1859, James DeKoven was named the President and Rector of Racine College. This was a position he held for the next twenty years. His work at Racine is studied in detail in chapter 5. The emphasis was on a family-like atmosphere where students were leaders and where they were encouraged to "work hard, play hard, and pray hard." Under DeKoven's leadership, the campus expanded and the school attracted students from throughout the United States.

The next three chapters (6, 7, and 8) are thematic in their content. Chapter 6 explores the different ways in which it is possible to characterize and envision James DeKoven. Several photographs of DeKoven exist that were taken at different points in his life. These photos are priceless in confirming an image of who he was. There are also different written descriptions of him and records of his actions and interactions with people and events. All of these images help in understanding the man, James DeKoven.

Chapter 7 deals with James DeKoven as storyteller, preacher and orator. He had a powerful ability with words and he used this ability to educate, defend, inspire and amuse. The next chapter, 8, is both thematic and chronological. It covers the last ten years of his life and what was a most difficult and public period. It deals with several religious controversies and his increased role in the leadership of the Episcopal Church.

In the winter of 1879, although DeKoven seemed to be recovering from his broken ankle, he died quite suddenly on March 19, 1879 at the age of forty-eight. The final two chapters of this biography deal with his death and burial as well as his legacy. At the time of his death, without a doubt he was the best-known Episcopalian in the United States. His fame at his death did not come primarily from what he had done, but rather from what he was not able to accomplish: get elected a bishop of his church. The several elections where he was a candidate, and eventually defeated made national news. The debates about his ideas on church ritual and religious beliefs were publicized, praised and criticized. On his death, obituaries and articles appeared in major newspapers throughout the country. Memorial services in his honor were held in large and small cities. Although the majority of what were his controversial ideas have become accepted in his own church, the role he played in formulating and defending them is for a large part forgotten. He became famous during his brief lifetime, yet is essentially unknown today.

My primary goal in writing this detailed biography is to portray as fully as possible the complicated, yet at the same time, simple human being who was James DeKoven. He was dedicated to his ideas and beliefs and tolerant of those of others. He loved his family, his friends, his students, and his enemies. He was generous with his time and his fortune. He was saintly but not aloof; he loved to laugh. He cared deeply for those around him, recognized his own failings, loved the beauty of this world, and dedicated his life to being worthy of the next one.

1

An Accident in Milwaukee

On Friday morning, January 31, 1879, James DeKoven got up very early in order to catch the first "train of cars" from Milwaukee to Racine.[1] He moved as carefully as he could, so as not to disturb the others sleeping in the Clergy House on the corner of Division and Cass Streets.[2] Father DeKoven had come to the city to attend a meeting at the cathedral the day before and spent the night as a guest of the bishop.[3] Clergy House was a large, two-story wooden home in the Italianate style that served as residence and office of the bishop, as well as lodging for priests visiting or working with the Episcopal Diocese of Wisconsin.

Since no sounds came from the kitchen below, it was apparently well before 6 a.m. After splashing some cold water on his face from the ewer and bowl, he dressed in the dark while reciting his morning prayers. He had packed his valise the night before, so he didn't need to light a lamp. His familiarity with the house enabled him to make his exit quietly. DeKoven's involvement in the work of the diocese of Wisconsin

1. In January 1879, the first daily train on the Milwaukee, Green Bay and Lake Superior Line originated in Milwaukee and left the Union Depot at 7:15 a.m. The train was scheduled to arrive in Racine Junction fifty-five minutes later at 8:10 a.m. (Timetable, 13). The language of the day referred to "taking the train of cars" or "the cars."

2. Clergy House was part of the complex of buildings that was developed on the property of All Saints Cathedral in Milwaukee. In 1879, the street in front of the house was Division Street, and the name changed to Juneau in 1885.

3. Edward Randolph Welles (1830–88) was the third bishop of Milwaukee. He was chosen as a compromise candidate in 1874 after the sudden death of Bishop Armitage.

was significant, but nothing was as important to him as his life-work at Racine College. For this reason, he was anxious to get back to Racine as quickly as possible.

Going out of Clergy House, he noticed immediately that the weather had turned colder overnight. The "January thaw" of the last few days, which had played havoc with the ice rink created by the older boys at the Racine school, had given way to the return of the typically bitter cold weather of a winter in Wisconsin.[4] There were no lights in the large homes of businessmen which lined Cass Street on either side.

Taking the early train after an evening meeting the night before was not an unusual decision for DeKoven. The story is told that at the Diocesan Council, held two months earlier in November 1878, DeKoven had also stayed at Clergy House. The stress of the discussions and debate relating to the cathedral question caused him to decide to leave before the close of the session. In the early morning of his departure the next day, he knocked on Bishop Welles' door and was told to enter. DeKoven told the bishop, who was still in bed, that he was going back to Racine on the first train. According to Bishop Welles, DeKoven said, "The strain and worry is more than I am able to bear. I must go home. I do not believe that I shall come to the council again."[5]

However, he had returned for another meeting, and this morning in January 1879, he did not wake anyone else but left the house silently. His goal was the Union Depot on Reed Street, which was a good twenty to twenty-five minute walk down Yankee Hill on Cass Street. The melting snow from the previous days' thaw had refrozen overnight and covered the slightly sloping sidewalks with a sheer coating of ice. Not long into his journey, going down the incline of Cass Street, DeKoven slipped, fell, and broke his right ankle. At first, he was stunned by the sudden impact of his fall on the icy pavement. It took him a few moments to regain his orientation and calm his nervous reaction to the accident. Because of the intense pain that he felt in his right leg, he realized that his injury was serious. He tried to get up, but the slippery incline of the spot where he fell made it impossible for him to get to his feet. He called out, but there was no one

4. Letter to Bishop Hobart of Fond du Lac, written as a thank you for his recent visit. Dated January 29, 1879. "We are in the midst of the thaw and suffering on the whole from the heat and the destruction of the new rink for the present at least." James DeKoven Collection, DeKoven Center Archives.

5. This encounter with Bishop Welles is first recounted by William Cox Pope in his biography of James DeKoven published in 1899. Pope, *Life of the Reverend James DeKoven*, 88.

nearby to hear him. He remained in this prone position for a full half hour, the throbbing in his ankle intensifying with each passing minute.

There was little traffic, neither carriages nor walkers so early in the morning. Eventually a housemaid in the neighborhood noticed him lying on the sidewalk as she unlocked the household doors. She attempted to help him stand up, but it was obvious the injury to his right ankle was serious and he couldn't put weight on it. She returned to her house, called for assistance, and directed the arriving rescuers in their efforts to carry him back to Clergy House. Once there, he was made as comfortable as possible, and a doctor, E. B. Wolcott, was summoned.[6] James DeKoven insisted that the injury was slight and he needed to continue his return to Racine. The doctor put a temporary dressing on the injured ankle and provided him with some pain medicine to drink. DeKoven began orchestrating his return to Racine. He dictated a telegram that was sent to his personal physician, John G. Meachem, Sr., of Racine, informing the doctor of the accident and of his arrival at Racine Junction Depot on the 1 p.m. train. A coach was ordered, and DeKoven was taken to the Union Depot.

He was helped onto the train by the coachman and settled onto the rather uncomfortable seat for the fifty-five minute trip from Milwaukee. The progress of the train must have seemed especially slow, as well as painful for DeKoven. Railroads were still a relatively new form of travel, but their newness did not mean smoothness; every movement of the rail car was jolted to his injured ankle. Dr. Meachem did meet the train at the Junction Depot, and his presence brought a sense of relief to James DeKoven.

Over the years, DeKoven and John Meachem had developed a mutual respect based on their work together. DeKoven was impressed by Meachem's solid faith, allegiance to the Episcopal Church, and his dedication to incorporating charity into the life of the community. Meachem respected DeKoven as a man of religion but also an individual with a business sense not common in ordained ministers.[7] Together they had

6. Information provided by John G. Meachem's manuscript autobiography is the source of much information about DeKoven's fall and recuperation (*Autobiography of Dr. John Goldesborough Meachem*). Dr. Meachem gives a fairly detailed account of DeKoven's accident. He indicated that DeKoven had broken his leg at the "ankle joint." This description led to two different interpretations of DeKoven's injury: 1) a broken ankle and 2) a broken leg. Meachem also indicates the name of the doctor who was called to attend to DeKoven in Milwaukee: Dr. W. B. Walcott. Racine Heritage Museum Collection.

7. "Dr. DeKoven's whole heart and soul was given to the work of the prosperity of

worked on the founding of St. Luke's Hospital in Racine. Meachem served on the board of trustees of Racine College beginning in 1872. DeKoven regularly relied on him for advice and help with the governance of the college. He also had great faith in him as a man of medical science and confided in him about his own health concerns.

Dr. Meachem took the warden[8] of Racine College in his own personal carriage to the college campus. This large Victorian Gothic building had several functions in the campus community. It was the administration building, the college students' residence hall, and the home of DeKoven and his two sisters. Dr. Meachem had alerted the college about what had happened and when he would be returning with DeKoven. One can imagine the scene of organized chaos that reigned on the entry stairs to the college building. The sisters, Margaret and Elizabeth, awaited this arrival while attempting to maintain a calm demeanor, though worried about their younger brother's accident.[9] There had been an attempt to disperse the curious students and workers away from the front of the building but to no avail. Racine College was a small community, and James DeKoven was its mayor, police chief, and leading citizen all rolled into one. What happened to him mattered to everyone.

Taylor Hall had become a refuge for James DeKoven. He had supervised its construction in 1867 and its rebuilding after a devastating fire on February 5, 1875. These had been years of growth in the college and years of controversy for DeKoven as his role in the national Episcopal Church took on added importance. The role did not distract him from his primary concern as rector of Racine College. Under his guidance, Taylor Hall was fashioned into a more modern and comfortable college building with a central steam heating system and indoor plumbing. No longer were the rooms heated by individual wood stoves or fireplaces. Fire hazards had always been a great concern for DeKoven, and he admitted to frequently

---

Racine College. Nothing connected with it escaped his notice. He was wealthy himself, and knew how to manage his own business as well as that of the College. It was my good fortune to be his own physician, as well as that of the institution, and consequently I was placed in more or less intimate relation with him, and I enjoyed the association greatly. At the end of any period that you spent with him, you felt elevated by that communion." Meachem, *Autobiography of Dr. John Goldesborough Meachem*, 99–100.

8. The title of "warden" had been given to DeKoven in 1867. Prior to this date he was called rector and president of Racine College.

9. Elizabeth Dyer and Margaret Casey were two of the ten children born to Henry Louis and Margaret Sebor DeKoven.

patrolling the campus at night to make sure the many stoves in Kemper and Park Halls were properly vented and regulated.[10]

His residence within Taylor Hall was that of a college president, not that of a scholarly monk. He enjoyed having people around him, and his well-furnished rooms in the college building made this possible. In September 1875, his sister Margaret Casey, widow of Dr. William Casey, left her home in Middletown, Connecticut, and joined her brother in Racine. In his journal DeKoven wrote about this change in his lifestyle: "My sister is coming out to keep my rooms for me instead of a matron as heretofore. This is a comfort, I trust."[11] Then their eldest sister, Elizabeth Dyer, joined Margaret in 1876. The two sisters formed the core of the support group that looked after DeKoven following his accident. A young man, Charles O. Olson, who served as a manservant, coachman, and caretaker for DeKoven's apartment, helped as well. Added to these three primary caregivers was the matron who supervised the infirmary, Miss Van Deusen. The forty-four students enrolled in coursework in the college who lived in the north section of Taylor Hall did their best to maintain a calmer household for his recuperation. Additionally, several servants and laborers lived in the building.

The building was reconstructed so that the warden and sub-warden lived in the south one-third of Taylor Hall. There was a separate stairwell in this section. DeKoven's rooms were on the first and second floor; the rooms of the sub-warden, at this time occupied by the head of Taylor Hall, F. S. Martin, were on the third floor. The principal room of the warden's suite was a large library that occupied the entire end of the first floor. It had a fireplace and was impressive in its decoration and housed

10. DeKoven wrote on several occasions about his concern for fires: "I am so anxious about fire that I cannot sleep well at night . . ." DeKoven, *Journal*, P02, 115. *The Story of a College* was a journal kept irregularly by James DeKoven. He started writing entries in this journal on July 31, 1862, during a visit to his mother's home in Middletown, Connecticut. His goal was to record the history of Racine College. DeKoven kept this diary in a bound ledger called the *Index Rerum*. It did not have page numbers but rather had pages identified by letters of the alphabet. In my references to the journal, I've given the actual page indication from the ledger and the page number from the typed script.

11. DeKoven makes two additional remarks about the presence of his sisters and the impact on his life, "My sisters have been here this winter, and for the first time I have had something which seemed like a home," DeKoven, *Journal*, R01, 127. Their presence also impacted his relationships with the boys, "My home is very comfortable with my kind sisters and I am able to be very hospitable to the boys and kind to them." DeKoven, *Journal*, Sa, 128.

his personal collection of books.[12] There were eight large bookcases in this study/library and an assortment of chairs, tables, and desks. It was in this library that DeKoven held the Sunday gatherings that were called the Warden's Receptions. There were many windows, and from here one could see the gardens and other buildings of the campus.

On their arrival at Taylor Hall, Dr. Meachem redressed DeKoven's ankle and gave specific, stern instructions for his recuperation. He was to limit his activities, and under no condition was he to leave his rooms until permission was given. Dr. Meachem confided the supervision of this recovery to DeKoven's two sisters. They arranged a temporary bedroom in the first-floor parlor, so that DeKoven would not have to negotiate the narrow stairwell to his second-floor sleeping quarters. Dr. Meachem's diagnosis of the injury led to some confusion in newspapers and later stories. According to Meachem, as he reported in his unpublished autobiography, DeKoven slipped and fell, "breaking his leg at the ankle joint."[13] This diagnosis resulted in different reports, some indicating that DeKoven had broken his leg, others that he had broken his ankle. Both were correct in a sense, and DeKoven used both explanations in different letters.

Life in the warden's home resumed its normal pace as quickly as possible. James DeKoven insisted that he continue to meet with students and faculty as often as they wished. He was a hands-on administrator and didn't want this to change. His energy, however, did not allow for a complete return to normal, and his sisters, backed by Dr. Meachem, did succeed somewhat in limiting his activities.

The physical arrangement of Taylor Hall allowed him to keep track of the college-aged students, and he made certain that his accessibility to them was not completely cut off. They were his lifeblood and reason for being. They were used to consulting freely with him, and it was important to him that this continue. It was common for him to meet with each student at least once during each academic year. He continued these sessions as best he could during this period of recuperation. It must be said that his style of advising was very directive and at the same time supportive. He knew each student by name and had a strong idea of what he thought

12. An estimated two-thirds of his personal library was saved during the fire of February 4/5, 1875. The students formed a book brigade to move the thousands of volumes from Taylor Hall to the Chapel of St. John. They did this despite the below-zero temperatures. A leather-bound ledger, titled "Library of the Rev. James DeKoven, D.D., Warden of Racine College," is located in the DeKoven Center Archives. This listing is by title of the book or collection.

13. Meachem, *Autobiography of Dr. John Goldesborough Meachem*, 101–2.

best for each of them.[14] He was especially insistent on religious obligations for students and strongly encouraged confirmation preparation for those who had been baptized in the Episcopal Church. If he thought an individual had an interest in the priesthood, he doggedly pursued this topic. Two students who spoke of their discussions with DeKoven about the priesthood were William Cox Pope and Alexis du Pont Parker. DeKoven explored his belief in Pope's suitability for ordination in letters that still exist. Parker wrote about getting "a general overhauling of my inner self" in a meeting with the warden.[15] He also indicated that the day following their discussion DeKoven explained that it was out of love and concern that he pursued his encouragement for theological studies.[16]

DeKoven was in the unusual position of being both the spiritual and academic leader of the institution. Reportedly, students were often surprised at the amount of information he knew about each of them. He was able to maintain his sense of humor when facing a well-placed challenge to his dual role.

From his recuperation quarters he could hear the movement of students to and from their classes and tutorials: he knew when they awoke in the morning, exited the building, went to the gymnasium and to Kemper Hall to eat their meals, and when they quieted down for the evening. Sounds from the campus outside his windows also kept him tuned in to the activities of the many students. In February the winter weather had returned, and the ice on the skating rink had reformed so that this sport was once again available. He could hear the younger students, who lived in Park and Kemper Halls, going from their grammar school classes in the school room on their way to the new gymnasium and laboratory; they always made twice as much noise as their numbers warranted when

14. Student (Anonymous), "Racine and Dr. DeKoven III." *The Church Scholiast*, Vol IV, No. 2, 19–20.

15. One letter, "Reasons for Entering the Ministry," was addressed to "Willie Pope" and dated Delafield, October 8. 1857. It was first published in the *Nashotah Scholiast*, Vol. II, No. 3, January 1885, 37–38.

16. A relatively small number of letters written by James DeKoven have survived. The largest two collections are housed in the National Episcopal Archives in Austin, Texas. They are the Street Collection (MS: COL, 70:82. Street) and the Eckels-Cox-Pope Archives (RG137 1–9). The DeKoven Center Archives possesses thirty-six letters written by James DeKoven to John Henry Hobart Brown from 1852–79. Hobart Brown Letters, James DeKoven Collection, DeKoven Center Archives.

they were heading to an activity that they enjoyed. This made him happy because it reflected his philosophy of work hard, pray hard, play hard.[17]

DeKoven's accident was a significant happening in the life of the city of Racine. Coverage of this event by the local press is evidence of the important role that Racine College played in its educational and economic development. James DeKoven was also a personage of local celebrity because of his position in the school, his association with various projects in the city, and the press coverage he had received during the Episcopal elections in Wisconsin and Illinois. He was also well-known in the active religious community because of his work with the mission churches, as well as his leadership in founding St. Luke's Hospital. The following article, under the headline "Accident to Dr. DeKoven," appeared in the *Racine Journal* for Wednesday, February 5, 1879, six days after his accident:

> Last Friday as Rev. Dr. DeKoven, warden of Racine College, was passing down Cass Street in Milwaukee on his way to the depot to take the cars for Racine, he slipped on the sidewalk and fell, breaking one of his ankles. He was unable to arise and lay on the sidewalk for some time. Finally, he was relieved and placed on board of the train. He arrived home and is now at Taylor Hall, where his injuries are being cared for.[18]

As much as possible, DeKoven continued with his daily duties including a significant correspondence not only about college-related activities but also about events in the Episcopal Church and the political concerns of the day. He took to writing his letters in pencil because of the difficulty of juggling an inkwell perched on the improvised desk on his wheelchair. A letter written to his close friend, Bishop Hobart Brown of Fond du Lac, illustrates his continued involvement in events of the day:

> My dear Bishop, I sent a copy of a Bill introduced into the legislature by Fulton & the St. Paul People—Does it mean mischief? Mr. Hall, Hon. E. C. Hall, one of my old boys sent it to me. I'll send it to Milwaukee & I hope you will prevent its passage if necessary. It is a shame that any private person can get legislation for a whole state without consultation. With best regard to your family, affectionally, yours, JdeKoven.[19]

17. This motto was well-known by the students in the college. DeKoven believed that these three activities were essential. He encouraged sports, allowed a billiards table in Taylor Hall, did not forbid card playing, etc.

18. "Accident to Dr. DeKoven."

19. Hobart Brown Letter. Feb. 19, 1879. James DeKoven Collection, DeKoven Center Archives.

A more personal letter, also written in pencil, was sent to his friend, Canon J. H. Knowles of Chicago, rector of the cathedral in that city. DeKoven was obviously replying to an invitation to preach. He and Knowles had studied together at General Theological Seminary in New York City. DeKoven uses Dr. Meachem's diagnosis of his injury in this undated note. It was most probably written early during his recuperation hiatus in February 1879:

> My dear Knowles—I have broken my leg & am laid up so please excuse pencil. When I can preach, I cannot tell. I will do so when I am well—I will gladly give $20 when the time comes for your altar. I can only write a line. Do come up & see me. Evr. Affect yrs. Jdekoven[20]

This note also gives a slight indication of DeKoven's generosity. For the time he was considered a wealthy man and was willing to share his wealth with many who called on him for donations. His friends benefited from this generosity, as did Racine College and other institutions.

As the month progressed, the status of his health and recuperation continued to interest the people of Racine. The following notice was published in the *Racine Daily Herald* for Saturday, March 1: "Dr. DeKoven will soon be able to be out of doors, and attending to his duties. He has suffered severely but very patiently."[21] This good news about his health probably was the result of a positive report from Dr. Meachem that was shared with the community.

The enforced calm that came with his being unable to walk was taxing, as he was very used to visiting all parts of the campus on a regular basis. His inability to participate in the daily services in St. John's Chapel undoubtedly caused him serious anxiety. He was impatient to end this period of confinement. Dr. Meachem wrote about DeKoven's accident and his recuperation in his unpublished autobiography: "I . . . attended him daily for four weeks, and no patient could be in a better condition after such an accident in the time. He had increased considerably in weight and was the very picture of health."[22] When Meachem ventured to tell DeKoven that it was no longer necessary for him to visit daily, DeKoven replied, "If you stop coming, I shall miss your visit so much, so

20. A660, Letter to Canon Knowles. Letters of James DeKoven, St. James Cathedral, Archives of the Episcopal Diocese of Chicago.

21. *Racine Daily Herald*, Mar. 1, 1879, 4.

22. Meachem, *Autobiography of Dr. John Goldesborough Meachem*, 102.

come every day until I tell you to stop."[23] Dr. Meachem obliged his patient and continued his daily visits. It was about this time that DeKoven made complete and detailed plans for his own funeral service and burial.[24]

James DeKoven understood his body well. He had expressed his fears of suffering a lingering illness due to stroke similar to that which his mother endured for several years. He had watched her confined to bed and had talked this over with Dr. Meachem. He had experienced the years of fragile health of his father which had begun even before James's birth in 1831 and ended in his father's death in 1840. His brother William's sudden death due to a heart attack and the many years of his brother Henry's weakness due to heart disease weighed on his mind. His own experiences of stress-related illness throughout his life were significant. He remembered the interruptions of his own schooling even if no one else did: the absences in Middletown, the year-long absence from Columbia College during his junior year, the excused withdrawal from the final months of his senior year at General Theological Seminary.

He confided his concerns to others, too. John Henry Hopkins, friend and fellow clergyman, recounts a conversation he had with DeKoven during the general convention in 1877 in Boston:

> In walking from our hospital quarters to General Convention he would take my arm, and now and then, notwithstanding his smiling face and cheerful talk, I felt an uncontrollable nervous twitch in his arm. On speaking to him about it he said he could not help it; and then, in language I can never forget, he said that no one could realize the weight of the burden that was perpetually upon his mind and heart and conscience. The entire work of Racine College rested upon him—educational, religious, disciplinary, and financial. And beside this was the share he had been driven to take in the affairs of the Diocese and the general controversies of the Church. "God alone knows," said he, "How long I shall be able to stand it."[25]

23. Meachem, *Autobiography of Dr. John Goldesborough Meachem*, 102–3.

24. A long article in the *Racine Advocate* dated March 22, 1879, contains this statement about the ceremonies of his funeral: "These celebrations, and the interring of the remains was an expressed wish of the Dr.'s which he made on last Sabbath [March 16], when he little thought that before another Sabbath should dawn, he would be deposited in this earthly tabernacle ("Racine College Mourns Her Beloved Warden").

25. Hopkins, "Few Recollections of James DeKoven, No. VI." *Nashotah Scholiast*, Vol. II, July and August, 1885, Nos. 9 and 10, 151.

Dr. Meachem's final diagnosis provided a positive outlook for a return to health. This undoubtedly encouraged DeKoven as he continued to take care of the many challenges that faced him at Racine College. In a typical gesture of understanding and love, he ordered an Episcopal ring for his friend George F. Seymour, who had been elected bishop of Springfield, Illinois. This election undoubtedly brought bittersweet thoughts to his mind, thoughts that he directed toward buying a symbolic gift for a longtime friend.

DeKoven did not continue with the regular Sunday evening receptions during his recuperation.[26] These events were generally organized by him and often included storytelling, an impromptu homily on some event either local or national, and a poetry recitation or reading of a short passage. However, on Sunday, March 16, DeKoven did hold a reception for the college students. This summary was provided by a former student in an article written eight years later:

> He was full of his usual fun and good spirits, and all were anticipating his speedy reappearance among us. He told us, I remember, that he thought of being wheeled to the chapel on the following Sunday, which would be mid-Lent, and preaching to us while seated in his chair; or, as he expressed it, "turning my chariot into a pulpit."[27]

DeKoven was at a point where he needed to make decisions about his own life. He saw developments unfolding which promised a more positive future. In the last entry in his journal, he mentions this possible positive change in organizational arrangements:

> Steps have been begun to make the Board of Trustees at Nashotah the same as that at Racine. Should this be accomplished, a union will be accomplished at last. How strange if this were to take place at the end of my 25th year of work in the west.[28]

The years of work and struggles seemed to be paying off. He had also made the decision not to leave Racine. He knew his future was tied to the future of Racine College, and he continued to turn down offers for pastoral positions in the Episcopal Church. The latest was as rector of

26. The receptions were divided into three categories: the grammar school reception, the college reception, and the general reception.

27. Student (Anonymous), "Racine and Dr. DeKoven. VIII," *Church Scholiast*, May 1887, 123.

28. DeKoven, *Journal*, Ua, 144. This is part of the last entry he made in this journal.

the Church of St. Mark in Philadelphia. He mentions the gift to Bishop Seymour and the offer in a letter, written in pencil, to his niece Mary Beach Johnson, who arranged for the design and fabrication of the ring:

> Dear Mary: The ring arrived and is beautiful. I have sent it today to Bp. Seymour. I thank you for your trouble. The bill has not arrived, but no doubt will appear in due time . . . I suppose you have heard that I have been elected to St. Mark's Phil but do not intend to accept it. All are well here. With love to the sisters and to your mother, I am affectionately yours, James de Koven.[29]

It requires no great stretch of biographical imagination to envision these six weeks of enforced confinement following his accident in Milwaukee as ones during which James DeKoven took stock of his life and work. He was not one who dealt easily with change in his routine. It is natural for a person of high motivation, if not always high energy like DeKoven, to find ways of adapting to a new situation with its limited physical activity and seemingly idle hours. James DeKoven had been in Wisconsin for almost twenty-five years when he had his fall; twenty of those years were spent at Racine College. His routine at the college had assumed a fairly regular pattern, although there were always crises and difficulties arising in the administration of an educational institution. In these twenty-five years he had also assumed greater responsibilities in the functioning of the Episcopal Church in Wisconsin and earned a reputation in the national church. He had long worried about his personal role in the life of the school as being too central.[30] He did not want to be thought irreplaceable, and this accident, though not life-threatening, brought the question of succession to his mind. It seems perfectly understandable that during this time of relative peace he would look back over these years and assess his accomplishments and his future, whatever it might be.

DeKoven was aware of the importance of celebrating milestones and helped organize and actively participated in the twenty-fifth anniversary

29. This letter and one other that were written to his niece Mary Beach Johnson are included in the collection of letters and documents called the Eckels-Cox-Pope Archives, RG137 1–9.

30. This is one of two themes that DeKoven repeats in the last pages of his journal. The idea that someone else should be chosen to take over the College is even one he introduces to the board of trustees. This idea of the school being too closely associated with him is mentioned in the long article in the *Racine Advocate* published a few days after his death. The other theme is that of his weariness. Ultimately, he resigns himself to the continuation of his role at Racine College

celebration of the founding of Racine College. He began his sermon, "Preached at the Collegiate Church of St. John," on June 26, 1877, with this insightful comment about what such an anniversary represents: "Long to look back upon, though it may have been longer to look forward to, is at any time a period of five and twenty years." He provided a summary of the accomplishments of the school during this period and devoted the final thoughts of this sermon to the importance of Christian education. One of these ideas could well be applied to his own life and work in Wisconsin. In speaking about the histories of Oxford and Cambridge universities in England he said, "Twenty-five years is a brief period in a country where centuries of civilization have come and gone; it is a long time on the shores of Lake Michigan." It is this long time that he could contemplate and review during his recuperation period.

As he looked at his journal, he could quietly review the entries that had started seventeen years earlier. His "Story of a College" had become, in many ways, the story of a college president. He undoubtedly could ask himself, how was this man of forty-eight years of age different than the young man who arrived in the wilderness of Wisconsin in 1854? How was he different than the young priest who took over Racine College five years later? What was there in his family life in Middletown, Connecticut that prepared him for the paths that he had followed? How had his education and early experiences prepared him for the tasks he had set for himself? Who were the people who had played central roles in his life? Had he always made the best or wisest decisions regarding the college, its students, and his own life? Why had he been chosen to lead and yet not been given the highest authority to fulfill the difficult tasks of leadership in the church? Had he always expressed his ideas in the clearest and most direct manner? Had he dealt with adversity, controversy, and criticism in a way that reflected true Christian values? Why had he become embroiled in these debates and controversies?

James DeKoven was used to examining his thoughts and deeds. Even though he didn't answer the particular questions asked above in any one autobiographical writing, he did answer many questions as he shared his beliefs in the documents he wrote, as well as in the sermons and speeches he made over the years. In the following pages an attempt is made to provide some additional insight into this remarkable man of faith as we examine his life in detail.

2

The Family of James DeKoven

THE HENRY L. DEKOVEN FAMILY AT HOME IN MIDDLETOWN, CONNECTICUT

James DeKoven's Parents

Henry Louis DeKoven + Margaret Yates Sebor

Henry: Born June 16, 1784; Married February 24, 1813; Died August 7, 1840

Margaret: Born August 15, 1790; Died December 8, 1874

ON SUNDAY, DECEMBER 21, 1834, Henry L. DeKoven wrote the following words in a letter to his eldest daughter, Elizabeth, then living in Chicago, Illinois: "I am writing Sunday evening in the Parlor, Mary writing her French exercises, Mother reading, Miss Hannah Moore & the children at play upstairs."[1] He presents in the simplest terms the tranquil scene of a merchant-class family in early nineteenth-century New England. However, this is much more than a father writing his daughter: it is an indication of the fundamental changes that were occurring in the social structure of the United States. The new frontier for the country was now

1. Letter from H. L. DeKoven, Middletown, Connecticut, to Mrs. Elijah K. Hubbard, Chicago, Illinois, December 21, 1834. DeKoven Letters & Accounts, Walter Steding Material, Wadsworth Archive, Middlesex County Historical Society.

the great Northwest Territories. The DeKoven Family, firmly established in the business and financial world of the East Coast, was writing to the first member of the family to go west with her husband, Elijah Kent Hubbard. Elizabeth and Elijah were married on September 15, 1834, in Middletown and soon after left for Chicago where Elijah had established a partnership with Gurdon Hubbard,[2] a well-known pioneer entrepreneur in the Northwest.

It was from the comfort of the front parlor of their house on Washington Street in Middletown that Henry wrote his letter to his daughter. It is easy to imagine this family gathered around the fire in this drawing room, undertaking their different tasks at the end of a wintery Sunday. Other members of the family also wrote to Elizabeth on this day on the same large sheet of paper. Only two letters written to Elizabeth by her family have survived. These letters are remarkable documents. They consist of folio-sized sheets of paper that are folded in half and then in thirds, and there is writing on both sides of the paper. Additionally, the writing is doubled: there are lines of writing not only horizontally on each side but also written vertical lines overlaying the horizontal script. This was a fairly common practice to economize on paper and reduce postage costs. Different members of the DeKoven family contributed to these long letters; the one discussed here had four different authors and runs to approximately 2,800 words.

Elizabeth was the first child of the DeKoven family to marry and move away from the Middletown family home. She had turned twenty-one in November of that year. There was an obvious attempt on the part of the writers of this letter to provide an upbeat communication to "Lizzie" at this holiday season. In addition to parts written by her father, Henry Louis, there are sections written by younger sister Mary Charlotte, younger brother Henry Louis, and an unidentified writer who signed a segment of the letter "EHS." This could possibly be Elizabeth's aunt, Harriet Emma Sebor, a favorite of the children and grandchildren of the Sebor and DeKoven families.[3]

2. Gurdon Saltonstall Hubbard (1802–88), a prominent nineteenth century citizen of Chicago. A land speculator, fur trader, insurance underwriter, and developer of the first stockyard in Chicago. He also opened the first meatpacking plant, as well as the first warehouse in the city.

3. Both Henry and his wife were direct descendants of Jacob Sebor; they were first cousins.

Mary Charlotte begins her section of the letter to her older sister by giving advice about what type of information Elizabeth should include in her letters from Chicago to the Middletown family: "We expect to hear something of the society & manners of the place itself . . . whether it has any streets, whether the houses are made of brick, wood, etc. 2ndly the Society—is it refined or not? Are there many Gentlemen & if the Ladies are equal to those in the East?" (Dec. 21, 1834).[4] Elizabeth had already sent several letters back home, but the readers in Middletown were disappointed by the lack of detailed information they contained. Mary then provides more questions that could help "dearest Lizzie" in satisfying their curiosity. Chicago was the wild frontier; this family was seeking first-hand eyewitness from one of their own now living in this frontier community.

Mary also supplied much gossipy information about family, friends, and goings and comings in preparation for Christmas in Middletown. She displayed a touch of petulance in announcing her decision "to refuse Grandma's invitation to dine at Christmas . . . I know they don't like me there" (Dec. 21, 1834). Mary admits she is lonesome and misses her sister very much. They all await the letters from Chicago and obviously share theirs with members of Elijah's Hubbard family who reciprocated when they received similar communications:

> Jane Wilkinson & myself took tea with Margaret Hubbard the other evening & Margaret related the particulars of your letter . . . We were delighted to hear that you were so contented & happy. It gives us sincere pleasure. (Dec. 21, 1834)

The section of the letter written by the father, Henry Louis, gives updated details about the lives of the family members. Even though he states that "I shall be a dull correspondent," he does provide information about the other children. Henry L. (Junior) is preparing to leave for New York City, and Willie (William), ten, is studying at the school run by Mr. Eliot. Margaret, fourteen, and Cornelia, seven, attend a school kept by the Misses North and Hurthhust. Frances (Fanny), five, will join her sisters at the school soon. The next to the youngest, James, is mentioned using his nickname. He obviously had had some skin disease (possibly childhood eczema): "Jamie's face is quite well. We had to give him a course of blue

4. All additional references to this and other letters will include the date of the letter after the quotation.

pills before we could accomplish a cure."[5] The youngest child, John, is not mentioned in the letter. He had turned one year old on November 25. The father's droll sense of humor emerges in his prose, as in this excerpt: "Mrs. Thaddeus Nichols was buried last Sunday from which you will infer that she is dead. I thought I would tell you one piece of news" (Dec. 21, 1834). Fatherly advice is found in several places in his message to Elizabeth. He mentions church attendance, what he calls "so important a duty." He asks this pointed question: "What sort of church have you at Chicago or have you given up the good old fashion of attending Public Worship?" (Dec. 21, 1834). It seems that Elizabeth had already demonstrated definite independence as far as her religious beliefs and practices were concerned. The subject returns later in the letter. He relates that he has asked "Mother" if she had anything to add to his letter:

> She says, tell her not to neglect her Sunday duties. You can understand whether she merely means to have your hair well combed & be neatly dressed to see company or if it means to go to church twice a day. (Dec. 21, 1834)

Her sister Mary even raises the issue: "In particular what Church do you attend? Are you a regular Presbyter?" This question will be one that returns several times during Elizabeth's life in relationship to other members of her strongly Episcopal family.

It is apparent that this is a family much concerned with business affairs and very aware of the opportunities represented by Chicago and the growing importance of the great Northwest. Henry Louis mentions that he and partners are ready to launch a new company called "General Silk Jobbing." This was related to trade arrangements he had already established with China. His commitment to the start-up funds for this new company was $20,000, a significant investment in a new business for this period.

Several questions remain unanswered because of a lack of context that previous letters or conversations would have provided. Mr. DeKoven refers to Henry getting ready for his departure to New York to avail himself "of this opportunity." A similar reference is made about Mary who "has a most excellent opt to improve herself and she is disposed to improve it [sic]" (Dec. 21, 1834). Records show that Henry had returned

5. The blue pill was a common medication used in the eighteenth and nineteenth century for skin diseases. It contained mercury chloride, and it was sometimes used to treat depression and "melancholia."

from London in April of 1833.[6] At the time of this letter, almost two years later, he is leaving for New York City. Were these two events for the DeKoven children connected? Henry was definitely being groomed for a productive future.

The concern expressed by Henry Louis DeKoven for his daughter's welfare is genuine. He demonstrates a fatherly love that he probably missed during his own childhood. One is left to wonder who provided him with ideas about parental roles. His concern, found in the earliest part of his writing to Elizabeth, reveals an endearing sensitivity and human warmth.

> I was much gratified to hear that your husband, in a letter to his sister recently rec'd, spoke of you in terms of increasing affection. From that of the first of your own letters I am led to believe that you are very happy & you may be assured the conclusion is to me a very delightful one. (Dec. 21, 1834)

It is apparent, from the different references to letters, that there was a steady stream of communication between Middletown and Chicago. An earlier and perhaps first letter to Elizabeth was penned on October 12, 1834, not long after the departure of the young couple for their new life in Chicago. The most significant part of this first communication is the section written by Elizabeth's mother, Margaret Sebor DeKoven.[7] It is not only a touching message of love and concern to her daughter but also one of realization that life has taken a sudden and definite change. It is important to note that Mrs. DeKoven managed a large household that included nine children, ranging in ages from one to twenty-one, at least three live-in servants, and a husband who was experiencing the first signs of heart problems and paralysis that plagued his final years of life. It is easy to understand that after the turmoil of the wedding of her eldest child and amid the activity of daily life of this large family, Margaret DeKoven would suddenly realize that a major change had occurred in her family. She wrote openly and honestly of her feelings:

> I can assure you, my beloved child, that I never realized how much I should miss you & what a void my heart would feel. I did

6. Henry DeKoven, age 13, arrival date Apr. 17, 1833. Ship Ontario, New York, Passenger and Immigration Lists, 1820–50.

7. There were at least three individuals who contributed to this letter. Elizabeth's mother, Margaret Yates Sebor; Elizabeth's uncle, Charles Robert Sebor, younger brother of Margaret; and Elizabeth's sister, Mary Charlotte.

> not know how much I love you and how necessary you were to my comfort and happiness. I believe now you have gone [that] the house has lost its charm and no one comes to enliven us of an evening and we are a dull set. (Oct. 12, 1834)

In the section of this letter written by Mary Charlotte, she mentions her brother James. Elizabeth had apparently played an important role in his life, and now he has transferred his affection to Mary Charlotte. She provided the first quotation we have recorded of the later-in-life great orator:

> Little Jamie is sitting by the side of me & I asked what I should tell sister Lizzie for him. He says to tell her to come home & . . . that I love her. Dear little fellow he has taken a great fancy to me & is with me most of the time. (Oct. 12, 1834)

The charming nature of these letters, the sincere expression of concern and care found in them, and the type of family details they contain are a source of positive information as well as frustration. The frustration results from the fact that there are so few letters available to provide additional insight into the thoughts and feelings of the members of the DeKoven family.[8] None of the letters written by Elizabeth to her family have survived.

The two letters written in 1834 to Elizabeth in Chicago also provide a very clear idea of the nurturing atmosphere in which James DeKoven spent the first years of his life. It was this same nurturing attitude that led his two older sisters to come to Racine to take care of their brother many years later (1876) at a most stressful time. The strong bonds of the DeKoven family were established in the early years of the century, before the older children began to create their own lives. These connections continued throughout their lifetimes and lasted well beyond the death of their younger brother, James.

The DeKoven family history is closely linked to the trading history of the American colonies, the turmoil and division of the American Revolution, and the eventual westward expansion of the United States. Although the DeKoven name does not figure prominently in the political realm, the involvement of family members in commerce, banking, religion,

8. Such primary source documents for the DeKoven and Sebor families are rare. Helen Beach provides the following bit of information in a "Prefatory Note" to her genealogical work *The Descendants of Jacob Sebor, 1709–1793*: "There were few written records and no family letters at all, all such having been destroyed." She based her 1923 work on the personal recollections of family members of the "fifth generation." 6.

education, and the arts for more than a century was significant. The social and financial links established by different members of the DeKoven family created an enlarged circle of influence both in East Coast cities, as well as the new cities and states of the upper Midwest.

THE ANCESTORS OF JAMES DEKOVEN

On April 8, 1781, Johann Ludwig (John Lewis) de Koven, age thirty-three, married Elizabeth Sebor, age eighteen, in Christ Church, Middletown, Connecticut. They were married by Rev. Abraham Jarvis, rector of the church and later Episcopal Bishop of Connecticut. This was the first instance of the de Koven name being used in an official document in America.[9] John Lewis was born in Verden, Hanover, on August 20, 1748.[10] He served in the army of the Elector of Hanover and came to America in 1778 as an ensign in the mercenary Hessian troops who fought with the British Army. He was listed in the von Stolzberg Regiment. On October 9, 1779, he was on a ship, *The Badger*, captured by an armed American revolutionary vessel. DeKoven and two other officers were taken prisoners and detained for two years "on parole" in Middletown, Connecticut.[11]

During his internment he became involved in the social life of the Middletown community, where he is known to have played a role in the Masonic lodge there.[12] His marriage to Elizabeth Sebor, one of the five children of Jacob Sebor and Jane Woodbury, marked a connection with one of the established merchant class families of the community. One child, Henry Louis de Koven, was born to this couple three years later on June 16, 1784.

In March 1785, John Lewis left the United States, effectively abandoning his young family. It is here that versions of the family story begin to diverge. One version has him returning to Europe and never coming back.[13] Another variation says that he had to return to Hanover to look

9. There are two versions of the last name that were used by members of the family. In Germany the name was simply Koven. The "de" was added in America. James DeKoven used both versions: de Koven and DeKoven.

10. Beach, *Descendants of Jacob Sebor, 1709–1793*, 63.

11. Beach, *Descendants of Jacob Sebor, 1709–1793*, 64.

12. Case, "American Masonic Roots in British Military Lodges," 21.

13. In fact, Ensign de Koven returned to England, married again in 1798 (indicating falsely on this second marriage document that his first wife had died), had two more children, and was eventually sent to Canada where he died in 1821. His English

after family property there, and when he did finally return to Connecticut, he found that his wife had remarried. Because he heard that his wife was happily married, he sought dispensation from his marriage vows and moved to Canada where he died, having lived "in lonely sadness."[14] A final and more salacious story claimed that an irate husband chased him out of town because de Koven was involved in a dalliance with this man's wife.[15] Whatever the truth behind the abandonment, documents do show that "on July 7, 1788 the Superior Court Middlesex County granted to Elizabeth de Koven a divorce from her husband, John L. de Koven, on the grounds of desertion dating from March 17, 1785."[16]

The rest of the story of Elizabeth Sebor de Koven reveals a strong character, as well as an entrepreneurial spirit, unusual for a woman of her era. Living with the stigma of being a divorcee in a very conservative environment, she decided to make her own way in the world. At approximately the same time as she sought her divorce she opened a general merchandise store on Main Street in Middletown. An ad in the *Middlesex Gazette* for November 8, 1788, announced the following:

> Just received, and ready for Sale at the Store lately occupied by William Richards, . . . by Eliza d'Koven, A large and general Assortment of European GOODS suitable for the approaching Seasons, which she is determined to sell as CHEAP as can be purchased in any Store in the State.[17]

Elizabeth Sebor came naturally to the business world through her father Jacob Sebor (1709–1802), who had operated a general store in Middletown with her brother, also named Jacob (1755–1847). Her brother traded in imported goods primarily from England but also from throughout the expanding British Empire. Elizabeth owned her store for over a year and announced the closing sale in October of 1789, following her marriage to Ralph Isaacs, an attorney, who lived in New Haven. She eventually gave birth to five more children.[18] Elizabeth and her second husband remained

---

children returned to England, where their descendants now live. Bill Daley, "Descendants of deKoven visit Middletown," *Hartford Courant*, Oct. 19, 1996, 39.

14. DeKoven, *Musician and His Wife*, 86. There is no record of this dispensation.

15. Case, "American Masonic Roots in British Military Lodges," 21.

16. Cited in Beach, *Descendants of Jacob Sebor, 1709–1793*, 12.

17. Quoted by McCain, "Colonial Woman Rises Above Scandal."

18. Different documents indicate that the Connecticut Sebor and DeKoven family stayed in contact with the Isaacs family. James DeKoven visited these cousins and mentions this in his journal. Some descendants moved to Beloit, Wisconsin.

in Connecticut until 1806, when they moved to Augusta, Georgia, where she died in 1809.

Henry Louis DeKoven was only a year old when his father left the country and five years old when his mother remarried. From the circumstances of his life, it appears that he remained close to the Sebor family, and it was through this relationship that he became a merchant sea captain. His uncle Jacob Sebor and his cousin William Shirreff Sebor were both actively involved in the English, China, and India trade.

There is no specific information available about Henry Louis's education other than what can be surmised from the records of the time about educational institutions or rather their lack. Although Connecticut has a long history of requiring education and supporting schooling with public funds, enforcement varied from community to community.[19] Primary schools for boys were the most common and were generally small. Oftentimes such schools were privately operated, like those mentioned by Henry DeKoven earlier in this chapter, and much education took place at home. Secondary schooling was almost nonexistent.[20] A review of the surviving business documents of Henry Louis shows that he wrote well, was good at business mathematics, and understood legal matters. For the most part, his education seems to have been based on life experience and native intelligence.

Uncle Jacob Sebor operated the family business of importing and selling goods from New York City until about 1805, when he returned with his family to Middletown. Henry Louis's ties to the Sebor family became even closer, and the resulting relationships more difficult to follow, when he married his first cousin, Margaret Yates Sebor on February 24, 1813. His uncle became his father-in-law, and his cousin and business partner, his brother-in-law.

Shipping records and business papers which have survived in relatively large numbers provide some insight into the success of Captain Henry L. DeKoven as sea captain and trader. The records of his trading voyages show him commanding different ships to chief trading posts including Cadiz, Spain; Havana, Cuba; Buenos Aires, Argentina; Montevideo, Chile; Goa, India; Lisbon, Portugal; Lima, Peru; and Canton,

19. Mandatory school laws date back to colonial times in Connecticut, some dating from as early as 1680.

20. The first high school for boys in Middletown opened in 1841 and was housed in the basement of Christ Church. This information comes from the history of Christ Church. James and his brother John attended this first high school in 1841 and 1842.

China.[21] He had at least one successful trading mission that involved the shipment of silver from Peru to China. A receipt from his purchase of silk in Canton has survived. Captain DeKoven had sufficient success from his trading activities to make other investments.

He retired from the active life of a ship captain in the late 1820s. On June 29, 1830, he was one of the founders and served as president and director of the Middlesex County Bank, holding this position from 1830 through 1835.[22] In 1831, he was listed as one of the incorporators of Wesleyan College in Middletown and served on the board of trustees of this institution from 1831 to 1839.[23] During this period of his life his association with the Russell family of Middletown became important. The Russells were among the earliest manufacturers in this Connecticut city and also among the first speculative investors in Chicago real estate.[24] The ties between the two families were close. Samuel Russell succeeded Henry Louis as president of the Middlesex bank from 1835 to 1840 and again from 1841 to 1846. Henry and Margaret named their eighth child Frances Russel DeKoven to honor Samuel's wife, Frances Ann.

The cooperation between Henry L. DeKoven and the Russell brothers was a small part of a larger phenomenon involving Eastern entrepreneurs in the development of the Northwest Territory. More specifically, investors began seeking opportunities in Chicago and the surrounding territory. The first formula was relatively simple: Easterners with money would buy land in a new area and then as the market improved would sell it for a profit. Edward A. Russell and his brother Samuel were encouraged to invest in land by a distant relative, Gurdon S. Hubbard (1802–86). Hubbard was originally from Vermont, but his mother lived in Middletown. He had first arrived in the Chicago area in 1818 and had success as a fur trader, land speculator, and meatpacker.[25]

Hubbard served as the agent of the Russells and bought land for them close to the centers of commerce and transportation, such as the sites for future railroad and canal development. He eventually entered into a business partnership with Elijah Kent Hubbard, husband of the

21. Coggeshall. *Voyages to Various Parts of the World.*

22. Whittemore, "Town and City of Middletown."

23. Wesleyan University, "Charter of Wesleyan University."

24. Whittemore, *History of Middlesex County*, 169. See also Schultz, "Businessman's Role in Western Settlement."

25. Schultz discusses in great detail the life of Gurdon Hubbard and the challenges he faced in frontier Chicago.

eldest DeKoven daughter, Elizabeth. It is probably through this connection that on June 25, 1835, Henry L. DeKoven purchased 280 acres of prairie land in Illinois near the burgeoning community of Chicago, which was formally incorporated in 1837.[26] This land that was the basis of the DeKoven family's Chicago property holdings. Henry L. DeKoven was relatively late in entering land speculation because by this date the Russell brothers had begun to sell out and had earned significant sums on their investments. In addition to the Chicago land, Henry L. DeKoven also invested in real estate in Augusta, Georgia, where his mother had moved early on in the century with her second husband. More investments included banking in Connecticut and New Orleans. Other records indicate that he invested in a limited co-partnership in the dry goods business under the name Foster & Easten in New York City.[27]

From business records and legal transactions, Henry DeKoven's success and activities continued up until the time of his death in Middletown on August 7, 1840. He was survived by his wife of twenty-seven years and nine children. All the children were living in Middletown when he died, and young James DeKoven was only eight years old. Elizabeth, the eldest, had returned to Connecticut with her two young sons; her husband, Elijah Kent Hubbard, had died the previous year. Mary and her husband, Hunn Beach, would eventually move back to New York City. Henry L. DeKoven Jr., had been in Europe during the year and had just returned to the United States from England four days before his father's death.[28]

Church records indicate that his funeral took place on Sunday, August 9. According to a notation in the church records, he died of paralysis after a succession of attacks that began in 1833.[29] He would eventually be buried in a family plot in Indian Hill Cemetery in Middletown. He left his estate to his wife Margaret, who was to be an executor along with Samuel Russell and Elijah K. Hubbard. Settlement of the estate was a

26. *News* (Chicago), Apr. 15, 1984, 118.

27. Limited co-partnership announced in the *Evening Post*, May 23, 1835. H. L. De Koven listed as contributing $20,000 towards the capital stock.

28. Henry DeKoven, arrival date Aug. 3, 1840, Ship St. James, New York, Passenger and Immigration Lists, 1820–50.

29. In the letter that Margaret wrote to her daughter on October 12, 1834, she mentions her husband's illness and the results of paralysis: "Father felt as if he had had so much excitement for the last two months that he wished to be alone. The more quiet he is, the better his hand and arm feel . . ." She also points out that she is trying to make Henry Jr. understand the importance of keeping his father calm and free of stress.

complicated matter because of the extent of his financial interests. Some issues were not resolved until the death of his wife thirty-four years later.

What was the impact of Henry's death on his young son James? DeKoven never mentioned his father in any of his surviving writings. More importantly, what was the relationship between father and son? Again, no relevant information is available. James was one of four boys in the household. The eldest, Henry Jr., was almost thirteen years older than James and had traveled to England for studies on at least two occasions. William, seven years older, had started studies at Wesleyan University. John was two years younger than James. Several maternal Sebor uncles lived in Middletown as well as the grandfather, Jacob Sebor, who perhaps provided some fatherly help and guidance to these boys. The Henry Louis, Senior, revealed to us in the two letters written to Elizabeth in 1837 was obviously a loving, caring man. The loving and caring man that James became is a reflection of such a person. In these early years James was surrounded by men involved in two worlds: the world of business and the world of the church. Although not actively involved in the business world of his family, James DeKoven was comfortable in dealing with financial investments and business arrangements. According to Dr. Meachem he was a "thorough business man,"[30] which made him unusual in the administration of the church and church institutions. Trading and finance were an essential part of the culture of the DeKoven/Sebor family.

James DeKoven's mother, Margaret Yates Sebor, was born in New London, Connecticut, on August 15, 1790. She was the third of the eleven children born to Jacob Sebor (1755–1847) and Elizabeth Winthrop (1766–1847). By 1791, the family had moved to New York City where Jacob took over the merchant business started by his brother James. They remained there until 1805, when the family returned to Middletown. According to Helen Beach, Jacob "owned ships which traded to China and India and he sold the goods they brought back. Probably he did not go to sea himself, but his eldest son and his son-in-law were merchant captains for many years."[31]

Margaret spent the first years of her life in New York City, returning to Middletown with her family at age fifteen. On February 24, 1813, at the age of twenty-three, she married her first cousin Henry Louis DeKoven, the son-in-law mentioned above. He was six years her senior and

30. Meachem, *Autobiography of Dr. John Goldesborough Meachem*, 99.

31. Beach, *Descendants of Jacob Sebor, 1709–1793*, 8.

was already engaged in the merchant service of her father. The first of their ten children, Elizabeth, was born on November 28, 1813 and the last, John, was born in 1833. When Henry Louis died in 1840, he left his widow with a family that included seven unmarried children, one daughter, Elizabeth, widowed in 1839, and one married daughter, Mary Charlotte Beach.[32] Margaret became the central focus of the family. Helen Beach includes this statement in the family history: "She brought up all her children and had the pleasure of seeing all her grandchildren and several of her great-grandchildren and welcoming them to her home in Middletown."[33] The home became a gathering spot and refuge over the years for members of the family.

The DeKoven House, Middletown, CT
Built in 1792 by merchant captain Benjamin Williams, sold in 1818 to Henry L. DeKoven for $3,600. Remained in the family until 1941 when it was given by DeKoven descendant Clarence Wadsworth as the headquarters for the Rockfall Foundation and a Middletown community center.

32. Several writers have indicated that following the death of Captain Henry Louis, the DeKoven family moved to New York City. I can find no documentary evidence to support the contention that Margaret DeKoven moved to New York City with her family. Religious records that list the DeKoven family continue to be noted in the registers of Middletown Christ Church from 1840 on. There is no record of the house on Washington Street being sold or vacated. During his enrollment at Columbia College and the General Theological Seminary James lists his home address as Middletown, Connecticut.

33. Beach, *Descendants of Jacob Sebor, 1709–1793*, 13.

The house in Middletown on Washington Street was home for James DeKoven, a place of comfort where the worries and responsibilities in Wisconsin were distant and he could relax with family. It was here that he began to write his journal that he called *The Story of a College*. The first page has this heading: "July 31st 1862, Middletown, Conn." Although DeKoven's references to his family in the journal are rare, he does mention his mother on several occasions, especially toward the end of her life.

One of the earliest mentions of Middletown as home is this one written in the third person, before he moved to Racine: "The Rector went home for his vacation like the rest, and before the holidays were through had returned to Delafield and Nashotah."[34] His trips to Middletown and the East Coast were regular and frequent, and he noted when they did not occur. On June 27, 1867, he wrote the following: "For the first time for thirteen years I spent my vacation in the West this year and did not go home."[35] This reference was to the longer school holiday in the early summer months because in an entry written on October 22 of the same year, there is this statement that links home and his mother. "I have finished my visit at home and will leave again (D.V.) in the morning . . . Mother is so lovely and beautiful in her old age, that it is a blessing to see her."[36]

His most complete reference to his mother is in an entry from October 29, 1870. His compassion is seen in the reference to her memory loss and the positive impact this has had on her well-being:

> I went back to Middletown, as usual. Mother in her 81st year is better than she was a year ago and calmer. She just forgets enough not to be troubled at the afflictions of her children as she would have been a year ago. She is pleasant and lovely. She is more at peace too religiously. It is a fault of our communion that she [our religion] does not give a sufficient assurance of pardon by her priesthood, that we see people of singularly innocent and beautiful lives like my mother who yet do not seem to have the assurance of pardon.[37]

Religion obviously played an important role in Margaret DeKoven's life. Two of her four surviving sons were ordained Episcopal priests. She was a member of the Church of the Holy Trinity, which was also the parish church of many of the members of her extended family. In her will she

34. DeKoven, *Journal*, Fa, 28.
35. DeKoven, *Journal*, Le2, 77.
36. DeKoven, *Journal*, Li1, 41.
37. DeKoven, *Journal*, Ni2–No1, 99–100.

left a last payment of $625 to finish her commitment for the erection of a new church for this parish. This payment was the final one of her pledge of $2,500. She also left the sum of $1,000 to be reinvested and managed by her sons Henry, James and John until a new church was built or the current church building repaired. She wrote her will in February 1869. The new church was finished the year of her death, 1874.

James DeKoven's last references to his mother came during the year of her death. Her physical and mental condition obviously had deteriorated greatly:

> My dear mother has been thought to be dying this summer. She no longer knows her children. I administered the communion to her last All Saints Day, November 1873. My sister, Elizabeth, is with her, my eldest brother and his family are in Europe.[38]

Margaret DeKoven died on December 8, 1874. DeKoven learned of the death of his "beloved and venerable mother" via telegram. He left immediately for Connecticut and was the priest celebrant at her funeral. He points out that "there had been no recovery of her mind before she died, but when death had come she looked as she had looked fifteen years ago."[39] He was proud of the fact that there were four generations of the DeKoven family present in Middletown the day of her funeral. Margaret Yates Sebor DeKoven is buried next to her husband in Indian Hill Cemetery in Middletown, Connecticut.

The picture that emerges from the rare mentions of Margaret DeKoven by her descendants is that of a caring and competent *mater familias.* Apparently she had the natural inclination to worry, commonly associated with the head of a large and disparate family. As seen above, her son James found her memory loss later in life a relief from this tendency to worry.

The care and concern demonstrated by Margaret is evident in her last will and testament written on February 10, 1869. Obviously a wise business woman, her investments were made in a variety of companies and financial institutions. In the 1870 Federal Census, the value of her property is listed at $250,000 and her personal property is valued at $80,000.[40] Her three surviving sons were named as executors, although

38. DeKoven, *Journal*, Pe1, 111.

39. DeKoven, *Journal*, Pi2, 113.

40. Helen Beach makes this comment about her grandmother and the property left: "Mrs. De Koven was left with small means at her husband's death. He had a large tract of unproductive land in the environs of Chicago, and she managed so well that she was able to keep this for her children until it was in the city and valuable. Beach,

James and Henry legally ceded this responsibility to the youngest, businessman John. She provided bequests for a long-time personal servant, a name-sake granddaughter, and a less fortunate cousin. She directed that her daughters receive their inheritance in their own names, not that of their husbands.[41] As one of the two surviving executors of her husband's estate, she took care of some unfinished business with her own will. She directed that minor debts owed by Mary Charlotte, Henry, James and John to the estate of Henry L. DeKoven, their father, be paid for from her resources. She wanted no "loose ends" when she died. She took care of her children to the very end.

THE TEN CHILDREN OF THE DEKOVEN FAMILY

Elizabeth Sebor DeKoven + Elijah Kent Hubbard, + Thomas Dyer

Elizabeth: Born November 28, 1813; 1st Married September 15, 1834; 2nd Marriage, March 11, 1844; Died June 3, 1896.

Elijah: Born October 8, 1812; Died May 26, 1839.

Thomas: Born January 13, 1805; Died June 6, 1862.

William DeKoven

William: Born April 22, 1815; Died August 28, 1815.

Mary Charlotte DeKoven + Hunn Carrington Beach

Mary: Born June 1, 1817; Married August 10, 1836; Died April 18, 1891.

Hunn: Born September 18, 1794; Died January 22, 1873.

Descendants of Jacob Sebor, 13.

41. An article about the tenth child, John DeKoven, in the *Encyclopedia of Biography of Illinois*, includes the following statement about Margaret and the land holdings and other investments that she had inherited from her husband: "After his death his widow and mother of our subject, Margaret Sebor de Koven, by economy and wise management, kept the property intact until her decease in 1875 [sic], when over a million dollars was divided among the nine [sic] children—and the share which fell to John deKoven became the nucleus from which developed his own splendid fortune."

Henry Louis DeKoven + Charlotte Le Roy

Henry: Born January 24, 1819; Married February 10, 1852; Died July 10, 1884.

Charlotte: Born 1826; Died October 12, 1885.

Margaret Marston DeKoven + William Bryan Casey, M. D.

Margaret: Born December 3, 1820; Married October 5, 1854; Died March 24, 1900.

William Bryan Casey: Born December 25, 1815; Died March 25, 1870.

William Sebor DeKoven

William: Born May 9, 1824; Died May 30, 1852.

Cornelia DeKoven + Julius Wadsworth

Cornelia: Born March 20, 1827; Married November 25, 1856; Died April 2, 1895.

Julius: Born March 19, 1815; Died May 28, 1887.

Frances Russel DeKoven + Hon. Hugh Thompson Dickey

Fanny: Born June 21, 1829; Married April 18, 1850; Died October 12, 1900.

Hugh: Born Circa 1812; Died June 2, 1892.

James DeKoven

James: Born September 19, 1831; Died March 19, 1879.

John DeKoven + Helen Hadduck, + Annie Larrabee Barnes

John: Born December 15, 1833; 1st Married February 16, 1858; 2nd Marriage, April 8, 1890; Died April 30, 1898.

Helen: Born March 19, 1835; Died March 18, 1886.

Annie: Born March 20, 1854; Died May 30, 1948.

Nine of the children born to Henry and Margaret DeKoven survived to adulthood, and seven of them played important and different roles in James DeKoven's life. They were all active in different ways in the society of their time as they participated in the evolution of their social class. Several lived their lives on the new Northwest frontier of our country, representative of the evolution of America from its East Coast focus.

FIVE SISTERS

On May 1, 1884, Anna Farwell, daughter of Senator Charles Farwell, married Reginald DeKoven, son of Rev. Henry Louis DeKoven. Their wedding was the social event of the early season in Lake Forest, Illinois. Anna eventually wrote about the members of the family that she joined on this day in her autobiographical work, *A Musician and His Wife*. She provides rare portraits of the family members she came to appreciate. Among other comments, she wrote this one-sentence statement about her many in-laws: "All the de Koven family possessed qualities of marked individuality."[42]

She was especially insightful in her description of the five sisters.[43]

> The five aunts of my husband had delightful old-fashioned manners and a naive and delicious humor. They adored one another's society, and when, as a new member of the family, I made relationships outside the charmed circle, it was considered a curious and unnecessary proceeding.[44]

42. DeKoven, *Musician and His Wife*, 88.

43. The search for photographs or portraits of the sisters as well as other members of the family has been frustrating and seemingly futile. It is hard to imagine that they did not sit for such a record at some point in their lives.

44. DeKoven, *Musician and His Wife*, 88–89.

These five sisters played different roles in James DeKoven's life story; they were there for him at various points in his life, and each had an interesting life story of her own.

Elizabeth, the first child of Henry Louis and Margaret Yates DeKoven, lived her early life in the relative comfort of a long-established New England community and family group. On September 15, 1834, she married Elijah Kent Hubbard, also of Middletown. Elijah was one of those enterprising young New Englanders who saw the opportunity for personal development in the Northwest Territory. In a very honest and straightforward letter dated June 26, 1834, Chicago, written to his fiancée Elizabeth, he affirms his love for her and describes the place where he had traveled in the spring of that year and where he hoped to make his fortune.

> The people here are rough in their manners, fond of swearing, horse racing, etc., not neat in their appearance, of all nations, French, English, half breeds and Indians. They are very different in all respects from anything you have seen, nor is the novelty pleasing. Their houses are small and generally dirty. Little houses with one small room and a little loft above are rented for 100 dollars a year and families are obliged to content themselves with such. I sleep in a room with sixteen other persons. The room is neither lathed or plastered, nor is there any ceiling but shingles. But I am more favored than any other person I know of for I have a bed to myself. Do not think I am disappointed here. I expected to find a disagreeable place and I have found one.[45]

If Elijah had planned on discouraging Elizabeth with this bleak description of the people and place, he did not succeed. Soon after their marriage they moved to Chicago. The newlyweds already knew people in this frontier city, including Juliette and John Kinzie. Among the Middletown families who came with their support were E. K. Hubbard and his wife, Elizabeth Sebor De Koven, one of Juliette's childhood friends. The women remained fast friends for the rest of their lives and spent many happy times together as their children grew up together in Chicago.[46]

45. Elijah Kent Hubbard, letter to Elizabeth DeKoven dated Jun. 26, 1834, Hubbard Collection, Middlesex County Historical Society.

46. Keating, *World of Juliette Kinzie,* 71. Juliette and Elizabeth both had ambitions of being novelists. They shared their writing efforts as they worked toward their goals. Juliette published a novel, *Walter Ogilby*, in 1868. She dedicated this novel to Elizabeth, "Mrs. E. DeKoven Dyer, the friend whose words of encouragement first suggested [the volume] . . . and whose genial, sympathizing smile has beamed on its progress and completion." Even though Elizabeth moved back to Middletown, the two remained close friends.

In a letter she wrote forty-four years later in 1878, Elizabeth described the conditions of life in Chicago when they arrived. She emphasized her husband's "prophetic eye" in foreseeing the great possibilities of life and work in Chicago: "He seemed to see, as in a glace, the great future of this city, and became speedily identified with its interests seeking its prosperity."[47] In this spirit Elijah obtained the charter for the Galena and Chicago Railroad, which he began constructing in 1836. He also invested heavily in real estate. However, the financial crisis of 1837, and his own poor health, brought his efforts and life to an early end. He died of typhoid fever on May 23, 1839, leaving Elizabeth a young widow of twenty-six, with two sons, Elijah Kent and Louis DeKoven Hubbard.

Over the years Elizabeth DeKoven Hubbard appears to have spent time in both Middletown and Chicago. On March 11, 1844, she married Thomas Dyer in Middletown. Like Elijah Kent Hubbard, Thomas Dyer had gone to Chicago from Connecticut and quickly established a role in the nascent business community, investing early in the grain shipping and meatpacking businesses. For several years Dyer was president of the Chicago Board of Trade. "By 1850 he was counted among the forty-four richest men in Chicago . . . Dyer thought of himself primarily as a businessman and used politics as a tool for commercial ends."[48] A pro-banking Democrat, he was elected the eighteenth mayor of Chicago on March 10, 1856. After Thomas Dyer died on June 6, 1862 in Middletown, Elizabeth devoted many years of her life to caring for her mother who died in 1874.

Elizabeth maintained both personal and professional contacts in Chicago, overseeing rental property both for herself and her mother. Unfortunately, she lost her home and other possessions in the great fire of 1871. In 1876, Elizabeth joined her sister Margaret Casey in Racine, Wisconsin, at the recently rebuilt Taylor Hall on the Racine College campus, taking over the supervision of James DeKoven's household. He mentions the positive effect of their presence on his life: "My sisters have been here this winter, and for the first time I have had something which seemed like a home."[49] They served as hostesses, providing a family presence that he valued greatly. They were with him when he died on March 18, 1879.

47. Letter written by Elizabeth Dyer, Dec. 20, 1878, and published in the *Biographical Memoranda of Yale College for 1831*.

48. Schultz, "Businessman's Role in Western Settlement," 157.

49. DeKoven, *Journal*, R01, 127.

By 1881, three of the five sisters were living back in Middletown, with the other two in Newport and/or New York. Elizabeth died on June 30, 1893, survived by her son Elijah K. Hubbard, who had become a very successful businessman in Middletown, as well as mayor of that city. Elizabeth's second son, Louis DeKoven Hubbard had died of consumption on April 15, 1866, in Paris, having been sent there as a military attaché after the Civil War.

Mary Charlotte, four years younger than Elizabeth, also received her formal education at a private "young ladies school" in Middletown. In the letter already cited that Mary wrote to Elizabeth, who was traveling to Chicago, we have a good insight into their sisterly love and care. Mary expresses concern in the midst of telling the daily gossip of the town in 1834: "I miss you very much now since it was about this time last year you had the scarlet fever & Elijah was taking care of you. I feel very lonesome sometimes, particularly when Father reads his paper and Mother sews."[50]

When she was seventeen years old, Mary left for a position in New York City. Her mother, Margaret, mentions this in a letter to Elizabeth dated October 12, 1834: "Mary is going to New York next week to live with Miss Shirley." We can assume that this opportunity was as a companion or tutor in a private household. Within eighteen months she married Hunn Carrington Beach, a successful New York merchant, twenty-two years her senior.

Mary and Hunn Beach had six children, one son and five daughters. Although the couple spent the first years of their marriage in Middletown, the Beach family resided primarily in New York City, living there during the years that James attended Columbia College and the General Theological Seminary. DeKoven was always very close to his Beach nieces who visited him in Racine and wrote about their visits with their beloved uncle. They also spent time with him when he came to visit his mother, their grandmother, in Middletown. His niece Mary's story about their dinner conversations while staying in the DeKoven House is one that is often repeated. This version comes from DeKoven's journal and is written about her:

> As it is, my niece, who is full of life, and I amuse ourselves in the dullness of the town in making believe that all sorts of great people are visiting us. Sometimes they are poets and literary men, sometimes the Pope and Louis Napoleon favor us. We

50. Mary Charlotte DeKoven to Elizabeth DeKoven Hubbard, Dec. 21, 1834.

> converse with them as though they were there and are much disturbed at the disputes that go on between Cardinal Antonelli and the Holy Father.[51]

Mary Charlotte was devoted to her brother James and upon his death worked with her daughters on assembling the scrapbooks of obituaries as a tribute to him.

James DeKoven's third sister, Margaret, was the caregiver of the family. She looked after her mother, and when she married she looked after her stepchildren as well. Eventually, she cared for her beloved brother, James, at Racine College during what would be the last years of his life. Margaret's early life in Middletown was much like that of her sisters. She lived with her mother and unwed sisters until her own marriage to William Bryan Casey, a graduate of the University of Pennsylvania Medical School. Dr. Casey had his first practice in New York City before moving to Middletown in 1839. He and his first wife, Cornelia Beare, had six children; she died in childbirth in 1852. He and Margaret married in 1854, and she assumed responsibility for her stepchildren.

Dr. Casey was highly respected in the Middletown community, serving two terms as mayor and as an Army surgeon during the Civil War. Starting in 1852, he edited a local newspaper, the *Daily News*. He was a warden of Christ Episcopal Church in Middletown, where there is a stained-glass window donated in memory by Margaret.

In 1875, after the death of her mother and husband, Margaret moved to Racine and oversaw her brother's household in Taylor Hall on the Racine College campus. This task included attending to the many guests from around the country who visited the college and DeKoven after his rise to prominence in the church. Their sister Elizabeth joined

51. This particular version is from DeKoven's journal, entry dated Oct. 29, 1870, DeKoven, *Journal*, No1, 100. This is a version of the story, from a letter written by Mary to William C. Pope, 64–65:

> I especially recall one visit, when Grandmother was an invalid upstairs, and he and I had our meals together alone. We used to entertain imaginary visitors, the Archbishop of Canterbury, Tennyson, various cardinals of note, Thackeray, Dickens, etc, etc. and the conversation was always adapted according to the rank or profession of the guest of honor. When 'the Laureate' was with us, we talked entirely in rhyme. I remember, one day, Uncle James came hurrying in, and said he had 'just met Queen Victoria and the Pope at the stations, and had asked them up to take a bite.' I shall never forget the horrified look of a new domestic, who heard him make this pronouncement to me with a perfectly grave face, and saw me receive it as a matter of course, and state that I would "have two extra chops put on to broil at once."

them in 1876. In April of that year James made this entry in his journal: "My home is very comfortable with my kind sisters and I am able to be very hospitable to the boys and kind to them."[52] Having family members with him helped support his continued work with the college, as he faced some difficult decisions about his professional life and his role in the Episcopal Church. He was devoted to his sisters and their presence in his daily life brought him great comfort.

After her brother's death, Margaret returned to New York City, where she lived among her stepchildren. She divided her time between New York City and Middletown, where her sister Cornelia had given her use of the DeKoven House for as long as she lived. Margaret Marston Casey died in 1900.[53] Her care for others continued even after her death with her endowment of $6,000 for the poor of the parish of Holy Trinity Episcopal Church in Middletown.

There are few specific details about Cornelia and her early life, other than what can be determined from official records such as census data. In the 1850 Federal Census she is shown to be living with her mother and her sister Margaret in the house on Washington Street in Middletown. It is safe to assume that she spent some time in Chicago at the home of her sister Elizabeth and Elizabeth's second husband, Thomas Dyer. Thomas had become very successful in the growing meatpacking industry, joining forces with the Wadsworth brothers of Connecticut, Elisha and Julius. These brothers went first to South Carolina to make their fortune but soon saw the golden opportunity that the great Northwest offered and relocated there. As early as 1841, Julius Wadsworth and Thomas Dyer had purchased 160 acres of land in the Chicago district.[54] That same year they also purchased land in the Milwaukee district. In 1856, the same year that Elizabeth's husband, Thomas Dyer became mayor of Chicago, Cornelia married Dyer's business partner, Julius Wadsworth. By this time the Wadsworth brothers had expanded their land speculation interest into railroad construction and operation. The railroad investments became more and more important in their business life and resulted in

52. DeKoven, *Journal*, R02, 128.

53. The following notice is from an obituary published at the time of her death: "The funeral services will be held in the home of her daughter, Mrs. C. J. Bacon, at 25 West 38th Street." Mrs. Bacon was her step-daughter, the second child of Dr. Casey and his first wife.

54. Chicago District, Land Title Certificate 4884, May 20, 1841.

the creation of the Chicago, Milwaukee and Saint Paul Railroad. Julius Wadsworth served as vice-president of this railroad throughout his life.

The Wadsworth family lived primarily in New York City as Julius's business interests expanded to national enterprises. Cornelia and Julius had two sons, William Seymour, born in 1858, and Arthur Philip, born in 1860. A tragic accident ended the life of the eldest, William, at the age of eleven. The two brothers were playing in the large brick barn behind the DeKoven House in Middletown, when William fell down a feed chute and broke his neck.[55] His brother, Arthur, was with him, and according to the family story, suffered a broken heart and never recovered psychologically from his brother's death. Arthur died one year later at the age of ten. James DeKoven, quite unusually, comments on the second son's death in his journal: "My own pleasure in commencement was marred by the sad news of the death of my poor sister's only surviving son, leaving her childless and sorrowing."[56]

All hope was not lost, however. Cornelia and Julius had another son, born in 1871, Clarence Seymour. In 1875, Clarence's father Julius purchased the DeKoven House from Cornelia's siblings, and it remained in the family until Clarence's death in 1941. Meanwhile Clarence consolidated the family fortune, became the largest landowner in Connecticut, gave many acres of protected and scenic land to the state of Connecticut for parks, built a new home for the family in Middletown—the Wadsworth Mansion at Long Hill Estate—and created one of the first environmental preservation endowments, the Rockfall Foundation. This foundation still operates from offices in the DeKoven House.

Cornelia divided her time between her homes in New York City and Middletown. Her Christian generosity especially benefited the orphanage of Holy Trinity in New York City and the St. Luke's Home for Destitute and Aged Women in Middletown. Upon her death in 1895, she left a very detailed will which included sixty-seven named beneficiaries. These personal bequests totaled more than $175,000. The two institutions mentioned above were to benefit from an endowment to be called the "Cornelia Wadsworth Dole." The DeKoven House received special attention: "To my sister Margaret DeKoven Casey the free and unrestricted use and occupancy of the property in Middletown, Connecticut, known

55. This story was told me by the lead docent at the Wadsworth Mansion in Middletown. I have not been able to find any published record of this story, although I have found brief death notices of both boys.

56. DeKoven, *Journal*, Ni2, 99.

as No. 37 Washington Street and grounds and contents for the term of her natural life."[57] In her will Cornelia provided for maintenance, insurance, and taxes for the property, which upon Margaret's death would go to her son Clarence. She seemed determined to keep the house in the family; it was a special place for all of the family members to whom she was devoted.

Much like her sisters, Frances Russell, the youngest girl, remained in her mother's home in Middletown until the time of her marriage in 1850. It is no surprise how she met her husband, lawyer, judge, and Chicago investor, Hugh T. Dickey. He moved and operated in the same social and business circle as Thomas Dyer and Julius Wadsworth. In 1850, Hugh is listed as living in the home of Thomas Dyer and his wife, Elizabeth. He brought his young bride, Frances, to live with him in her sister's household.

Hugh T. Dickey graduated from Columbia College, New York City, in 1830. He practiced law in New York for several years before heading west to Chicago, where he gained fame as a lawyer and began investing in the booming economy. He remained on the board of the Chicago, Milwaukee and St. Paul Railroad his entire life, the railroad connected from its inception with the Wadsworth brothers.

Fanny was known for her outgoing and positive personality. A devoutly religious person, she frequently donated to various church projects and activities.[58] Her brother James sometimes called on her for financial help for needy students. She was known for the bible study gatherings she sponsored at her Newport home which were followed by tea and dancing.

The Dickeys had four children; two predeceased their parents. Their youngest son, Hugh Thompson Dickey Jr., died at twenty-seven and was survived by a daughter, Cornelia, who married an Episcopal priest, George Douglas.

The five DeKoven sisters demonstrated the grace and bearing of individuals who were raised with a set of values and a code of accepted behavior. All five married well and each in her own way. They each attached great importance to family and standards of communal relationships. They had families with their own children or stepchildren. They knew the joys of a comfortable upper middle-class life. They suffered

57. Ancestry.com. *Illinois, U.S., Wills and Probate Records, 1772–1999.*

58. She paid for an addition to Trinity Church in Newport, RI, as a memorial to her two sons (*Churchman*, Nov. 3, 1894, 548) and left a bequest of $5,000 in her will to Holy Trinity Church in Middletown for a set of chimes (*Hartford Courant*, Nov. 5, 1900, 2).

from tragedies and faced challenges of living in a rapidly changing world. They respected each other, admired and watched over of their younger brother, James, and formed a bedrock for their involved families.

FIVE BROTHERS

The lives of the five sons born to Henry and Margaret DeKoven do not create a neat parallel with the lives of the five daughters. Symmetry in life is not realistic: life is not neat. The DeKoven family did not escape tragedy or sadness associated with accident and illness. These two themes appear in the stories of two of the sons and probably played a more important role in the life of the others than is first apparent.

The second child born to Henry and Margaret on April 22, 1815, was named William and lived only four months. The rector of Christ Church in Middletown recorded that baby William died "of a bowl [sic—bowel] complaint. 4 ms." This short life and painful death must have been an especially difficult time for the DeKoven family.

The life story of the fourth child, named after his father, Henry Louis, is one that raises some interesting questions about unfulfilled and changed plans. Most of the questions cannot be answered. Henry Louis was born on January 24, 1819, and baptized on the next day. His daughter-in-law, Anna, wife of the composer Reginald DeKoven, writes very warmly about her father-in-law and tells an unusual story about an experience Henry had while still a young boy:

> My husband's father was more distinguished in his appearance and manner than any American I ever saw. In his early youth he was sent to England to visit Sir William and Lady Farquhar, to whose house on a week-end visit came no less a person than Talleyrand, then ambassador to England. The young American was brought down from his bed to be exhibited to Talleyrand as a sample of what America could produce.[59]

Anna does not provide an explanation for the young DeKoven boy's trip to England other than to visit Sir Farquhar. Henry Louis returned from London on April 17, 1833, on the ship *Ontario*. He was listed as a "gentleman" aged thirteen.[60] The importance of Farquhar in the East India trade

59. DeKoven, *Musician and His Wife*, 91.

60. Henry DeKoven, age 13, arrival date, Apr. 17, 1833. Ship *Ontario*, New York, Passenger and Immigration Lists, 1820–50.

and establishment of the British presence in Singapore and other areas of Asia provides one possible answer. As the eldest son of the DeKoven family, it is possible that Henry Louis, Junior, was destined for a life as a sea captain or at least one as a merchant trader. Was this trip seen as an introduction to the seafaring world and the world of the merchant class? In any case it is fairly remarkable that a young boy of thirteen would be sent by himself to travel to England. The passenger list does not indicate anyone traveling with him.

There seems to be a change in the direction of his life sometime after 1834. Additional information about Henry appears as it relates to his studies at Wesleyan College in Middletown. In several school publications he is listed as a member of the class of 1836, and his name appears on the roster of juniors in 1838. His place of residence is his father's house, "Captain DeKoven's." In 1837, he is listed as a teacher of modern languages at Wesleyan Academy and thus began his life-long association with teaching. Was this change brought about by his return trip to England sometime before 1840? Did his interest in studying for priestly ordination result from his experience with the new ideas of the Oxford Movement? Whatever the cause, he does make a major change in his life after the death of his father.

There are several references in different documents to his studious nature. He served as tutor to his younger brothers and sisters "at a time when the family could not afford a private school or tutor for the children."[61] After graduating from Wesleyan College in 1842 with a master of arts degree, he studied theology with Dr. Samuel F. Jarvis, rector of Christ Church in Middletown. In 1843, he was ordained deacon in Christ Church and priest at Ascension Church in New York City in 1844. Henry began his priestly career as an assistant minister of Christ Church in New York City and then as rector of St. Paul's Church in Red Hook, New York. It was in Red Hook that he met the woman who was to be his wife, Charlotte Le Roy. They were married on February 12, 1852.

During his time as priest in Red Hook, Henry continued his teaching career at an academy in Tivoli, New York. Henry and family returned to Middletown in 1861, when he became the professor of homiletics at Berkeley Divinity School. He continued in this position until 1873. The fact that James was known as a great preacher and Henry taught homiletics would seem to have provided common interests and reasons for

61. Beach, *Descendants of Jacob Sebor*, 19.

association. There is no mention of Henry ever visiting Racine College or traveling to Chicago to visit family there. James did visit his brother and stayed with his family on several occasions when he returned to New York.

Henry DeKoven and his family lived in Middletown until 1871, when he left his position at Berkeley Divinity School for health reasons. According to Anna Farwell DeKoven, his heart condition was worsened by "too many walks up the hill to the seminary" where he taught.[62] In 1873 the family lived in Newport, Rhode Island, close to his sister Frances and her husband, Judge Hugh Dickey. In 1874, the Henry Louis family made the permanent move to Europe. They first established their residence in England where the two younger boys were put in school. They traveled to different countries, including extended stays in Germany and Switzerland. Their final place of residence was in Florence, Italy, where they leased the Villa Camerata in the hills overlooking the city. It was there that Reginald brought his wife Anna, on their honeymoon in 1884.

Reginald and his bride found his father in declining health and returned to the United States "with heavy hearts." Despite his condition, Henry undertook one more trip to Switzerland. It was there at Engleberg that he died on July 10, 1884, and was buried in the cemetery of the Benedictine Abbey in that village. His wife, Charlotte, died on October 12, 1885, in Florence and was buried beside her husband in Engleberg. Anna wrote this summary paragraph describing her parents-in-law:

> No standard of breeding, no ideals of duty and conduct, were ever more clearly expressed and exemplified by any American gentleman than by my ever-to-be remembered father-in-law. His relation to his wife, with whom he never ceased to enjoy endless conversations of mutual delight and interest, was itself a standard of all that a marriage of distinguished and intelligent people may and should be.[63]

Henry and Margaret DeKoven named their sixth child and third son William Sebor. He was born on May 9, 1824, in Middletown and baptized August 22, 1824, at Christ Church in that city. Following a common practice in large families, he was named in honor and memory of the

62. There is a slight error in her statement: the seminary was located on Main Street in Middletown, at the bottom of the hill. The Henry DeKoven home was up the hill; it was the return trip that was a major climb for him. One interesting fact that she does reveal is the fact that he was never paid a salary for his work at the divinity school.

63. DeKoven, *Musician and His Wife*, 94–95.

first son who died in infancy. His name is listed in the 1835 catalog of the pupils of Isaac Webb, Esq., proprietor and director of a private boarding school in Middletown where he studied for two years. In 1840, he is listed as a freshman at Wesleyan College, living on campus.

In 1840, the year his father died, William left Wesleyan and began work in an office in New York City. His destiny, however, seemed to call him to become a sailor, although not a sea captain like his father. On September 9, 1841, he formally entered service in the United States Navy as a midshipman and began studies at the Naval School in Annapolis, Maryland. He was in the first graduating class at Annapolis, and upon graduation he passed the lieutenant's examination and became eligible for promotion. His various assignments recorded in the registers of the U.S. Navy and Marine Corps included service on a receiving ship, *North Carolina*, for three years off the coast of Africa.[64]

He died suddenly on May 30, 1852 on board the United States surveying schooner *Ewing*, docked at San Francisco. The following description of his final day appeared in the *Philadelphia Inquirer* on July 21, 1852:

> Passed Midshipman William DeKoven, of Connecticut, died very suddenly on board the surveying schooner Ewing, at San Francisco. He was about 24 years old. *The Alta California* says:—He was on shore on Friday, was taken with neuralgia of the stomach, seemed a little better in the morning, went to sleep at eight o'clock, and at twelve when the physician, who had been up with him all night, went to his bed he found him dying, probably from apoplexy.[65]

Apparently, he suffered from the heart disease that was so common in his family. He was buried in Yerba Buena cemetery in San Francisco on May 31.

Over the years William's body was moved three times. This inscription is on his tombstone in Indian Hill Cemetery in Middletown, Connecticut: "Wm DeKoven after resting in three San Francisco cemeteries each in turn closed is buried here in 1939."

John DeKoven, the last child of the family, was only seven years old when his father died in 1840. We know little of his childhood or youth. We do know that James and John attended the Middletown Male High

64. "DeKoven Family of Middletown."

65. *Philadelphia Inquirer*, Jul., 21, 1852.

School in 1842. A search of census records has failed to identify his place of residence in 1850.

John's active life began with his move to Chicago in the early 1850s about the same time that his brother James came to Nashotah, Wisconsin. John first worked on the Galena and Chicago Railroad and then, through family and business connections, found employment as a bank teller.[66] Eventually he became cashier of the Merchants' National Bank and was at this institution when the great fire of 1871 swept Chicago. He played a heroic role in saving the assets of the bank and his employer.[67] According to the biography printed in the *Encyclopedia of Biography of Illinois*, John de Koven was part of a "band of influential citizens through whose zeal and energy the work of succoring the helpless and restoring the devastated city was carried forward."[68] During these years he launched into private investments, achieving great success. Connections from the family of his wife as well as his brothers-in-law, definitely helped in these financial matters and he became director of many corporations.

John married twice, the first time to Helen Hadduck in 1858. She came from a long-established Chicago family with extensive property holdings as well as interests in the financial world of Chicago. Her father was president of the Merchants' National Bank, where John DeKoven first worked in the banking sector. John and Helen had one child, Louise, who became known as a leader in social reform and philanthropy. Helen died in 1886. In 1890, John married Annie Larrabee Barnes, a widow with one child. Annie lived until 1948. The family home at 1150 North Dearborn Street still stands.

John was active in the governance of Racine College, serving on the board of trustees during the time of his brother's leadership. His name appears as sponsor of different awards at the school. In 1874, he established a $50 prize for athletic achievement in both the grammar school and college.[69] John was also very active in the social and business life of Chicago. For twenty-five years he served on the vestry of St. James Episcopal Church, to which he gave generously during his lifetime. He died

66. "Mr. de Koven came to Chicago when a lad of some nineteen years and accepted employment on the old Galena railroad." "John de Koven," *Encyclopedia of Biography of Illinois*, Vol. 3, 38.

67. His daughter, Louise deKoven Bowen, describes her father's role in saving the Merchants' Bank resources in her book, *Growing Up with a City*, 31–32.

68. "John de Koven," *Encyclopedia of Biography of Illinois*, Vol. 3, 39.

69. *College Mercury*, May 30, 1876.

on April 30, 1898. Among the honorary pallbearers at his funeral were famous Chicago businessmen Marshall Field and George Armour. His detailed and frequently changed will contained many provisions. Among other items it created a trust estate.

> The largest single item under this provision of the will is that of a bequest of $50,000 to St. James Episcopal Church. This fund given by Mr. DeKoven is to be known as the "John DeKoven fund," and is to be expended under the direction of the rector of the church for the benefit of the sick and deserving poor persons of the parish.[70]

The ten children of Captain Henry Louis DeKoven and his wife Margaret Yates Sebor present a fascinating story of upper-middle-class success in the antebellum and post-Civil War period of the United States. Although a family with very strong ties to New England and the colonial history of our country, the majority of these very strong individuals found their success, or at least their future, in what was known then as the Great Northwest Territory. They also embodied in their lives so many of the developments that came with the financial, intellectual, and territorial expansion of the era. They were involved in land investment, agricultural development, and transportation expansion on the Great Lakes and the rapidly expanding railroads as the United States became a marketer to the world.

From these family stories we learn that James DeKoven belonged to a warm and supportive family. He was involved in the lives of his siblings, nieces, and nephews through visits and, it can be assumed, letter writing. The lack of more family correspondence is frustrating to the biographer. It was a letter writing society. James often mentioned in his journal, as well as in those few letters that we do have, that he had many letters to write. What happened to them? Those that have survived are rich in their portrayal of a close family with a great deal of compassion and understanding for each other.

70. *Inter Ocean*, May 11, 1898, 7.

3

The Education of James DeKoven

On Wednesday, July 30, 1851, the *Evening Post* of New York City ran an article entitled "Columbia College Commencement."[1] This relatively detailed article gave a synopsis of the event, including a summary of the different addresses that were made by graduating seniors. The fact that critiques of certain presentations were included in the description demonstrates the seriousness with which these ceremonies were viewed. These exercises were open to the public and considered an important standard of the educational level of a community. The anonymous article writer was not delicate or hesitant in expressing an opinion. About a presentation on "Rest" as the "English Salutatory" address there was this comment: "The oration was tedious from its great length and the monotonous tone in which it was delivered."[2]

This was the graduation ceremony for the class of 1850–51, of which James DeKoven was a member. He was ranked second in the class and participated in the ceremony as described in the following excerpt. DeKoven fared much better than his classmate in the estimation of the reviewer:

> 'The Inner Life,' a philosophical poem, was pronounced by James De Koven, with much grace and ease of delivery. The subject was well treated, in an effective manner, and the versification was flowing and easy.[3]

1. "Columbia College Commencement."
2. "Columbia College Commencement."
3. "Columbia College Commencement."

This event marks the end of the first four years of DeKoven's higher education in New York City. Although DeKoven did not write about his time at the college, it is possible to reconstruct what he experienced during his three years as a scholar there. The lack of a "fourth year" will be explained later. It is more difficult to recreate the nature of his earlier education due to the very limited amount of information. This commencement ceremony also marks the progress of James DeKoven to the final three years of his formal education at the General Theological Seminary, located in New York City. An information gap exists between his attendance at the Middletown Males High School in 1842 and his enrollment at Columbia College, New York City, in the fall of 1847.

EARLY EDUCATION

One aspect of James DeKoven's early education is mentioned by his niece, Helen Beach, in her historical work on the descendants of Jacob Sebor.[4] According to Beach, Margaret Yates Sebor, James DeKoven's mother, could no longer afford outside instruction for her younger children after the death of her husband. She also could not afford to send them to a private academy for their education. At this time her eldest son, Henry Louis, stepped in to serve as tutor for Cornelia, thirteen, Fanny, eleven, James, nine, and John, seven.[5] Such an arrangement can be explained in part by the complicated settlement of Henry L. DeKoven's estate, as well as the year-long period of mourning observed by the family. This was a busy time for the younger Henry, as he was studying at Wesleyan College while working with Rev. Samuel Jarvis in preparation for his ordination. Henry Louis was ordained deacon at Christ Church, Middletown on June 4, 1843, and on October 29, 1843, was appointed minister of St. Stephen's Church, East Haddam in Middlesex County.

Henry's role as family tutor did not last very long. The first indication of formal schooling for James appears in the *General Record of Middletown Male High School* dated March 2, 1842.[6] James DeKoven is listed as student no. 113 and is enrolled in the session from February to April 1842. According to the registration listing, he received instruction in arithmetic, grammar, and Latin. He was also given marks in conduct.

4. Beach, *Descendants of Jacob Sebor.* 6.
5. "DeKoven Family of Middletown."
6. *General Record of Middletown Male High School*, Mar. 2, 1842.

There is also an indication, in this very limited entry, of his number of absences: seventeen during the twelve weeks of the term. This is the first record of formal education and also the first evidence of either illness or some difficulty about attendance. His grades did not seem to suffer, as he received mostly nines in arithmetic and grammar, and eights and nines in Latin.[7] John DeKoven, student no. 114, joined James for the May–June session for instruction in reading and writing. Once again James is absent frequently, thirty-eight times, while John has only three absences. No grades are marked for this session. The frequent absences leave unanswered questions as to their cause: was he seriously ill? This difficulty with attendance is repeated in his later educational experiences.

Another intriguing question for which there seems to be no satisfying answer relates to the decision of James DeKoven to go to New York City for more formal education. The association of the DeKoven family with Wesleyan College in Middletown seemed to be an important connection. Henry Louis, Sr. was on the founding board of directors of that institution. Both of James's older brothers, Henry and William, attended the school. Henry graduated from Wesleyan before he began his private studies for the priesthood with Rev. Jarvis. Was James guided in this decision to go to New York City by his elder brother, family friends, or his own desire to be educated at two institutions closely affiliated with the Episcopal Church?

Between July 1842 and October 1847, when James DeKoven enrolled as a freshman at Columbia College, he had undertaken more serious studies than known records would indicate, thus enabling him to meet the admission requirements of this school. These standards emphasized what was a traditional classical formation:

> No student shall be admitted into the Freshman Class, unless he be accurately acquainted with the grammar of both the Greek and Latin tongues, including such rules of prosody as may be applicable to such of the poets as he is to be examined upon; be master of Caesar's Commentaries, on the Gallic War, except the last book; of the Orations of Cicero against Catiline and for the Poet Archias; of the first six books of Virgil's Aeneid; of Sallust; of the Gospel According to St. Luke and St. John, and the Acts of the Apostles; of Jacob's *Greek Reader;* of the first three books of Xenophon's *Anabasis*, and the first three books of Homer's *Iliad.*

7. A ten-point grading scale was used in this school, where ten was the highest possible mark.

> He shall also be able to translate English into grammatical Latin; and shall be well versed in the first four rules of *Arithmetic* . . .[8]

These stringent and limiting guidelines for admission were in effect for many years and had an impact on who could plan on attending Columbia College. From what we know of the formal education that DeKoven had received, the question remains, "Where did he gain his preparation to meet these very specific admission standards?"

There is the possibility that James DeKoven spent the years prior to his enrollment in Columbia College at the Columbia Grammar and Preparatory School. This institution had been established in 1764, under the "superintendence of the Faculty of the College." Its creation took place just ten years after the founding of King's College. The curriculum of this school was geared toward preparing students for a curriculum as outlined in the King's College statutes.

Attempts to determine if there was a connection between James DeKoven and Columbia Grammar have proved inconclusive. There are no records of enrollment lists of students at the grammar school prior to the 1890s.[9] The fact remains that DeKoven obviously had pursued a serious preparation before enrolling in the college. Another question that is raised if he did attend Columbia Grammar and Preparatory School concerns his living arrangements. The school was not a boarding school; students generally lived with their families. Although some writers have indicated that the DeKoven family moved to New York City after the death of Henry Louis, Sr., there is no proof of this move.[10]

8. "Of Admission, Extract from the College Statutes," *Catalogue of the Officers and Students of Columbia College*, 22.

9. Communication from Elaine Kingman, Assistant to the Head of School, Columbia Grammar & Preparatory School, dated March 4, 2020. Search in the archival collections of Columbia University have not resulted in any evidence of DeKoven's attendance at the preparatory school.

10. As far as I have been able to determine, Mrs. DeKoven never moved from Middletown. References made by Morgan Dix in a footnote, do suggest that some of the early writing efforts of James were known by the pastor of Grace Church in Brooklyn Heights. This does not prove that the family lived or had moved to this neighborhood. There are two letters written by James DeKoven from New York City that support the fact that he lived in the city prior to attending Columbia College. The first is dated May 1846, and the second, to Ellen Woodward of Middletown, dated December 16, 1846. Both of these letters are in a private collection in New York City.

COLUMBIA COLLEGE

The college that James DeKoven entered in the fall of 1846 when he was barely sixteen years old was a small, classically oriented school. Founded in 1754 as King's College, it was a city institution that differed in several ways from its chief rivals in New England. It was not a residence college like Harvard and Yale. Students at Columbia lived off campus, most frequently with family. Although not officially connected with any one religion, the preponderance of students and faculty were Episcopal in belief. The curriculum that James studied in 1847 was essentially that described in a review in 1809: "By 1810 the early Columbia College faculty had stabilized at five full-time members: one each to teach Greek, Latin, Moral Philosophy, mathematics and natural philosophy, and experimental science. It would remain at five for the next half-century."[11] The men who filled these positions were remarkably stable, too. Three of the faculty members who taught during DeKoven's enrollment averaged thirty-three years of teaching at Columbia. This longevity, combined with the physical continuity of the institution over a century in the same location, helps explain in some way this hesitancy toward change. As Robert McGaughey states in his work on the history of Columbia, "A student in the 1850s would have had little need to describe his schooldays to his father, an 1820s Columbia graduate, or even to his grandfather, a 1790s graduate: nothing much had changed."[12]

The building where DeKoven attended classes was the original College Hall, opened in 1760, which had undergone several renovations and additions over the years. When DeKoven was a student, College Hall was one of the city's oldest buildings. The school year and school days were amazingly predictable. There were two terms each lasting fifteen weeks, the first from early October to January and the second from February to June. Commencement usually took place in mid-July. The school week was even more established, each day beginning with a half-hour chapel service at 9 a.m., followed by four one-hour class periods.[13] All students in the same year took the same subjects. Students had no choice in the courses they took. Each day they had four classes. Classes ended at 1:30 P.M. and students returned home by 2:00 P.M. There were no free periods and no free time because there "was no place to put students not in

11. McCaughey, *Stand Columbia*, 98.

12. McCaughey, *Stand Columbia*, 104.

13. McCaughey, *Stand Columbia*, 106.

class."[14] Although students did not live on campus, faculty members did, taking up a large portion of the available space in the building.

The curriculum was as firmly established and inflexible as the daily and weekly schedule. In order to graduate, students had to complete thirty-two required semester units; each unit consisting of five class hours per week throughout the semester. The heavy emphasis on classical studies is reflected in the fact that fourteen of the thirty-two units required of each student were in Greek and Latin. Of the remaining requirements, eight units were in mathematics and sciences and eight units in the humanities, including English literature and rhetoric. A course in political economy was added for the third year in 1826 and moral and political philosophy was added to the final year curriculum. The contents of each year's courses were carefully described in the college catalogs, which were published annually. This prescribed classical curriculum at Columbia lasted into the 1880s, well beyond that of comparable colleges.[15] In many ways James DeKoven was the consummate classical scholar. He continued many aspects of this classical training both at St. John's Hall and Racine College, where for many years he was one of the instructors in the Latin language and classical literature.

Although Columbia College was not officially an Episcopal institution, the fact remains that Episcopalians were the largest denomination among the trustees, as well as the faculty and the student body. DeKoven was thus surrounded by members of his own faith and undoubtedly felt comfortable with the ideas and religious practices of his teachers and fellow students.[16] The faculty members during DeKoven's years at Columbia included two ordained Episcopal priests, two avowedly devout Episcopal laymen, and one ordained Lutheran minister, who taught German.

The small number of faculty, and their amazing longevity in their positions, added to the fact that they lived in the college building, all point to the impact that teachers had on the students at Columbia. Several were exemplars who influenced the thinking and the beliefs of their

14. McCaughey, *Stand Columbia*, 106.

15. McCaughey, *Stand Columbia*, 156.

16. In 1830 the Columbia trustees announced that, for a one-time gift of $20,000, any New York City Protestant church could thereafter send up to four sons of church members to the College annually without further payment of tuition or fees. This was an attempt to broaden the religious affiliation of the student body. McCaughey, *Stand Columbia*, 85. This offer was not taken up by any churches in the city and the student body remained predominantly Episcopal.

young scholars. Among these men there are four of special importance in the intellectual development of James DeKoven.

DEKOVEN'S TEACHERS AT COLUMBIA

John McVickar became the professor of moral philosophy, rhetoric, and *belles lettres* at Columbia College in 1817 at the age of thirty. An ordained Episcopal priest, he played a significant role in the religious life of this denomination in New York City, as well as in the early history of the General Theological Seminary.[17] He taught at Columbia until 1864 and died in 1867. He was notable for introducing "political economy" to the curriculum.[18] This was one of the first examples of a social studies discipline being introduced into a college curriculum in the United States. This did not, however, lessen his devotion to and insistence on the traditional classical curriculum. He taught almost all courses in the college, and the notes from his courses that James DeKoven kept reflect the thoroughness of his teaching.[19] Like most of his colleagues, he was a graduate of Columbia College.

Charles Anthon, called "Bull" Anthon by students, was the professor of the Greek and Latin Languages and Literatures for thirty-seven years, beginning in 1820. During twenty-five of these years, he also served as rector of Columbia Grammar School. He had studied to be a lawyer, but his true love was being a professor. He had been a brilliant student at Columbia, never married, and was dedicated to Columbia and its students, who respected and feared him, too. He was a devout Episcopalian and was known for his editorial work with textbooks for Latin and Greek studies.[20] Two of the notebooks that DeKoven saved reflect the influence of Anthon on the classical studies that DeKoven pursued throughout his life. His ability in the Greek language is evident in the meticulous transcriptions in his notebooks on Greek literature and history.

17. Dawley, *Story of the General Theological Seminary*, 120.

18. McCaughey, *Stand Columbia*, 85.

19. Included in the notebooks that DeKoven saved from his time at Columbia College are four that are clearly identified as originating in the lectures given by "Professor McVickar—Columbia College." These are the titles given to the items, "Notes on Modern History, Professor McVickar, D.D., Vol. 1, but last written"; "Political Economy"; "Notes on History for professor McVickar, Vol. 2, but first written"; "Greek/Roman history, Notes on Dr. McVickar lectures, second part of notebook."

20. McCaughey, *Stand Columbia*, 98–99.

Anthon had an amazing collection of Greek and Latin authors, as well as commentaries on these works. In many ways, Anthon's influence on DeKoven continued throughout his life, especially in the personal library he created.

James Renwick was another long-serving faculty member of Columbia College, being the professor of natural and experimental philosophy and chemistry from 1820–53. In this position he taught chemistry, geology, and physics. He created a laboratory for his own experiments as well as those of his students.[21] DeKoven was thus introduced to a broader conception of higher education through the teaching of Renwick, another Episcopalian and Columbia graduate. His influence can be seen in DeKoven's insistence that students at Racine College have a thorough grounding in the sciences. The construction of the laboratory wing of the new gymnasium in 1875 at Racine College continued the influence of this professor.

Another long serving faculty member at Columbia during DeKoven's years was Henry Drisler Jr., adjunct professor of Greek and Latin languages. He was appointed in 1843 and would eventually serve for fifty-four years. He first taught at the Columbia Grammar School and over the course of his career filled almost every position at Columbia, which he loved passionately. He was a bachelor, a deeply devout Episcopalian, and a tireless editor of educational texts.[22]

21. McCaughey, *Stand Columbia,* 100.

22. McCaughey, *Stand Columbia,* 101.

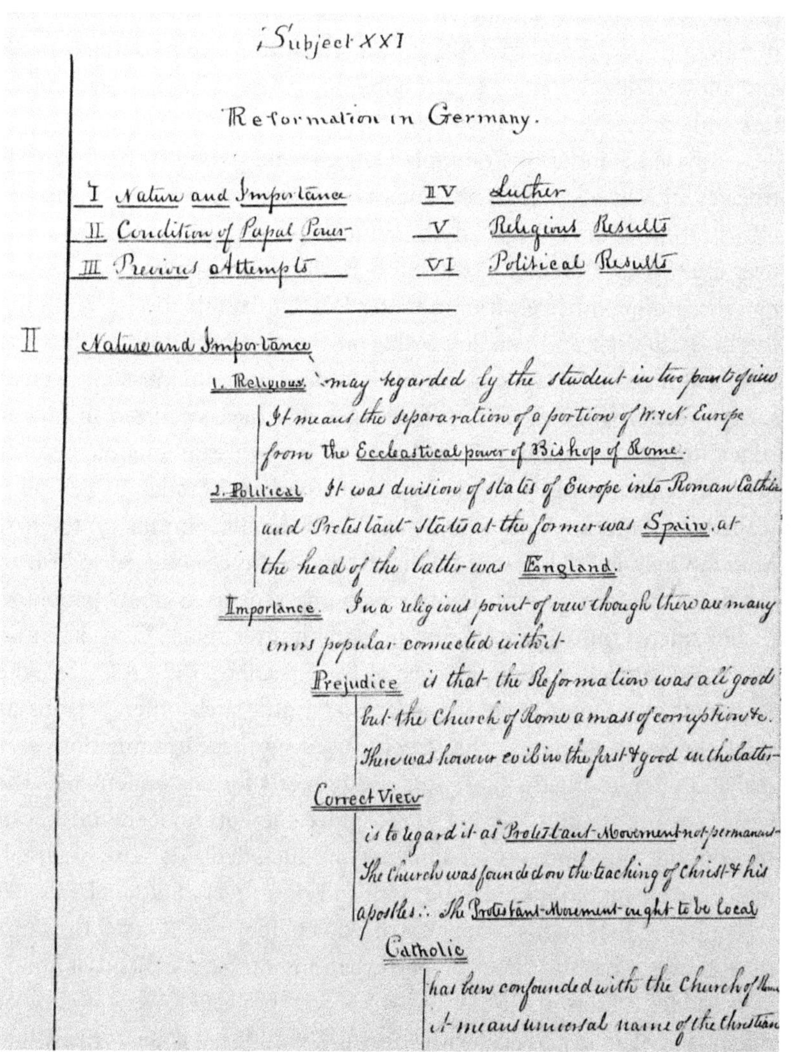

Subject XXI

Reformation in Germany.

I Nature and Importance — IV Luther
II Condition of Papal Power — V Religious Results
III Previous Attempts — VI Political Results

II Nature and Importance

1. Religious. may regarded by the student in two points of view
It means the separation of a portion of W. & N. Europe
from the Ecclesiastical power of Bishop of Rome.

2. Political It was division of states of Europe into Roman Catholic
and Protestant States at the former was Spain, at
the head of the latter was England.

Importance. In a religious point of view though there are many
errors popular connected with it

Prejudice is that the Reformation was all good
but the Church of Rome a mass of corruption &c.
There was however evil in the first & good in the latter

Correct View
is to regard it as Protestant Movement not permanent
The Church was founded on the teaching of Christ & his
apostles ∴ The Protestant Movement ought to be local

Catholic
has been confounded with the Church of Rome
it means universal name of the Christian

Notes on History for Professor McVickar, D.D. Vol 2

These summaries of the faculty with whom James DeKoven studied give some insight into the type of dedication he found among the teachers during this first experience of higher education. These years of study and working with different types of instruction and different competencies also prepared him to some extent for the administrative tasks he would encounter at St. John's Hall and Racine College. In many ways Columbia College was not too different than Racine College as far as instruction, faculty competency, examinations and student issues. The numbers of faculty and students at both institutions were relatively small and allowed direct contact that resulted in a close bond between educators and educated.

Revised Statutes of Columbia College were passed by the board of trustees in May 1848. The revision's twenty-five chapters cover the administration of the college, admission to the college, the course of study over four years, attendance, student behavior and discipline and examinations, among other topics.[23] Chapter IX, "Of Examinations," is among the most specific and detailed listing in the statutes. It also differs the most from current-day ideas about education; for this reason, it gives today's reader some ideas of the changes that have occurred in higher education in our country. There were to be two examination periods in each academic year: one to begin on the first Monday in February (called the "intermediate" exams) and the second beginning on the first Monday in July. These were public events, to be announced in two of the daily newspapers with invitations being sent to as many people as the President "thinks proper." Sub-paragraph three states, "The examinations shall be held in the presence of the President, the Professors, the Students, of a Committee of the Trustees, and such other persons as shall choose to attend."[24] The stress caused by these examinations was real and often resulted in absences and requests for postponements. The writers of the statutes seemed to recognize the nature of the impact of these public questionings on students and included this sub-paragraph five: "The examinations are to be close and rigid; every Student being left to stand or fall upon his proper merits; due tenderness being at the same time shown, that the effect or perturbations may be avoided as much as possible."[25] From the little that is known about DeKoven's ability, or rather lack of ability, to deal with stressful situations, it appears likely that these examination periods were difficult for him.

Several of the chapters of these statutes provide insight into the life of the institution, especially those dealing with attendance, student behavior, and as listed in chapter VII, "Of Crimes and Punishment." Interestingly enough, it was the board of trustees who administered the discipline and not the faculty or president.

23. *Statutes of Columbia College.*

24. "Of Examinations," 19.

25. "Of Examinations," 20.

The student body at Columbia College was never very large until late in the nineteenth century. Class sizes during the years that James DeKoven attended the college averaged thirty-four students. Once in a while there was an increase to perhaps fifty. Interestingly enough, the size was similar to that of Racine College's total student body when DeKoven was in charge. DeKoven's class had thirty-three students when he was a sophomore and thirty-four when he was a senior.[26] The total school enrollment during his sophomore year was 135. The Columbia Grammar and Preparatory School had larger numbers, with 225 boys enrolled during the same period. The entire student/faculty orientation of Racine College was in many ways the polar opposite of Columbia College. There was no way that the student body and faculty formed a family at Columbia, and this was the main objective of James DeKoven in elaborating his policies and philosophy at Racine College.

Most students who attended Columbia College and the General Theological Seminary lived in New York City or its suburban areas. In DeKoven's sophomore class there were two students from Connecticut, including James, and one from New Jersey. The class enrollment remained relatively stable from the sophomore to the senior year: one student did not continue after the sophomore year, and two students were added in the senior year.

When DeKoven began his freshman year at Columbia College, he was barely sixteen years old. He did not have the security of campus housing but had to negotiate a city of almost 500,000. Did his experience in New York City already include some years at a preparatory institution in the city? His family life in the small city of Middletown did not compare with what he would experience in the nation's largest urban area.

We do know of two addresses where DeKoven lived during his years at Columbia. During his sophomore year, his place of residence was listed as 69 Irving Place, and during his senior year the address given is Third Avenue, near Twenty-third Street. For the three years of catalogs that are available, his hometown is listed as Middletown, Connecticut. Other than the two published addresses, nothing is known about his living arrangements while at Columbia. There is a possibility that he lived with the family of his older sister, Mary Beach, whose husband was a businessman in the city. Another possibility is the very successful boarding house operated by Elizabeth Sebor Isaacs Smedes, his father's half-sister and

26. A school catalog for the first year of DeKoven's enrollment at Columbia College has not been located.

mother of his classmate and cousin John Esten Cooke Smedes. Another close family member who lived in New York was his uncle and business partner of his father, Charles Robert Sebor.[27]

The lack of information concerning DeKoven's junior year at Columbia is due to the fact that he was absent for the entire year because of illness. (The information after his name in the college catalog indicates his residence—Middletown, Connecticut—with an asterisk. At the end of the listing there is this notation: "*Left College"). The fact that he missed his junior year at Columbia is also noted in the obituary provided in the *College Mercury* at the time of his death. No additional information is provided in either source. The fact that DeKoven did return for his senior year and graduated second in the class provides positive indication of his intellectual abilities.

There are no letters or journal entries in which DeKoven commented directly on his education at either Columbia College or the General Theological Seminary. However, there do remain fourteen carefully written and organized school notebooks that clearly bear witness to DeKoven's hard work and diligence. He obviously attached great importance to these notebooks, as they were saved over the years and are now housed in the archival collection of the DeKoven Center. Most of these notebooks are from his time at Columbia; several contain notes and information from both institutions. Some are dated, and the instructor of the course where the notes originated is indicated. The handwriting is generally very clear and precise; DeKoven obviously took great care to make the notebooks neat and attractive. Several of the notebooks were created from other notes and sources. Taken as a whole, they form a remarkable artifact of the higher education of a dedicated student and scholar.[28]

James DeKoven was no different than many eighteen-year-old students; he liked to doodle and frequently drew and wrote on the inside pages of his carefully filled-out notebooks. He provided several versions of his name: J de Koven; James de Koven, Esquire; James DeKoven. The last version became the most frequent. He also did some drawings and wrote the names of two classmates on these cover pages: George Seymour and J. E. Smedes. Seymour was his roommate at General, a good friend and colleague of many years; Smedes was a cousin from his grandmother

27. The presence of these close relatives in the city at the time that DeKoven was a student provide some assurance of a support network for this young student.

28. The content of the fourteen notebooks include notes on the Gospels, philosophy, modern history, political economy, and Greek and Roman history.

DeKoven's second marriage. At one point, for no known reason, he even writes his brother's name using this form of the signature: John de Koven, Esquire.

There is one interesting note found in the back of notebook fourteen: "Received 3 trunks for Middletown for Mr deKoven, May 28, 1851." It is signed: Redger. Was James DeKoven planning his move back home after graduation from Columbia? Why would he have three trunks? Perhaps his book collection was already beginning to grow. The space he would be moving to next at the General Theological Seminary would be very small. The search for a piece of paper to write a receipt could have been done hurriedly; the back of this notebook served in a pinch.

GENERAL THEOLOGICAL SEMINARY

The three years from 1851 to 1854 that James DeKoven spent at the General Theological Seminary in New York City fell between two of the most troubling periods in the early history of that institution. The 1840s had witnessed the accusations and incriminations connected with the Oxford Movement and its purported influence on the faculty and students at the seminary.[29] The mid-1850s were a period of financial crisis for the school as a result of the earlier turmoil, and its future was much in doubt. Although DeKoven did not seem personally involved in these two controversies as they occurred, similar issues eventually played an important role in his own professional life. He, too, would be frequently condemned for what were considered his "romish" ideas, and he also would know the challenges of leading an Episcopal institution that received little or no financial support from its denomination.

The training of priests in the early American period of the Episcopal Church resembled that used for the law profession: candidates studied/read with a mentor and were eventually recommended for ordination, or not, by that person and other presbyters. This was the manner by which DeKoven's older brother, Henry, prepared for his entry into the priesthood. This lack of seminaries and organized seminary training was a regular topic of discussion at annual conventions in the early dioceses and at the triennial General Convention. A formal resolution was adopted at

29. An early nineteenth-century movement which reasserted the apostolic and catholic heritage of Anglicanism. It began among members of the Church of England at Oxford University who sought to incorporate some older Christian traditions into Anglican liturgy and theology.

the meeting of May 1817 to create a theological seminary to be located in New York City. The first year of operation began in the spring of 1819. Six students constituted the seminary's enrollment in its first academic year.[30]

During its early history this seminary definitely had its share of problems, generally financial, resulting in debates about the true value of such an institution. The struggles associated with the seminary can be ascribed, in part, to the unwieldiness of the board of trustees. Since it was designated the seminary for the Protestant Episcopal Church of the United States, all dioceses were given a role in its governance. A byzantine formula for allotting membership on the board was established, "By 1838, when the board included 138 clerical and lay members in addition to the bishops, 57 represented the diocese of New York."[31] The real work of overseeing the seminary fell to the standing committee of the board, whose membership was made up of individuals from the city. This almost exclusive association with New York City led to a "let them do it" attitude on the part of others in the church.[32]

During the first years of its existence, classes met at different locations in the city. There was even a period of five years that the school, its faculty and students, as well as administration, moved to New Haven, Connecticut (1820–25). In 1826, thanks in part to the generosity of Clement Clarke Moore, the General Theological Seminary became a residential college in the Chelsea district of New York City. The first seminary building was built on land donated by Moore and provided living quarters for students and faculty, recitation rooms and a library. This East Building brought about a change in the concept of the preparation of priests for the Episcopal Church. The positive impact of a community of men residing, working and learning together caused a positive extension of the normal period of candidacy to three years.[33]

By 1834, the student body had outgrown the original building and the trustees voted to build a second structure: the West Building. It was designed to accommodate sixty students in double rooms. It also had classrooms and offices for the administration of the institution. The two buildings could comfortably house ninety students; this capacity was reached in the 1835–36 academic year.[34]

30. Dawley, *Story of the General Theological Seminary*, 48.

31. Dawley, *Story of the General Theological Seminary*, 99

32. Dawley, *Story of the General Theological Seminary*, 99–100.

33. Dawley, *Story of the General Theological Seminary*, 97.

34. This number was not reached again until 1879–80. Dawley, *Story of the General*

As indicated earlier, the 1840s were a decade of turmoil brought about by developments both in England and the United States. Two significant factions had developed in the American Church.

> The churchmanship controversy between the High Churchmen and the Evangelicals, which had been smoldering with increasing intensity for a half-dozen years, was suddenly fanned into a flame of partisan strife that had disastrous effects upon the welfare of the Seminary.[35]

The event that brought the situation to a boil was the challenge made at the diaconate ordination of a candidate sponsored by New York's high church bishop, Benjamin Onderdonk. The candidate, Arthur Carey, was accused of holding views in "close conformity with those of the Church of Rome."[36] The ordination took place on July 2, 1843, at St. Stephen's Church in New York City. The impact on the church was amazingly swift. Sides were taken; editorials and books written. The controversy had been growing slowly since the publication in 1839 of an American edition of the ninety pamphlets called *Tracts for the Times*. These tracts had launched the Oxford Movement in England, and when published in the United States had received the enthusiastic support of Bishop Onderdonk.

The effect of this division within the church was especially harmful on the morale of faculty and students, as well as the reputation of the General Theological Seminary. Its status as an institution of theological learning had been growing.[37] Now the evangelical faction of the church became convinced that General was a hotbed of romish beliefs and practices. Bishop Onderdonk was probably the most visible of the professors of the seminary, but he was not the only one who was challenged by the various inquiries launched by the board of trustees and the House of Bishops of the General Convention. A committee of inquiry was created by the trustees, and questions were written by the House of Bishops. A set of forty-three questions was sent to each professor, who was directed to provide answers to these questions regarding his beliefs and teaching. An example of the type of question asked is the following:

> Third. Whether in the intercourse between the Professors, or any of them & the Students, either in the Seminary apartments

Theological Seminary, 123.

35. Dawley, *Story of the General Theological Seminary*, 145.

36. Dawley, *Story of the General Theological Seminary*, 146.

37. Dawley, *Story of the General Theological Seminary*, 176–79.

> or elsewhere, any influence, direct or indirect is exerted with a view to inculcate any errors of the Romish Church, or any doctrine inconsistent with the articles of the Prot: Episc: Church, or having a tendency to encourage of palliate any such errors or doctrines.[38]

Students were also challenged concerning their religious practices and goals. Two students were expelled and two withdrew from the seminary. The enrollment at General declined rapidly.

When James DeKoven enrolled in 1851, he entered an institution that was still dealing with the fallout of the tempests of the mid-forties. Fewer than half the number of students attended during his years as had been enrolled twenty years earlier. Although he had not been directly involved in the divisive events, he undoubtedly knew of them; his own beliefs and leanings were more in keeping with the high church faction. He obviously knew of the Oxford Movement and supported many of the practices and doctrines championed by this group. In his later life, at general conventions he was called upon to explain and defend many of the issues that had already been broached during the turmoil surrounding this decade of institutional strife. Given the bitterness that resulted from the affair surrounding the Carey ordination, the resulting persecution of Bishop Onderdonk, and his eventual disgrace, it could not have come as a surprise to James DeKoven when he was attacked so consistently and thoroughly on many occasions during the public years of his life.

The curriculum at General was fixed by the statutes of the institution and based on books prescribed in the authorized "Course of Ecclesiastical Studies" of 1804.[39] It was possible for new titles to be added or substituted from time to time with approval of the faculty. However, this was a relatively rare occurrence, and the list as approved in 1804 was essentially the list in use during the years of DeKoven's attendance. In the twenty years between 1835 and 1855, fewer than a half-dozen books were discarded and a like number added.[40] The only area where there was change was in the discipline of ecclesiastical history, which, by its nature, was an evolving field of study. In effect, course work was not defined by subject matter but rather by the name of the professor and the day and time of his recitation

38. Dawley, *Story of the General Theological Seminary*, 162.
39. Dawley, *Story of the General Theological Seminary*, 87
40. Dawley, *Story of the General Theological Seminary*, 134.

period. This system continued through the 1850s, when course listings began to be described as they are now in college catalogs.

There were usually two periods of classes each day, each of an hour or an hour and a half. They usually consisted of recitations on assigned readings. The use of the lecture method of instruction was virtually unknown. Discussion of ideas or topics in the classroom was also not common. Different organizations and societies provided such opportunities for students. The monthly meetings of the Theological Society, in which all students were expected to participate, was viewed as the forum for expression of ideas.[41] Recitation periods were essentially a time for questions to be posed by the professor on an assigned reading and for answers to be provided by the students. Just as seen in the description of Columbia College where evolution was slow, students from one era would have felt comfortable in the classrooms of another because so little change took place. The same could be said of General. The lecture/discussion method of classroom instruction did not become commonplace until the 1870s. Its adoption was the source of serious discussion and much debate. There had, however, been some nomenclature changes in the classification of students from First, Second and Third Classes, to Junior, Middle and Senior years.

The college catalogs provide information about which professors provided course instruction for which of the three classes each year, but there is very little information about pedagogical standards. The examination periods continued to be feared:

> The examination had always been regarded by the students with considerable trepidation, and it appears to have become an increasing source of anxiety as the years passed. Students were sometimes too ill to attend, suffering perhaps from nerves and vapors, and more than one collapsed in despair.[42]

Chapter VI of the Statutes of the General Theological Seminary, "Of the Professors," spelled out who would be responsible for instruction at the Seminary. According to this chapter, there were to be professors of Oriental and Greek Literature; Biblical Learning and the Interpretation of Scripture; Evidences of Revealed Religion and Moral Science in Relationship

41. Dawley, *Story of the General Theological Seminary*, 89.

42. Dawley, *Story of the General Theological Seminary*, 135.

to Theology; Systematic Divinity; Ecclesiastical History; Nature, Ministry and Polity of the Church; and Pastoral Theology and Pulpit Eloquence.[43]

During his three years at General, James DeKoven studied under the following five individuals. The first was Samuel Hulbeart Turner, professor of biblical learning from 1821 to 1861. During his forty years of teaching, Turner slowly moved away from the recitation method to lectures and discussion. Turner was a consummate scholar, constantly learning and studying.[44] The next was Milo Mahan, professor of ecclesiastical history, 1851–64. Mahan succeeded John David Obilgy in this professorship in 1851, both of these men being fine examples of scholar/teachers.[45] Their influence on DeKoven was obviously important for the position he filled at Nashotah when he came to Wisconsin in 1854. Samuel Roosevelt Johnson served as professor of dogmatic theology, also called systematic divinity. He was a high churchman, much influenced by John Henry Hobart, and promoted daily Eucharist at the seminary. Benjamin Isaac Haight, professor of pastoral theology and pulpit eloquence, brought to his teaching his personal experience as rector of All Saints Church in New York City. He stressed proper methods of conducting religious ceremonies and provided examples of effective preaching to the seminarians. The instructor of biblical languages during DeKoven's years at General was George H. Houghton. He was rector of the Church of the Transfiguration in the City and an avowed proponent of the Oxford Movement. DeKoven's ability in Greek is evident in his notebooks and obviously shows the influence of Houghton.

Another individual listed as a professor at the General Theological Seminary during the DeKoven years was Bishop Benjamin Onderdonk. Although he did not teach after his suspension in 1844, efforts to have his name removed from the list of the seminary faculty failed. His leadership from afar was not enough to provide the stability needed during difficult times at the institution, but his wisdom and Christian charity in submission were wonderful examples for those associated with him. Students were known to visit him, and he welcomed them to his home.[46]

43. *Constitution, Act of Incorporation*, 19.

44. Dawley, *Story of the General Theological Seminary*, 191.

45. Mahan resigned his position in 1864 due to his support of the Confederate cause during the Civil War.

46. Dawley, *Story of the General Theological Seminary*, 173.

Requirements for admission to the General Theological Seminary are listed in Appendix C of the 1851 Statutes. There were several methods for meeting the qualifications necessary for acceptance.

> Every person producing to the Faculty satisfactory evidence of his having been admitted a candidate for Holy Orders, with full qualifications, according to the Canons of the Protestant Episcopal Church in the United States, shall be received as a Student in the Seminary. All others may be admitted, who shall produce satisfactory evidence of religious and moral character—of classical and scientific attainments—of attachment to the Protestant Episcopal Church, and in general such dispositions and habits as may render them apt and meet to exercise the ministry.[47]

The statutes also spell out competency requirements in Hebrew and Greek, biblical knowledge, and English composition. The annual report published the list of those admitted each year into the junior class along with the qualification they met for admission. Most frequently cited was the candidacy of an individual for a particular diocese. James DeKoven was admitted "on testimonial of moral and religious character."[48] He is not listed as a candidate for the Diocese of Connecticut, nor is his "attachment to the Protestant Episcopal Church" stressed. Other students admitted in the same year, 1851, had several qualifications listed to support their acceptance.

The seminary that James DeKoven attended at Chelsea Square in New York City had evolved into a very different institution from that first established in 1819. By the time of DeKoven's enrollment, the school had been on the campus at Chelsea[49] for twenty-five years and had grown to two almost identical structures called the East and West Buildings. The West Building, where DeKoven lived for three years, was designed with space for sixty students in double rooms. When compared with the East Building, the student rooms in the new structure were "lighter and pleasanter than those in the older building."[50] Each room had two sections, a study with a window, and a bedroom which was essentially a dark,

47. "Report of the Faculty," 25.

48. *Columbia College Catalog of 1852*, 25.

49. Professor Clement Clarke Moore, of "A Visit from St. Nicholas" fame, donated fifty-five usable city lots to the Seminary for the construction of a building. His summer home, called Chelsea Mansion, was next to this property. The first building was built in 1826; the second in 1836.

50. Dawley, *Story of the General Theological Seminary*, 124.

elongated closet. In the new building there were recitation rooms, a library, a large meeting area called the Long Room, and in 1845, the creation of a chapel on the floor above the Long Room. The decision to create a special place for worship reflects an evolution in the basic concept of the seminary:

> The prevailing notion of a quarter-century earlier, that the institution was a hostel for resident study, the advantage of which was chiefly convenient and companionable proximity, had slowly given way to a concept of the Seminary as primarily a group of men whose common life and vocation should find its empowering center in their regular corporate worship.[51]

In the early years of the institution, the faculty and administration admitted no responsibility for the religious life of the students but "assumed" that the spiritual duties of the seminarians would be fulfilled by their participation in the parish churches where they worked or with which they were connected.

One of the most successful activities of the students in the seminary were the Sunday school classes organized by the Sunday School Society. These classes were provided in association with local churches and grew to large numbers very quickly. The "Ragged School" that DeKoven and friends organized was designed for a more elementary-level student, most probably unschooled and unchurched.

Daily life and routine were established early in the existence of the Chelsea Square campus. The rising bell sounded at 6:30 a.m. during fall and winter and a half-hour earlier in spring. There were scheduled times for prayer, and eventually Holy Communion in the Seminary Chapel was instituted. What was effectively a "lights out" time occurred with the closing of the buildings at 11 p.m. By the time of DeKoven's enrollment, there was a "Boarding Club" which provided regularly scheduled meals in the basement refectory. There were two recitation periods scheduled each day except Saturday.

It was in this atmosphere of a "group of men with a common life and vocation" that James DeKoven developed several deep and rewarding friendships. His roommate during the three years at General was George F. Seymour. Like DeKoven, Seymour had studied at Columbia College. They traveled to Europe together in 1858, and their association continued through the years when both were responsible for educational

51. Dawley, *Story of the General Theological Seminary*, 125–26.

institutions. Seymour was eventually elected dean of General, and DeKoven served as a delegate from Wisconsin on the board of trustees of the seminary. Another close friend, who remained devoted to DeKoven throughout his life, was James DeWitt Clinton Locke, who served as rector of Grace Church in Chicago for thirty-five years and founded St. Luke's Hospital in that city. Clinton Locke defended DeKoven in many instances of controversy, served on the board of trustees for Racine College, and delivered what many consider the most moving tribute to DeKoven upon his death, entitled "The Upright Man."[52] A third classmate who remained a close friend through the years was W. Stevens Parker. He and his wife lived in Elizabeth, New Jersey, where DeKoven visited them frequently during his years at Racine College. Upon the death of his friend, Parker was elected warden of Racine College to succeed him. Parker's son, Alexis duPont Parker, was a student at Racine College and was with DeKoven when he died. Another member of the same graduating class was John E. C. Smedes, DeKoven's cousin, who eventually became rector of St. Paul's church in Beloit, Wisconsin. DeKoven maintained close ties with his friends, visited them whenever possible, and probably wrote to them frequently. We are fortunate that the letters he wrote to his classmate John Henry Hobart Brown were saved, justifying the assumption that DeKoven's letter-writing was frequent.[53] They maintained a close friendship over the years and became even closer when Hobart was elected first Bishop of Fond du Lac, Wisconsin.

Other friendships developed during these years of living in the world of the General Seminary. Among the individuals who played a role later in DeKoven's life were fellow students John Henry Hopkins Jr.; William E. Armitage, second bishop of Wisconsin; and Morgan Dix, rector of Trinity Church, New York, where he served for over fifty years. Evidently, James DeKoven was much appreciated by his colleagues and developed strong relationships with them over the years.

The years at General provided DeKoven with the opportunity to observe firsthand the controversies that developed in the Episcopal Church during the 1840s and 1850s. Although he may not have been an active participant in any of the disputes that took place, he was a keen observer and by these years had matured his own feelings and intellectual convictions. He would soon be called upon to defend his own positions on

52. Locke, "Upright Man."

53. Hobart Brown Letters, James DeKoven Collection, DeKoven Center Archives.

matters relevant to the issues of ritual and the Eucharist. His studies and interactions with professors and fellow students at General provided him with a solid background for such discussions. He had learned to present his ideas and defend them in a remarkably clear and forceful way.

There was also a very spiritual component of James DeKoven's personality. He believed strongly in the importance of prayer, and the following excerpt from the statutes of 1851 was an admonition he took very seriously:

> As mere Theological Learning, unaccompanied with real piety, is not a sufficient qualification for the Ministry, it is declared to be the duty of every student, with a humble reliance on Divine grace, to be assiduous in the cultivation of evangelical faith and a sound practical piety; neither contenting himself with mere formality, nor running into fanaticism. He must be careful to maintain, every day, stated periods of pious reading, meditation and devotion; and occasionally, special seasons for the more solemn and enlarged observance of these duties, together with that of such abstinence as is suited to extraordinary acts of devotion, have due regard to the Days and Seasons recommended for this purpose by the Church.[54]

The James DeKoven who finished his studies in New York City in July 1854 was a very confident and independent individual. Although his first plan for missionary-type work with two colleagues among the poor of New York City did not win approval,[55] he soon substituted a secondary plan and traveled to Wisconsin to explore his association with the school at Nashotah. The missionary spirit that was active at General definitely shaped his thinking and his actions. James DeKoven did not sit for the final exams of his senior year. There were twenty-three students who graduated, and DeKoven was ranked at the top of the class. In the final report for 1854, Dean Mahan made this statement as part of his summation of the year:

> Leave of absence was *granted.*
> On the 11th of April to James DeKoven of the Senior Class, to the end of the session, on account of infirm health.[56]

54. *Statutes of the General Theological Seminary*, 23.

55. Dix, "Preface," vii.

56. *General Theological Seminary Annual Meeting*, 878.

James DeKoven was ordained deacon in his home parish of Christ Church in Middletown, Connecticut on August 6, 1854, and arrived in Wisconsin just one month later, on September 15.

4

Mission to Wisconsin

JAMES DEKOVEN IN THE NORTHWEST

On May 18, 1854, James DeKoven was in Chicago, staying at the home of his oldest sister Elizabeth, and her husband, Thomas Dyer. He began a letter to his good friend John Henry Hobart Brown with this statement: "I received your kind letter the night before last on my return from Nashotah & hasten to answer."[1] Prior to writing this letter, DeKoven had traveled to Nashotah, Wisconsin, from Chicago, and in this letter provides impressions of this visit to his good friend and classmate.

This letter is the only written evidence that exists of DeKoven's impending decision to come to Wisconsin and accept a position at the seminary in Nashotah: "I wish you could have been with me at Nashotah. I am sure you would have enjoyed it."[2] We also learn from this letter that DeKoven had been suffering with some eye problems and explains his poor handwriting due to this condition ("for I have quite a weak eye"). He tells Hobart that he had begun the letter two days earlier but had to put off continuing it until his eyesight improved.[3]

1. Hobart Brown Letter, May 18, 1854. DeKoven Center Archives.

2. Hobart Brown Letter, May 18, 1854. DeKoven Center Archives.

3. Hobart Brown Letter, May 18, 1854. DeKoven Center Archives. "Indeed, two days having elapsed since I began this letter as I have had time to get much better." DeKoven indicates that he had heard that Hobart was also suffering from eye problems.

In general, James DeKoven did not deal well with the stress of the end-of-year academic activities, the examinations, and assignments. He had studied and read to the point that he had damaged his eyes. He was a dedicated student and his efforts resulted in his graduating first in his class at General in July 1854. However, at the end of his senior year he was granted a leave of absence from his classes. The following comment is from the annual report of the seminary's dean, Professor Mahan:

> The routine of study has been interrupted, however, to a greater extent than usual, by sickness and other causes, which have rendered it necessary to excuse several of the most diligent of the Students from the customary examination at the end of the year.[4]

On page seventeen of the same report, there is this notation under the heading, "Leave of Absence granted: On the 11th of April to James DeKoven of the Senior Class at the end of the session, on account of infirm health."[5] This explains why DeKoven could be in Illinois before the end of the academic year and why he was suffering from some inconvenience due to his eyesight. DeKoven benefitted from this dispensation to travel to Chicago and visit the mission school established by Bishop Kemper at Nashotah.

Why did James DeKoven come to Wisconsin to explore his future? He was ending a successful academic career at the General Theological Seminary, and looked forward to a future as a promising scholar and preacher. He also had good connections within the ecclesiastical organization of the established Episcopal Church. According to Morgan Dix in his preface to the DeKoven *Sermons* published in 1880, at the time of his diaconate ordination, James had offers in New York for positions in two parishes.[6] Pope repeats Dix's statement almost verbatim in his biography of DeKoven published nineteen years later: "He declined a call to a charming parish in Brooklyn, and another to an attractive work at Lower Red Hook, on the Hudson . . ."[7] James's older brother Henry was rector at St. Paul's Church in Red Hook at the time and had arranged a position

4. *Dean's Annual Report*, 13.

5. *Dean's Annual Report*, 17.

6. Dix, "Preface," In *Sermons Preached on Various Occasions*, vi. "Thereupon [after his diaconate ordination] he received a call to a charming parish in Brooklyn, and another to an attractive work at Lower Red Hook on the Hudson; but he declined them."

7. Pope, *Life of the Reverend James DeKoven*, 12.

for his brother in a neighboring community. No name is given for the "charming parish in Brooklyn" mentioned by both authors.

DeKoven's interest in coming to Nashotah was a natural consequence of his studies at the General Theological Seminary and the missionary movement that existed in the Protestant Episcopal Church at the time. In 1835, the General Convention of the Episcopal Church had decided to consecrate missionary bishops for the evangelization of the Western Territories of the expanding country. Jackson Kemper, who early in his career had demonstrated an interest in preaching to the unchurched in remote areas of Pennsylvania, was chosen to be the first bishop. His missionary diocese covered what was called the Northwest Territory and included the states of Indiana, Missouri, Wisconsin, Minnesota, and Nebraska. His efforts to attract ordained priests as well as seminarians to this "wilderness" area led him to undertake creative efforts in recruitment. Kemper was on the board of trustees of General and in 1840 had turned to the students of this seminary with his idea of establishing a school and mission in Wisconsin.[8]

In his diary, Bishop Kemper recounts his first meeting with four interested seminary students:

> January 20, 1841, New York—Were four students, Hobart, Breck, Adams and Miles. I saw them last night. They are ready to go to Wisconsin, or any other place, under or with me to open a Christian school and preach the Gospel. The prospect is highly promising and the step very important. May God for Christ's sake give it His blessing. I am to see them again the 21st.[9]

In subsequent meetings, the bishop and the four students outlined the details of the project they were to undertake. They chose as head of their mission Rev. Richard F. Cadle, who was already in Wisconsin, and established the requirements for their successful work. One of Bishop Kemper's main responsibilities, in addition to finding financing for this enterprise, was to obtain a release from the diocesan bishop of each of the young participants. He outlined the decisions made by these worthy "apostles" in a statement included in his diary entry for February 11:

> Messrs. Wm. Adams, J. Lloyd Breck. J. H. Hobart and James W. Miles, Members of the Senior Class of the General Theological

8. Bishop Kemper had established a training school in St. Louis that was not successful. "Story of Kemper College, St. Louis." *Nashotah Scholiast,* Vol. II, No. 3, 41.

9. "Extracts from Bishop Kemper's Diary," 1–3.

> Seminary, have after due reflection, determined with the consent of their respective diocesans, to devote themselves, as soon as they have received Holy Orders, to the Territory of Wisconsin, in the hope that they may be the humble instruments, under God, of evangelizing a portion of that interesting, beautiful and healthy country. In order that they may strengthen and animate each others' minds, amidst their arduous and trying duties and often unite in prayer for the blessings of the Great Head of the Church, they will have a common residence, where they can impart to the children of the neighborhood all the advantages of a thorough Christian education from whence they can go forth to preach the glad tidings of Salvation. To carry this design into successful operation, it is highly desirable to be in possession of funds to purchase lands, erect plain buildings, stock a small farm, and supply the establishment with necessary furniture and books. Deeply interested in the success of the undertaking, believing it may be productive of much good in the church of the Adorable Redeemer, and convinced of the sincerity and devotion of the parties concerned, I trust that the requisite aid will be cheerfully afforded by those who wish well to the Zion of our God.[10]

With this statement as a guide, three of the students did undertake the work of missionaries in Wisconsin; the fourth, James Miles, was not released by his bishop, Christopher E. Gadsden of South Carolina. The three did travel to the West in the summer of 1841, Hobart going alone to be followed by Adams and Breck traveling together.

The story of this missionary enterprise was published in 1873 and was written by Rev. John H. Egar, a colleague of these men at Nashotah.[11] Egar accurately described how they first established residence at Prairieville, now called Waukesha, about twenty miles west of Milwaukee. Following a money-raising appeal in the summer of 1842, the men were able to purchase a sizeable tract of land, twenty miles farther to the west on the Nashotah Lakes. On Thursday, September 1, 1842, they formally established their mission with a public religious service.[12] Here they began to put into effect the five principles they had outlined in the early discussions of their organization. The members of their group were to

10. "Extracts from Bishop Kemper's Diary," 1–2.

11. *The Story of Nashotah* was first published in England in 1873 and then re-edited in Milwaukee in 1874. The page references to the story used in this biography are to the Dodo Press reprint of 2009.

12. Details of this land purchase are found in Egar, "Appeal," in *Story of Nashotah*.

remain unmarried as long as they were associated with the institution. They were to yield implicit and full obedience to the rules and regulations of the group. Theirs was to be a community with possessions held in common and the catholic principles of the church were to be their guide. They also were committed to preaching from place to place on circuits to be determined by the bishop.

These early years in establishing Nashotah were filled with challenges, successes, and failures. They were dedicated preachers and on December 30, 1841, they published their first report of their missionary efforts. They traveled extensively throughout the region, preaching, baptizing, and conducting religious services. Their work at Nashotah involved building and agriculture. Because of their early efforts, other young men were attracted to this Christian outpost. A school was established "for general education, with a Divinity department for such as proposed to enter the ministry; the pupils to support themselves, in whole or in part by labor while pursuing their studies."[13] The lack of adequate financing was a perennial problem and appeals seldom brought in enough money to cover the costs of the effort. The harshness of the climate took its toll on the members of the community, for not all were equally capable of the hard work of farming and living in the rugged conditions of the buildings that they constructed.

The idealism of the early participants in this missionary experiment soon gave way to the reality of the differences and challenges of pioneer life when compared to the culture of the East. Bishop Kemper continued his annual visits to New York and the General Theological Seminary, where he preached the necessity of bringing the Catholic religion to the frontier. In the beginning, the first members of the brotherhood had hoped that each year a number of graduates of the seminary would volunteer to participate in the enterprise. In fact, only one other clergyman from New York came to join the group, and he only remained a year.[14] Egar described the situation most clearly:

> To gentlemen born and bred, men of university education, the hardships of pioneer life were particularly trying, and the triple labor, not only of carrying on an arduous mission, but also of establishing a school without adequate means, and at the same time of breaking up a farm, and reducing it to cultivation, together with the necessity of doing their own housekeeping,

13. Egar, *Story of Nashotah*, 12.

14. Egar, *Story of Nashotah*, 28. He was Rev. William Walsh.

> cooking and domestic work might very well weary the most devoted enthusiasm.[15]

By 1850, it became clear that the primary focus of Nashotah had evolved to become one of theological education. James Breck resigned his presidency, and Rev. A. D. Cole was chosen to lead the work of the mission. This was the fledging seminary which attracted James DeKoven in 1854 and which he visited in May of that year. The Nashotah of 1854, while still more rugged and primitive than similar Eastern establishments, was becoming more suited to his background than the earlier version as described by Egar. The story of Nashotah was well-known among the students at General, so James DeKoven was familiar with the life he was entering. In the same year that DeKoven made his exploratory visit, the first permanent stone and brick structures were built on the campus. The Episcopal Church in Wisconsin had been organized into a diocese and the population of the state, which entered the union in 1848, had grown rapidly.

What was in the background of this young, highly educated seminarian which led him to investigate the possibility of moving to Wisconsin and serving the church there? One story that is told by two writers, John Henry Hopkins and Morgan Dix, provides a little insight into this decision.[16] Both of these men studied at the General Theological Seminary at the same time as DeKoven. Hopkins used this story to illustrate DeKoven's "power of initiative." Dix felt it demonstrated how throughout his life, from beginning to end, "the work of teaching was always in his thoughts."[17]

THE RAGGED SCHOOL

According to the narratives of Hopkins and Dix, DeKoven and some of his fellow seminarians at General received permission to establish a Sunday afternoon "school" for boys from the neighborhood. It was called the "ragged school" because the students were poorly dressed and equally

15. Egar, *Story of Nashotah*, 28.

16. Hopkins, "Few Recollections of James DeKoven," 64. Other seminarians in New York conducted Sunday schools for different churches in the city. The clientele for these Sunday schools was obviously more refined than that of the "ragged school."

17. Dix, "Preface," v.

undisciplined. Dix refers to them as "uncouth ragamuffins,"[18] and Hopkins uses the expression "street Arabs" and calls them "neglected boys."[19] Together with his colleagues, DeKoven assembled a group of some forty-plus youngsters in the Long Room of the seminary. Because of his leadership role in the enterprise, James was given the task of the first attempt at educating this unlikely gathering. The religious nature of his lecture was understandable, but his poor choice of a passage from the New Testament spelled almost immediate disaster. The story he used to illustrate the power of God, and his importance in their lives, was that of the nations gathered together before the eternal judge with the armies of angels around him.[20] DeKoven described the majesty of God and the division of the assembled peoples into the chosen, good people, the lambs to the right, and the wicked, bad people, the goats, to the left. It didn't require much imagination for one of the young attendees to provide an accompanying "baa," which almost immediately was joined by a chorus of similar sounds: "blee," "baaa," etc. Regaining control was impossible. Fortunately, James DeKoven knew when he was beaten and called an end to the class that day. According to Hopkins, this experience "taught him a lesson in the art of reaching young minds that he never forgot."[21]

The ragged school continued throughout his time at General (1851–54) and the stories of this effort were long remembered. The participants, both scholars and instructors, grew in their knowledge and abilities. It is likely that this experience with the less fortunate was the fundamental motivation behind the request that James DeKoven and three of his classmates made of the bishop of New York when they were nearing graduation. They saw a need for a mission among the poorest and most abandoned areas of New York City and wanted to undertake this work. Their request was denied, not because of the lack of need, but because financial support could not be guaranteed.[22]

The story of the ragged school does not end with DeKoven's departure from New York to the wilds of Wisconsin. Toward the last years of his life, DeKoven became more and more involved in the national meetings

18. Dix, "Preface," v.

19. Hopkins, "Few Recollections of James DeKoven." *Nashotah Scholiast*, Vol. II, No. 4, February 1885.

20. Matt 25:31–46.

21. Hopkins, "Few Recollections of James DeKoven." *Nashotah Scholiast*, Vol. II, No. 4, February 1885.

22. Dix, "Preface," vi.

of the Episcopal Church. At one of the general conventions, he was approached by a younger clergyman who introduced himself. He explained to DeKoven that he had been one of the boys in the ragged school, and it was there that his love of learning and the church had begun. DeKoven was touched by this encounter, for no greater gift can be given a teacher than to hear years later of the positive impact of his teaching.[23]

THE HOBART BROWN LETTERS

Three letters from James DeKoven to Hobart Brown relate to his visit and decision to accept a position at Nashotah. In the first letter, mentioned at the start of this chapter, he writes of his visit there in May 1854 and shares his impressions with his seminary friend:

> I wish you could have been with me at Nashotah. I am sure you would have enjoyed it. Dr. Adams is a man of very great talent. His conversation was truly delightful and instructive. I should very much have liked to have heard his instructions in Theology.[24]

DeKoven feels that Adams compares most favorably with their professors at General and even surpasses them. He tells Hobart of others he met at Nashotah, including Bishop Kemper. Even a bit of ecclesiastical gossip is shared, and an observation by a mutual friend is added:

> I had a very interesting letter from Locke in which he describes the way in which the French clergy preach. Could we emulate them it would take away much of the dryness which I think of as characteristic of our clergy. They always learn their sermons by heart.[25]

Religious matters and improvement are never far from DeKoven's thoughts.

23. While doing research in Middletown, Connecticut, I discovered a fictionalized version of this story written by Joseph Formica, a student at Boston University. The details of the story are somewhat different, but the overall message is the same. Formica indicates that there were two young clergymen who introduced themselves as former "ragged scholars." "The Churchman," by Joseph S. Formica, for PR-341 Corporate Journalism, May 11, 1959. Unpublished manuscript located in the "Middletown Room," Russel Library.

24. Hobart Brown Letter, May 18, 1854. DeKoven Center Archives.

25. Hobart Brown Letter, May 18, 1854. DeKoven Center Archives. The Locke referred to in this quotation was a fellow student at General, James DeWitt Clinton Locke, who eventually served as an Episcopal priest in Chicago.

By the time of the next letter to Hobart Brown, dated August 1, 1854, from Middletown, James DeKoven had returned home and had decided on his future: "I have absolutely accepted the call to Nashotah on condition that they raise me a salary of $250 . . ."[26] He expresses certainty that this condition will be met, but just in case it isn't, he refers to a possible position at Janesville that Hobart had mentioned to him. He seems to still question his decision of accepting a teaching position when compared to parish work. He also mentions the prospect of a Wisconsin winter as not being inspiring. DeKoven wrote this letter on Tuesday and mentions that his ordination to the diaconate would take place on the following Sunday at the church in Middletown. He mentions that he will be leaving for the West in two or three weeks.

The final letter in this series is a quick note written on Saturday, August 19, from Middletown. DeKoven announces his intention to leave for New York City on the following Tuesday *en route* for Nashotah. He plans on spending two or three days at the seminary there and then will go on to his brother's home in Red Hook for ten days. He arranges to meet Hobart because, as he says, "I am very anxious to see you & have a great talk with you."[27]

Although James DeKoven does express some hesitancy about taking a position at Nashotah, he does not seem particularly worried about the move to the West. This was probably not the typical reaction of the average young man born and educated in the culture of New England. In many ways, this may reflect the particular experiences of DeKoven and his family.

THE DEKOVEN FAMILY IN CHICAGO

When DeKoven visited Nashotah in 1854, he was dealing with a comfortable situation: one brother, two sisters, two brothers-in-law, and four of his nephews were living nearby in Chicago. His sister Elizabeth had lived in Chicago since 1834 and was well-known in the social life of the city. Close to the time of her marriage, their father had purchased a large tract of land in Illinois that remained in the family until their mother's death in 1874. In 1839, Cornelia DeKoven married Julius Wadsworth,

26. Hobart Brown Letter, August 1, 1854. James DeKoven Collection, DeKoven Center Archives.

27. Hobart Brown Letter, August 1, 1854. James DeKoven Collection, DeKoven Center Archives.

who had invested in Chicago and land in Wisconsin. In 1844, widowed Elizabeth married her second husband, Thomas Dyer, who was president of the Chicago Board of Trade and would become mayor of Chicago in 1856. In the same year, Frances (Franny) married Judge Hugh T. Dickey of the Cook County Superior Court. These family members provided a welcoming environment for James as he began his professional career.[28]

The technological development of the United States also contributed to the ease with which James DeKoven could adjust to his new home. The new telegraphic network in the West revolutionized communication. By 1854, the telegraph had been available in Chicago for six years, making contact with the East fast and reliable. The telegraph also played an important role in the expansion of railroads.

Beginning on January 24, 1853, it had become possible to travel by train from New York City to Chicago. Prior to this date, the link between these two cities was haphazard at best, taking at least two weeks to complete if all went well. Earlier settlers made their way west via the Erie Canal, ship travel on the Great Lakes, stage coaches, and limited-distance railroads. The direct route, available with the completion of the Toledo, Norwalk, and Cleveland Railroad, still took almost two days.[29] The expansion of railroads played a significant role in the growth and importance of Chicago. Three of DeKoven's brothers-in-law, as well as his younger brother John, were actively involved in the development of this industry. Both Julius Wadsworth and Hugh T. Dickey were life-long members of the board of directors of the Chicago, Milwaukee and St. Paul Railroad.

James DeKoven traveled extensively by railroad. He made at least two trips each year to New York and Connecticut. It was also the preferred means of travel between Nashotah and Milwaukee. The railroad that linked Milwaukee with points west had been opened in 1852 with a station near Nashotah. During his years at Racine College, DeKoven often traveled to Milwaukee and Chicago for meetings. There was a train station, Racine Junction, located near the college. However, the rail link between Milwaukee and Chicago was late in development since passenger

28. The lack of any personal letters written by James DeKoven and his family members becomes even more troubling when their presence in the life of Chicago is considered. One or two letters written by members of the family in Chicago to their mother in Middletown have been found, but undoubtedly the correspondence was significant.

29. Keating, *World of Juliette Kinzie*, 126: "Where once the trip between New York and Chicago had taken weeks, but the late 1850's it could be completed in just under two days."

boat service on Lake Michigan was frequent and relatively convenient. As the railroads expanded, so did the frequency of the visits he made and those from people from around the country who visited him.

James DeKoven arrived at Nashotah on September 15, 1854, to take up his work as an instructor at the seminary. Two months later, on November 15, he made this entry in a now-lost diary, "My Parish School opened today. Thank God! May he bless it and make it succeed."[30] In addition to his duties as tutor in ecclesiastical history, he had been given responsibility for the Church of St. John Chrysostom in the village of Delafield, about two miles south of Nashotah. There is no documentation relating to this decision to name DeKoven rector of this lovely little church and parish. Although other instructors at the seminary had preaching responsibilities, none of the other priests or deacons had the charge of a parish and school. It is possible to turn to DeKoven's personal journal for information and insight into his years in Delafield and at Nashotah House.

30. Dix, "Preface," In *Sermons Preached on Various Occasions*, vii.

THE JOURNAL OF JAMES DEKOVEN

By Revd James de Koven of Racine College

July 31st 1862 Middletown Conn.

The Story of a College

I write this because there are many things which a time goes on one forgets but which are pleasant to recall in after years. I do so too because I have the hope that the College of which the story is told may do good work for God & the Holy Church beyond life when I have passed away, & then may be not without interest to others. Perhaps should it all prove a failure others in the narrative may find what has really been the cause of it in the unworthiness of the rectors, though now we hope and trust and pray that we are not seeking to do our own will but His - In the story I shall speak of myself as the Rector. Let it not be thought egotism that the prevailing thought all through is that in this work he has been guided by God's Providential Guidance, directed by His Love & following His leading That the work is God's work not his own - Without that thought his whole life would be a struggle - He believed that he has been doing the good works prepared for him to walk in. It is the one dread of his life lest some day he should discover, that he has been seeking his own will - May God forbid it & pardon him if in anything it has been so - Wherever he fails or shall fail he believes that this is the cause of it.

It is hard to know where to begin in the story but one must be as brief as possible & yet not brief enough to be clipped and uninteresting.

Nashotah was founded by the prayers and the labours of Mr Breck & Mr Adams and Mr Hobart helped but did not long remain in the year 44 or thereabouts. I cannot be accurate

First page of manuscript journal

On July 31, 1862, James DeKoven began keeping a journal that he called *The Story of a College.*[31] He did not write in this record on a regular basis and sometimes he made entries that were not directly related to the life

31. The handwritten manuscript of this "Story of a College" is located in the Archives Section of the Frances Donaldson Library at Nashotah House Seminary, Nashotah, Wisconsin.

of the school, Racine College, which he had begun administering three years earlier. The journal is a rare source for insights into his thinking and feelings about events and people in his life. It is significant that DeKoven began his diary-keeping during one of his stays at the family home in Middletown, Connecticut. Here in the comfort of his mother's residence, he had both the physical and emotional distance that allowed him to reflect on the work he was doing in Wisconsin. He does not record all the events that one might consider significant in the life of the institution, but the information he does include is incredibly valuable for a study of the life of this somewhat complicated man.

The physical history of the journal is almost as fascinating as the content. Sometime after DeKoven's death in 1879, Rev. Morgan Dix, rector of Trinity Church in New York City, had the journal, as well as an earlier diary, in his possession. Later on, the Morehouse publishing family owned it and at one point were considering its publication.[32] There exist various indications relating to its existence. In 1921, at a speech given after his retirement from Trinity College, Rev. Flavel S. Luther indicated that he had a copy of Dr. DeKoven's diary, "covering the years from the date he went to Nashotah to the time when his death was near at hand."[33] The location of the manuscript, after a typed transcript was made in 1932, was unknown until it was found in the archival collection of the National Cathedral in Washington, D.C., in 1996.

> The diary of Rev. James DeKoven, long thought lost, was discovered in December 1996, in the rare book collection of the Washington National Cathedral by the curator, Margaret Shannon. Richard G. Hewlett, Cathedral Historiographer turned the volume over to historian Thomas C. Reeves for study and eventual deposit at Nashotah Houses seminary. Reeves has discovered that a transcript of the diary, used by scholars up to this time, contains many errors. The diary has entries from 1862 to 1879, the year of DeKoven's death.[34]

32. The DeKoven Center Archives has a collection of letters that relate to the search for this important document. These include various attempts to locate the journal by the Sisters of the Community of Saint Mary as well as statements from different authorities about its assumed location.

33. Luther, "James DeKoven—Teacher," 172.

34. Mammana, "Journal of James DeKoven," 21.

DeKoven strongly valued the writing of a diary. His student and early biographer, William Cox Pope, indicated that his habit of keeping a diary was encouraged by DeKoven.[35]

Pope's first entry into his own diary, for what would be many years of journal keeping, was dated Monday, January 26, 1857. It was a very brief entry: "Mr. DeKoven gave me this book. Three new scholars at school. Hurt Worthinton's eye, went home with him." With this statement, Pope began the life-long habit that continued until his death in 1917.[36]

It would have been out of character for DeKoven to encourage diary-keeping for others and not to have pursued this memoir activity himself. He practiced what he preached in this and so many other ways. He realized that diary entries are often a way to clarify ideas and ask questions of oneself that lead to better and more defined answers. In the opening paragraphs for his *Story of a College*, he indicates his motivation for beginning this particular memoir:

> I write this because there are many things which as time goes on one forgets, but which are pleasant to recall in after years. I do so too, because I have the hope that the college of which this story is told may do good work for God and His Holy Church by and by when I have passed away, and this may not be without interest to others.[37]

What follow are pages that relate the history of Nashotah, the men behind its establishment, DeKoven's idea of a Christian college, a description of students at the school in Nashotah, the story of the creation of St. John's Hall, and resulting problems. The first long entry that he made in 1862, takes the "story" up to the departure of DeKoven and the students of St. John's Hall for Racine in 1859. DeKoven doesn't write in the journal again until almost two years later in 1864.

James DeKoven was not a consistent diarist. He did not write an entry every day. His all-encompassing duties at the college did not permit him enough leisure time for such an activity. Several of the longer entries were written during his vacation visits to Middletown. It appears

35. Diaries of William Cox Pope, National Episcopal Archives. These diaries cover the years 1857–1917.

36. This first diary is a small book with generally very brief entries. They do provide insights into the daily events of students at St. John's Hall and Racine College. Most valuable are the comments about the interactions of James DeKoven with students in the schools.

37. DeKoven, *Journal*, Aa, 1.

that there was a diary, mentioned earlier, in which he wrote with more regularity. Morgan Dix, lifelong friend and rector of Trinity Church in New York City, mentions this diary in his preface to DeKoven's *Sermons Preached on Various Occasions*, published posthumously in 1880. This diary did not survive. Dix gives a brief indication of its content:

> His diary abounds in memoranda which disclose the enthusiastic habit of his soul. At the close of each week something is sure to be found inscribed, as thus: 'The week is ended. Amen. Praise God for his mercies. May He preserve my health and strength to do this work! I am sometimes very, very weary; but, if my work succeeds, it matters not.[38]

The question of a "designated" audience for DeKoven's story of a college seems to be addressed in the first paragraph of his journal. In general, DeKoven doesn't seem concerned with identifying others interested in this story. He does address that reader directly on at least one occasion. When he does mention a possible reader, it seems to be more a literary conceit than an admission that he is writing for a specific audience. In describing the first attempt at establishing rules of conduct at St. John's Hall, he provides the following aside:

> (Here gentle reader, pause and listen—I am telling a story not making reflections on it. I am an historian, not a judge. I am not saying whether what was done was right or wrong, wise or foolish, nor what I think of it. I am only telling a story.)[39]

This posture of historical objectivity was very difficult for DeKoven to maintain.

DeKoven used a pre-printed, bound ledger for his journaling called the *index rerum* or subject index. The printed pages were not numbered with the traditional Arabic numerals but were designed to be filled in with subjects arranged alphabetically. The first page is "numbered" Aa, the next page, Ae, then Ai, etc.

The first thirty pages of the typed copy of DeKoven's journal are, in effect, a review that he makes as he looks back at the five years of his work in Delafield and the creation of St. John's Hall. He wrote this review in 1862, from the psychological comfort of his family home in Middletown. He made a serious effort at providing an objective view of what

38. Dix, "Preface," viii.

39. DeKoven, *Journal*, Co, 15.

were obviously five difficult and challenging years for him. They were also rewarding years. During these five years, he developed his abilities as a pastor and priest, further elaborated and applied his ideas about education, and dealt with the physical challenges of a lifestyle that were undoubtedly new for him. The situation he discovered at Nashotah was far from ideal, but he made the best of it. In his journal he presents a valuable summation of what he observed and what he tried to accomplish in the "tumble-down village" of Delafield with its picturesque church on the shores of Lake Nagawicka.

DeKoven appreciated the beauty of this new frontier where he had come to live. He describes Nashotah with its deep woods "thick with oak and young hickory." He calls the twin lakes "gentle, placid sheets of water." He compares this bucolic scene with the turbulence and danger he found later in Racine on "horrid Lake Michigan, shipwrecking sailors, tossing up dead bodies, raging at night."[40] He describes the physical setting that existed in 1854 at Nashotah Mission with its "ancient wooden houses full of memories and bed bugs.[41]

The buildings included the old chapel, the Blue House, and three brick houses occupied by some students and faculty members, as well as schoolhouse that was used for courses and the study rooms of the candidates.

At this point in his story, DeKoven reiterates that he is not planning on recounting the story of Nashotah, and he writes, "Nashotah has a grand history . . . but it is not mine to tell it."[42] He cautions that his references to Nashotah "may not appear altogether favorably on these pages." However, he emphasizes his firm belief that "N[ashotah] has been and is, I believe the work of God. It has done wonders for the Church, both in what it has accomplished and in the faith in which it has drawn forth to sustain it."[43] His efforts at objectivity and truthfulness can be seen in the descriptions he gives of the important characters in the history of Nashotah House.

DeKoven abbreviates the early history with this statement: "Nashotah was founded by the prayers and labours of Mr. Breck and Mr. Adams."[44] Even though Breck had left Nashotah in 1850, his educational

40. DeKoven, *Journal*, Ao, 5.

41. DeKoven, *Journal*, Ao, 5.

42. DeKoven, *Journal*, Ao, 6.

43. DeKoven, *Journal*, Au, 6.

44. DeKoven, *Journal*, Aa, 2.

ideas greatly influenced those developed by DeKoven during his work there and later in Racine. They were friends, and Breck visited both Nashotah House and Racine College during DeKoven's tenure. Breck's idea was to make Nashotah "a religious house, a 19th century convent."[45] DeKoven admired Breck and called him a man of great "earnestness, zeal and self-denial." Mr. Adams "wished to make a Theological Seminary" and his idea succeeded.[46]

According to DeKoven, "Mr. Adams is a very curious Irishman," but "certainly is a good man, a man of faith and integrity."[47] Their relationship was apparently not always a positive one. DeKoven states quite frankly that Adams "never altogether approved of" him as he began his work at Nashotah and Delafield. Adams did not like the changes DeKoven made, feared he was too "romish," and definitely did not help him much, even though "he threw no obstacles in his way." He was happy to conclude, "All that is over now,"[48] although the negative attitudes of Adams and others were a direct cause of his departure from Nashotah.

His description of a third person, the elderly Bishop Kemper, is relatively brief and direct. DeKoven states that Kemper "has faults and weaknesses," but he will not write them down. "If ever there was a saint on earth, or shall be one in heaven, it is he—a long life of the most simple-minded, pure-hearted missionary labors now drawing to its close."[49] Kemper lived close by and frequently visited the school at Delafield.

DeKoven's final description is of the one person who was consistent in supporting him in his efforts at Delafield, Dr. Azel Cole, then serving as president of the institution. Cole had the unenviable job of managing the funding and overseeing the different efforts of the clergy and students. DeKoven admits that Cole was not a popular man, but it was more important that he had real faith. In summation, referring to himself in the third-person as "the Rector," DeKoven writes, "He was ready to help any good work & always aided and sustained the Rector and was his best friend and supporter."[50]

DeKoven next turned his attention to the two categories of students at Nashotah, the candidates for ordination, and those in various degrees

45. DeKoven, *Journal*, Aa, 2.
46. DeKoven, *Journal*, Aa, 2.
47. DeKoven, *Journal*, Aa, 2.
48. DeKoven, *Journal*, Ae, 3.
49. DeKoven, *Journal*, Ae, 3.
50. DeKoven, *Journal*, Ai, 4.

of preparation for candidature: "The students were mostly supported by the alms and offerings of the Church—in return for this they were expected to study hard, devote their lives to the ministry, be self-denying and devout."[51] In his opinion, the students in general did not live up to these expectations for "there was not much discipline."[52] The lack of respect for others and their personal possessions bothered him. He tells the stories of his India rubber boots and a bottle of "very good brandy" that were used without his permission. He writes with firm conviction, "What one pays for, one values as one's own, one keeps with care because it is difficult to replace it. What one gets easily, one wastes and does not take care of."[53] Although he believed that the students were receiving a relatively good "intellectual training," even though it was a "Western institution," it was "by no means what it ought to be for the youth that were to be the future trainers of the next generation of the mighty West."[54] And it was with this spirit of a man with a mission that DeKoven began to make adaptations to the routine and regulations for the students in the preparatory classes he administered.

There is no written documentation to indicate when the decision was made to move the classes for the preparatory students from Nashotah to the school building across the road from the Church of St. John Chrysostom. However, this was the situation that existed for most of DeKoven's time at Nashotah. He felt strongly that the different age groups needed to be separated, and this was a policy he followed later at Racine College. He believed that the freedom allowed the older candidates had a negative influence on the younger boys, who needed more direction. He tried unsuccessfully to find lodging for those younger students in Delafield away from Nashotah House. Eventually the decision was made to build a separate dining room for them at Nashotah, and daily the students and rector made the slightly more than two-mile hike from Nashotah to Delafield for "morning Prayer and Recitation and back again for dinner."[55] This route from the church in Delafield to the Mission at Nashotah was the axis of James DeKoven's world and ministry for five years.

51. DeKoven, *Journal*, Au, 6.
52. DeKoven, *Journal*, Ca, 12.
53. DeKoven, *Journal*, Ca, 12.
54. DeKoven, *Journal*, Ca, 12.
55. DeKoven, *Journal*, Co, 15.

A CHRISTIAN COLLEGE

DeKoven devoted several paragraphs in the first part of this journal to explaining his ideas about the difference between an American college and a Christian college.[56] Whether or not he had written down these ideas before, these paragraphs are the only known source where he expressed them so completely. He does make the following statement at the end of his description: "It was with this idea of a Xn College, more or less developed, that the Rector undertook his work at Nashotah."[57] It is important to acknowledge that many of his ideas parallel those that came from the work of William Augustus Muhlenberg through the influence of James Lloyd Breck. Breck had studied under Muhlenberg at the Flushing Institute in New York before pursuing his training at the General Theological Seminary and then moving to Wisconsin. It is also possible to see the impact of the educational work of William Sewell in England and what has been called the Sewellian System.[58] It is important to remember that DeKoven is writing his description of a Christian college in July 1862. This is after the failure of his attempts to impose this ideal on a culture at Nashotah that he did not thoroughly understand or appreciate. He is elaborating on this idea while engaged in the hectic activity of realizing this vision at Racine College. His efforts along the shores of Lakes Michigan were having positive results, as evidenced by increased enrollment and the development of the campus.

In his opening statement about his ideal of a Christian college, DeKoven emphasizes that the most important principle to guide its development is the fact that "education without religion is an immorality."[59] The teachers, or at a minimum, the leadership of the school should be men in holy orders who join together to educate Christian youth in body, mind, and soul. The next most important principle is somewhat more difficult to achieve. Essential to the DeKoven philosophy is the goal that "they form one Family."[60] In order to arrive at this family spirit, they all live together in one building ("not Buildings"), eat in a common dining

56. DeKoven, *Journal*, Ba, 7.

57. In this instance the "X" is the Greek character chi, which represented Christ. DeKoven, *Journal*, Bu, 11.

58. Sewell created St. Peter's College, Radley, England, and later was the rector of this institution.

59. DeKoven, *Journal*, Be2, 9.

60. DeKoven, *Journal*, Bi, 9.

hall where there is "the same fare on all tables," and enjoy the pleasure of eating in a positive environment. "The dining hall ought to be the second best room in the college."[61] DeKoven goes on to describe the different rooms and facilities that should be available for the residents of this college: "There is a large Evening Room besides Reception Rooms and Parlors, where all meet together at stated times, especially on Sunday evenings, as one family."[62] A large gymnasium was essential for all sorts of activities including dancing and fencing.

In the midst of what he describes as large and spacious grounds is located the chapel which should be "all that Christian art can make of it."[63] This should be the site of daily services as well as the weekly Eucharist where the "Head is Priest and father to his family."[64]

DeKoven ends his theoretical discussion of this college with the issue of government. He boldly states that "the college should be governed by the students themselves in a certain measure. A system of self-government should be formed."[65] He doesn't go into detail about this system in his journal but insists once again that he is only stating general principles. It was the issue of student prefects and the imposition of a firmer standard of discipline that effectively brought the St. John Hall experiment to an end. There is an amazing sincerity in DeKoven's efforts to improve what he saw as a very imperfect situation. He had no dispute with the arrangement for the "Candidates" at Nashotah House. However, he wanted an opportunity to try the other system, his ideal of a Christian college, with the *preparatories*:[66]

> It would meet all the difficulties. The self-denial of its discipline, the obedience required would make a return for the alms that were given. It would preserve the students' self-respect. The intellectual training could be greatly improved, and the spiritually, the fatherly loving care of Presbyter living with them would make them holy and devout.[67]

61. DeKoven, *Journal*, Bi2, 9.

62. DeKoven, *Journal*, Bi2, 10.

63. DeKoven, *Journal*, Bo1, 10.

64. DeKoven, *Journal*, Bo1, 10.

65. DeKoven, *Journal*, Bu, 11.

66. These were the two categories of students: 1) Candidates, young men who had been accepted into the seminary to undertake their preparation for ordination; 2) Preparatories, young men and boys who were studying in order to enter the seminary eventually.

67. DeKoven, *Journal*, Ce, 12–14.

Armed with this conviction and the support friends and parishioners, James DeKoven made an amazing proposal to the board of trustees of the Mission on May 6, 1857, for the creation of St. John's Hall. This proposal outlined in detail how the "Training School" would be established and how it would be financed.[68] DeKoven committed his personal wealth to the enterprise. He had obviously been planning this move for some time, since the proposal involved other members of the Delafield community.

In the agreement, DeKoven gave approximately forty acres of land for the location and $2,000 for the construction of the school building. He also committed $800 a year toward the support of the institution. This annual support was contingent upon his continued association with the school. In a very practical move, he had already obtained the stone necessary for the building "free of expense." He and his associate, Rev. Mr. Hodges, agreed to work for the training school without salary "until such time as the Institution can afford to pay us one."

The trustees were asked to approve the name, St. John's Training School, and its existence as a distinct corporation. They were also asked to provide $8,000 toward the construction and furnishing of the school building by June 1, 1858. Other points related to the Church of St. John Chrysostom as the parish church of the school and the rector of the school as rector of the parish. Government of the school was to be the responsibility of the rector and associate rector, who in turn were to be responsible to the school trustees.

DeKoven requested a reply to this agreement by June 1, 1858. The board of trustees received the agreement on May 5, 1857 and moved approval on May 6. The only problem raised during the follow-up discussions of this agreement concerned the commitment of $8,000 toward the construction of the school building. DeKoven continued to move forward with his plans and completed the necessary legal work for the statutes of the institution.

At a meeting of the board of trustees of Nashotah House on July 13, 1857, the following commentary and motion concerning the work and dedication of James DeKoven were made by Rev. Azel Cole, the president:

> I would also call the attention of the Trustees to the insufficient return made to Rev. Mr. DeKoven. He teaches from one to three hours daily with no other salary than his board and room. His services are too many & too valuable to be left without some

68. *Agreement of James DeKoven and Trustees of Nashotah House.*

> further mark of esteem. I would propose that $100 be appropriated to him from July 1st.[69]

The first action undertaken after the approval of the St. John's Hall proposal was to authorize the building of a separate dining hall for the St. John's students and to formulate some disciplinary rules. These and other decisions were made during the 1858 academic year. DeKoven and Hodges still lived with the students on the Nashotah campus. Some of the conditions laid out in the agreement were met by the board, but other issues remained unresolved. DeKoven did not deal well or effectively with the stress of this uncertainty and became ill. In a letter to William Cox Pope on June 5, 1858, he wrote, "I have not been well for some time and I talk very seriously of going to England for the summer. In case I do I shall probably sail very early in July."[70] In a letter written three weeks later, DeKoven indicated the fact that Rev. Mr. Seymour, "an old friend and classmate" would be traveling with him.[71]

Years later George Seymour wrote the following about DeKoven and his physical condition: "The reason for his exhaustion in so brief a time as four years, was manifest to anyone who was much with him and saw him work. All his parishioners and pupils were in his heart."[72]

GEORGE FRANKLIN SEYMOUR

In many ways, the lives of George F. Seymour and James DeKoven ran on parallel tracks. They were both educated at Columbia College in the late 1840s. Seymour graduated in 1850 and DeKoven in 1851. They were roommates and studied at the General Theological Seminary and both graduated from that institution in 1854. They were ordained deacons in 1854, DeKoven in Connecticut and Seymour in New York, and priests the following year, both on September 23, 1855. Seymour was ordained in New York City and DeKoven in the Church of St. John Chrysostom, Delafield, Wisconsin, by Bishop Kemper. In spring 1858, DeKoven created a preparatory school for Nashotah House Seminary, St. John's Hall. In 1860, Seymour established a similar training program for the General Theological Seminary called St. Stephen's College. Seymour was the first

69. *Minutes of the Board of Trustees of Nashotah House*, 33.

70. Letter to William Cox Pope, Jun. 5, 1858, National Episcopal Archives.

71. Letter to William Cox Pope, Jun. 26, 1858, National Episcopal Archives.

72. Seymour, "James DeKoven," 16.

president of this institution at Annandale-on-Hudson. With the move to Racine in 1859, DeKoven became the president and rector of Racine College. It was apparent that the two stayed in close contact over the years because their ideas about the value and nature of education were amazingly similar. Seymour served as rector of three churches in New York City and eventually joined the faculty of the General Theological Seminary, where in 1865 he became professor of church history, a position very similar to that DeKoven occupied at Nashotah from 1854–59. They were both elected to the position of Bishop of Illinois: Seymour in 1874 and DeKoven in 1875. Both elections caused controversy and were effectively challenged. In 1875, Seymour became Dean of the General Theological Seminary and in May 1878 was elected Bishop of Springfield, Illinois. One of DeKoven's final acts was to have an Episcopal ring designed and created for his friend.[73]

TRIP TO EUROPE, SUMMER 1858

Bishop George Seymour wrote a short article entitled "Dr. DeKoven" that was published in the July 1884 issue of the *Nashotah Scholiast*.[74] In this brief reminiscence, Seymour indicated the reasons for DeKoven's first trip to Europe. According to Seymour, DeKoven had worked tirelessly on revitalizing the parish of St. John Chrysostom, Delafield, with its parish school, and creating the preparatory program that became St. John's Hall. Speaking of DeKoven, Seymour wrote, "He needed rest and change of scene to recruit his wasted energies. Relief was sought in a brief foreign trip across the sea in high summer."[75]

73. The ring was designed and created in New York City through the efforts of DeKoven's niece, Mary Beach. Bishop Seymour received the ring on March 19, 1879, the day that DeKoven died at Racine College.

74. Seymour, "James DeKoven," 16.

75. Before they could travel, however, these two young clergymen needed to procure passports. The archives of the Department of State retain the communications that were occasioned by their last-minute search for these travel documents. Seymour turned to his father, Isaac Newton Seymour, who in turn asked for the help of John Wurts, president of the Delaware and Hudson Canal and Railroad. Mr. Wurts turned to his friend, James Buchanan, president of the United States, indicating that two young friends were traveling to Europe for health reasons. The information was forwarded to Lewis Cass, Secretary of State. Cass filed passport applications for the two on June 25 but needed additional information which he sought from Seymour, Sr., who provided the requested documentation on July 15. DeKoven and Seymour had sailed already on July 7 aboard the steamer Persia.

The "brief foreign trip" resulted in three months of travel to several European countries where the two visited different cities and various institutions. Seymour commented on their renewed friendship with its added new common interest:

> To the many ties which united us in the past, were added now an identity of purpose in the work of ministry, and the same ideal which we both hoped to realize in the near future, the creation of a Church college of the highest order of excellence in the respective regions where God had assigned us out spheres of duty, the Northwest and the East. Racine and St. Stephen's are the fruits of this day dream of the two young priests, who then were looking with eager expectancy to the days to come.[76]

In all probability they visited St. Peter's College in Radley, England, because of the fame this school had already achieved in the Anglican educational world.

Dr. William Sewell, founder of this school in 1847 and eventually warden from 1853–61, seems to have had a direct as well as an indirect influence on James DeKoven. Three concepts were essential to the Sewell boys' school: "His idea was that the College should be a home; a kind of family."[77] A second feature was the dormitory system. This provided each boy with a cubicle which gave him privacy in a public space. The third concept was the prefectorial system, which was the government of boys partially by the boys themselves. At least two of these ideas were adopted by DeKoven for St. John's Hall and then Racine College. An indirect influence of Radley can be seen in the architecture of the buildings. The original chapel of St. Peter's College, erected in 1848, served as the model for the chapel that DeKoven had erected on the Racine College campus in 1864.

Together Seymour and DeKoven visited England, France, Belgium, Germany, Scotland and Ireland. During this trip DeKoven wrote many letters; he even mentions this fact in one of his letters, and twenty-six years later Seymour makes this comment, "He wrote many and many a letter to those whom he thought that his remembrance would bring pleasure, and so his life went out to his work."[78] Among the letters he wrote were nine directed specifically to the "Students of St. John's Hall." Eight of

76. Seymour, "James DeKoven," 16.

77. Bryans, *History of St. Peter's College*, 65.

78. Seymour, "James DeKoven," 16.

these letters have been saved. What is remarkable about these letters, in addition to the amazing amount of information he was able to pack onto a sheet of paper (his writing is very small), is the warm and caring nature of the writer. They also demonstrate his innate abilities as a teacher. The letters are not only informative, but they also show that he knows quite well how to capture the interest of his young readers. He tells great stories while at the same time teaching geography, history, cultural awareness, morality, and good behavior.

DeKoven shared many stories about the students and people of Delafield with his friend George during their European adventure. Twenty-six years later, Seymour could write, "Though absent from Delafield and Nashotah in person, he was not separated in spirit."[79] St. John's Hall opened officially on September 30, 1858, with Rev. Hodges as sub-warden and Rev. Shaw as fellow-in-charge.[80] DeKoven did not return until later in October, his last letter being one that he wrote from Oxford in September of 1858. It may be a question of twenty-first-century optics, but this absence simply didn't look good. James DeKoven and George Seymour came from a far different economic and social class than that of the average student and clergyman in Nashotah, Wisconsin in 1858. Wisconsin was still in many ways the western frontier of the country. Although travel to Europe for DeKoven and his family members, and most probably for Seymour, too, was becoming more common and accepted, it was far out of the reach of the vast majority of the people with whom they lived and worked. The situation that DeKoven found when he returned reveals one more occasion when he seems relatively "tone-deaf" as to what is going on around him. This is how he describes his return in the journal:

> It was about the middle or last of October when in the year 1858 the Rector returned from a summer trip to Europe, or rather England. Full of his work, he hastened to be at home again, with a heart full of love for all his boys and of zeal for the labor he had undertaken.[81]

One of the teachers had brought the children from the parish school to the Pine Lake railroad station to greet him on his return. He points out that they were accompanied by the clergy from Nashotah "and some,

79. Seymour, "James DeKoven," 16.

80. Diaries of William Cox Pope, 19.

81. DeKoven, *Journal*, Cu, 16.

though not all of the students at St. John's."[82] In his absence, with the opening of St. John's Hall, new rules had been put in place, and there were rumblings of discontent. DeKoven does point out that "at night the students sang under his window one of their songs to welcome him back and his heart was very glad.[83]"

One of the Sewellian ideas that DeKoven implemented upon his return involved the "governing of the boys by the boys."[84] This new system of prefects, as well as some more physical changes, led to an undercurrent of unrest. DeKoven does admit in his reflections written four years later that "like all Reformers, the Rector was somewhat unpopular. The boys naturally did not fancy discipline."[85] He appointed three students as prefects and established a system that involved a weekly report to the rector. The student prefects were the ones who bore the brunt of the displeasure of the other students. "Never were officers more unpopular. Pharaoh's task masters had an easy time when compared to them."[86] A more visible rebellion occurred with a change made in the dining hall. According to William Pope, who lived this experience as a student and was one of the first prefects of St. John's Hall, DeKoven brought back with him the idea that "forms," benches without backs, would improve behavior and posture for students at meals. This was the style at Radley but not at all popular in Delafield. "The students were quick to perceive that this was a piece of primitive medievalism, not proper to be transplanted to America. Consequently, one morning the "forms" were not to be found."[87] They had been dumped into a ditch behind the new dining hall.

DeKoven managed to deal with the student rebellions, sometimes with his good humor intact, but he found it more difficult to handle the criticism he received from his fellow clergymen and the older candidates in the seminary. He was accused of being too strict, of trying to impose an English system on an American school, of being "romish," etc. Matters came to a climax around November 1, 1857, with a struggle between the rector and a student accused of disrespect, who adamantly refused to apologize and was expelled.

82. DeKoven, *Journal*, Cu, 16.
83. DeKoven, *Journal*, Cu, 16.
84. DeKoven, *Journal*, De, 19.
85. DeKoven, *Journal*, Di, 19.
86. DeKoven, *Journal*, Du, 22.
87. The Diaries of William Cox Pope, 20.

In the midst of this turmoil, a letter of no confidence in DeKoven and his leadership was signed by all the candidates and some of the St. John's students. This was very hurtful to DeKoven and in many ways signaled the end of his commitment to St. John's Hall at Delafield. "The storm of course blew over . . . but there were seeds of evil left behind."[88]

Over the course of the academic year 1858–59, there were quite a few flare-ups relating to all that was new—and quite frankly all that was inherent in the administration of a boys' school. DeKoven and his colleagues weathered them all. It was natural for DeKoven to begin questioning his own convictions, and so he turned to his fellow clergy at the institution. He records in his journal that two of them "said that they thought he would be more useful in parochial life and as a parish priest."[89] Other colleagues in the seminary thought that the whole project was a failure. However, when he returned from the summer holiday and time away from Wisconsin, he faced a significant increase in enrollment. His efforts were being recognized outside of Nashotah. The main problem he now faced was finding housing for the younger students away from the mission campus in Delafield. It was at this point that the proposition of the merger of St. John's Hall with Racine College was made.

DeKoven indicates that this idea of the union was first presented by Robert H. Clarkson at that time rector of St. James Church in Chicago. Clarkson served on the board of trustees of both St. John's Hall and Racine College. He was well-acquainted with the management and academic difficulties that Racine College faced under the leadership of its first president, Dr. Roswell Park. Although Park was successful at first, he was not an effective administrator and failed to establish adequate rules and regulations for the operation of the school. Clarkson also knew of DeKoven's displeasure with the situation at Delafield. The proposal for a union of the two schools was made and DeKoven refused. He could not agree to work under Dr. Park, as he disagreed totally with him on how the school was organized. Park came to Nashotah to talk with DeKoven and urged him to take the position and agree to the merger. Park agreed to step aside from any role in the school, other than teaching, and convinced Bishop Kemper, among others, that this was for the best.

The "official story" used to explain the merger of these two educational institutions is not the one being given here. The financial panic of

88. DeKoven, *Journal*, Du, 21.

89. DeKoven, *Journal*, Fe, 29.

1857 was cited for the problems facing the two schools and union seen as the only way to save what had been established.[90] Although that was true for Racine College under Park's leadership, it was not true for St. John's Hall. The enrollment at St. John's was increasing, and the financial future seemed relatively bright, despite the economic woes of the country. This unexpected move to Racine gave DeKoven the separation of distance and ideology that he so greatly desired.

It is very likely that DeKoven would not have continued at Nashotah if this opportunity had not presented itself. He confided as much in his journal six years later, "How dark everything looked. Dr. Cole stood by the rector, but he knew not what to do."[91]

When James DeKoven decided to accept the position at Racine College, it impacted not only his relationship with Nashotah House but also his work with the parish of the Church of St. John Chrysostom. He had grown in his abilities as a pastor, having devoted much work and effort to the spiritual and intellectual growth of the parishioners of this small community. In some ways, the church and its school had provided a release, if not an escape, from the tensions that came from his work at the seminary and with the Nashotah community. The importance of his efforts is reflected in a letter written to him by the members of the vestry of the church and published the month after his departure:

> Rev. and Dear Sir: In accepting your resignation as our Rector, we must express our deep and heartfelt sorrow, that there should be any necessity for the dissolution of that connection, which has so happily and so profitably existed during the past five years. We desire to express also our deep sense of the great debt and obligations, we as a parish owe you. By your earnest and self-sacrificing labors, for the spiritual and temporal welfare of our parish, by your free devotion of yourself, your own private means and your prayers, you have raised us from being a weak and feeble parish to some degree of strength; under God, you have largely multiplied the number of our communicants, you have gathered a large Sunday School, maintained the Parish School, and conferred other material benefits upon the parish,

90. This explanation for the closing of St. John's Hall and the move to Racine has been repeated frequently: "A severe depression ravaging the country prompted a merger in 1859 between St. John's Hall and Racine College . . ." Reeves, *James De Koven, Anglican Saint,* 2. "The nation-wide Panic of 1857–58 (as depressions were then called) led to the merger of St. John's Hall with Racine College in 1859, with DeKoven as Warden." Crumb, "Biography of James DeKoven," 3.

91. DeKoven, *Journal,* Ee, 29.

> for which you will ever be kept in grateful remembrance. Our reluctance to your leaving us, is, only lessened by our knowing, that in God's providence, a way has been opened to you to carry out your great and long-cherished desire of establishing a Training School for Candidates for Holy Orders. We know that we should submit without a murmur, and we pray that God will bless your endeavors and grant you such graces of His Holy Spirit, as will enable you to conduct such an institution to the glory of God and the blessing of all its members.
>
> Signed: L. B. Seymour, A. B. Gumfry, Wardens.
> J. Kilmer, G. Thomas, S. R. Kemper, Vestrymen[92]

In a letter to "Willie" Pope, dated August 27, 1859, from Delafield, DeKoven wrote at length about the challenging situation as it existed and described the impact it had on him and those around him:

> You know, my dear Willie, what a troublous time we had last year in some respects, and how much of irritation there was among the boys. I lay it in great part to our unfortunate position. It is utterly impossible that the two institutions should go on in such close juxtaposition. Trifles became matters of importance, molehills were magnified in mountains, small restrictions became terrible privations, when there was a set of students ready to tell the S. John's students that they were being hardly treated. It was not surprising that many of them should believe that it was so, when told so on such good authority. Nor do I think it any ways surprising that some of the theological students should have felt and said so. It does not convince me of their evil condition; it only convinces me that the two institutions, under different systems of discipline, cannot go on well and safely close together.[93]

DeKoven points out the efforts that he and Dr. Cole had made to move the St. John's students to Delafield. He mentions the money he had set aside for the building which had not yet been matched by Nashotah. He makes a final statement about his state of mind before sharing his good news:

> Nothing would tempt me to go on as Warden of S. John's Hall with matters as they were during the past year, and I could see that the difficulties in which the S. John's students have been placed were to be increased rather than diminished.[94]

92. *Gospel Messenger and Church Record of Western New York 1859*, 2.
93. Letter to Willie Cox, "DeKoven Letters."
94. Letter to Willie Cox, "DeKoven Letters," 79.

DeKoven then outlines the proposal from Dr. Park and the arrangements that are being made for the move to Racine. He stressed that the "refectory arrangements will be admirable. Mr. and Mrs. Slengerfield will go on with us, and take entire charge."[95] He points out how difficult it will be for him to leave the Church of St. John Chrysostom and the community of the parish. He asks Willie to join him in the move to Racine:

> I feel that if my students will go there to work with me in this great work of Christian education which God's providence opens, while procuring great advantages and blessing for themselves, they will be doing also a good work for the Church of God by doing their part in building up a thorough Church college.[96]

The future was a challenge, but it was brighter than that at Delafield and had positive potential when compared to the past. Racine College presented a new and welcome chapter to DeKoven's Mission in Wisconsin.

95. Letter to Willie Cox, "DeKoven Letters," 79.

96. Letter to Willie Cox, "DeKoven Letters," 80.

5

James DeKoven, Educator at Racine College

On Friday, September 30, 1859, James DeKoven and twenty-eight boys and young men traveled by train from Nashotah to Racine, Wisconsin, to begin the renewed history of Racine College. "It was only a journey of 40 miles," he wrote, "but it seemed like a long pilgrimage."[1] DeKoven's use of the word "pilgrimage" in describing this move seems very appropriate. In some ways James DeKoven believed that he and his "pilgrims" were going to Racine to save an institution that had indeed fallen on hard times. He knew well the cry of the medieval crusaders, *Deus vult (God willing),* and he undoubtedly believed that it applied to his decision to leave St. John's Hall and Nashotah House.[2]

1. DeKoven, *Journal*, Fo–Fu, 30–31.

2. DeKoven frequently inserted the abbreviation DV in his writings—*Deus vult* ("God willing"), to indicate that he was putting a situation into God's hands.

The first two buildings of Racine College, Kemper Hall and Park Hall.

Although there is no description of the many hours of preparation that went into planning for the move, it is not hard to imagine the excitement and enthusiastic energy that the actual trek fostered. Earlier trips, either by train or horse and wagon, had probably been made to move equipment and goods from Nashotah to Racine. DeKoven's personal books alone would have required several large crates.[3]

As indicated in the preceding chapter, Rev. Roswell Park had traveled to Nashotah and encouraged DeKoven to take on the position of rector of the College. Park had agreed to step aside and assume the honorific title of chancellor. Although DeKoven did acknowledge that Park's humility in placing the college in another person's hands was commendable, he was very blunt in his private assessment of Park's abilities and the reasons for his ultimate failure at the college:

> Of information, the Dr. possessed a great deal. He had a wonderful memory and had read and studied well. He was thoroughly systematic, and yet his information was of the oddest and most uninteresting character. Of human nature, he knew but little, and was the last man fitted to have charge of boys.[4]

There was one particular failing that DeKoven saw as leading to the needed change in administration. This was linked to his belief that a Christian educational institution needed to be modeled on the family. From the very beginning of the new DeKoven regime and the creation of

3. The receipt mentioned earlier, found written in the back of one of DeKoven's notebooks, for a shipment of three crates of books, is evidence that his love of books started early in his career.

4. DeKoven, *Journal*, Fo, 30.

a new educational culture, it was made clear that faculty members would live in the college building with the students. "[Park's] college could not succeed . . . as he did not live with the scholars and every rule of prudence and care was unthought of, sin and wickedness abounded, and the place was a pandemonium."[5]

For DeKoven, this was also an opportunity to leave the unpleasant atmosphere in Delafield and at Nashotah. In his journal, DeKoven describes their arrival:

> They reached Racine at night, and for the first time together as soon as they arrived, celebrated the Service in Racine College Chapel.[6] Racine seems at first like fairy-land. Those first days in the beautiful October weather seem in memory like one of those fair landscapes the painters paint. There is a kind of romantic feeling about it. Our hopes were very high. We hoped to have very many new scholars, and pay all our expenses. The $2,000 finished off Kemper Hall.[7]

DeKoven had raised $2,000 for the construction of a new building for Saint John's Hall.[8] As part of his agreement with the Trustees of Nashotah, he was allowed to bring this sum with him; he applied it to the second building of Racine College, which had remained unfinished for almost two years. DeKoven had managed to raise both money and in-kind contributions for his school in Delafield; the enrollment at St. John's Hall was growing rapidly. He was a successful administrator, as witnessed by the letter of appreciation written by the vestry of the Church of St. John Chrysostom in Delafield.

Father DeKoven entered upon his new duties with the good wishes of those he had served in Delafield and was encouraged by those students who chose to follow him to the new site of his labors. There was also a certain sadness that accompanied this necessary change in his life situation.[9] Only twenty-eight years old, he had been ordained for just

5. DeKoven, *Journal*, Fo, 30.

6. This was the first chapel that occupied the third floor of the first building, Park Hall. This chapel burned in the fire of 1864.

7. DeKoven, *Journal*, Fu, 32.

8. DeKoven had advanced this amount to the trustees of Nashotah House in an agreement signed on January 10, 1858.

9. This move was emotionally difficult for DeKoven as he shared his memories: "St. Michael and All Angels' Day, 1859, was our last day at Nashotah. They laid the cornerstone of the Nashotah Chapel that day, and it was our last service there. Five years of work were over. The parish school, the beautiful church, the dear Sub Warden, all of the

four years; his organizational experience was limited to what he gained at Nashotah and Delafield. He was definitely relying on his natural instincts for order and efficiency. One of his fundamental beliefs, which had been confirmed at Nashotah, was that a solid educational experience was the answer to bringing the Christian message to the world of the frontier.

During his first five years in Wisconsin, DeKoven developed some specific ideas about how best to organize a Christian college. These ideas reflect the influence of others interested in new directions in education as well as new directions for the Protestant Episcopal Church in America. In many ways they built upon ideas advocated by William Augustus Muhlenberg, including the belief that an effective school should be organized after the model of a Christian family. Although Muhlenberg did not publish his theories, others very enthusiastically shared them in their writings: "Accordingly, master, teachers, and pupils, lived and slept under the same roof, ate from the same table, and felt equally at home in the school family."[10] This is how DeKoven expressed a similar idea in speaking of the students, their teachers and the administrators of the institution: "They form one Family. All live together in the college Building, Building not Buildings. Make it as large as you please, ten quadrangles if necessary, but let it be one Building for the sake of unity."[11] DeKoven stresses this idea of the unity of the collegiate family by pointing out that all should eat "the same fare on all tables."[12] For DeKoven, the dining hall was only secondary in importance to that of the chapel: "The dining hall ought to be the second-best room in the college."[13] He emphasized the importance of aesthetics in decorating the refectory as well as the chapel. DeKoven summarized this description with a concluding comment "In short, one family, older and younger, and eating together as one of the surest bonds that can bind it in one."[14] This was an ideal he first attempted to create at Nashotah and developed more fully at Racine.[15]

---

old friends, the many plans, the unaccomplished work, these all were said good bye to." DeKoven, *Journal*, Fu, 31.

10. Newton, *Dr. Muhlenberg*, 52.

11. DeKoven, *Journal*, Be2, 8.

12. DeKoven, *Journal*, Bi1, 9.

13. DeKoven, *Journal*, Bi2, 9.

14. DeKoven, *Journal*, Bi2, 9.

15. This concept of the family was one that influenced young men of the college and stayed with them throughout their lives. Writing in 1924, fifty-three years after his graduation in 1872, attorney Frank O. Osborne commented on the bonds he felt for his fellow students: "We boys of DeKoven's days were as members of a family after the flesh,

Although DeKoven never mentions Muhlenberg in his writings or presentations, several of his close associates in Wisconsin had a direct connection with this important educator. Bishop Kemper was influential in Muhlenberg's decision to be ordained an Episcopal priest. James Lloyd Breck, who played a crucial role in the creation and survival of Nashotah, studied and worked with Muhlenberg for five years at his Flushing Institute. Although Breck had left Nashotah by the time DeKoven arrived, they did communicate, and Breck visited Racine College several times. The schools and institutions he established during his work in Minnesota and California were founded on the principals he learned at Flushing.

An article in the *Church Journal* in 1859 does establish a direct link between the "new" Racine College and the ideas of Muhlenberg:

> Racine College has undergone somewhat of a change in its interior arrangement. The Students of S. John's Hall who are being trained to be candidates for Orders, will hereafter pursue their studies there; and the Church Education system, of which the Rev. Dr. Muhlenberg is the founder, and which has been so successfully carved [sic] out at S. James' College, will be inaugurated at Racine College at the commencement of the new term. Rev. Dr. Park becomes the chancellor, and the Rev. James De Koven the rector.[16]

An educator in England, Dr. William Sewell,[17] had published his ideas about Christian education that were influenced by John Henry Newman and the Oxford Movement. In 1847 he created Radley College, a school for boys based on the principle of brotherliness and emphasizing the importance of beauty in surroundings and decoration. The central idea was that the "college" was to be a home, a family community.[18] DeKoven knew of Sewell, Radley College, and had visited the school near Oxford in 1858.

James DeKoven was willing to take some risks in establishing the new order at Racine College. The following paragraph was published in the first college register after he assumed the position as rector. The Episcopal nature of the school was emphasized and disciplinary rules were established:

---

so strong were the ties." Osborne, "Letter to Claudia Winslow, 1924."

16. *Church Journal*, Vol. VII, No. 47, September 21, 1859, 2.

17. A search of the archives at Radley Hall have failed to produce evidence of the visit of DeKoven and Seymour in 1858.

18. Bryans, *History of S. Peter's College*, 54–59.

> The rector and three of the clergy reside with the students in the college building, and direct the internal government and discipline of the college. They devote their whole time and care to the duties of the institution, with the endeavor to realize the idea of a Christian family, where the teachers are elder brothers, and the scholars dutiful, obedient younger members, all working together for the good of each other and the glory of God. As a family they all meet together in a common dining hall, and as a family they all pray together, morning and evening, in the daily service of the church, in the college chapel. It is believed that in this way boys and young men are best shielded from sin and evil when away from the shelter of home and the care of parents.[19]

The information provided in this paragraph was sent to various church-related publications. DeKoven also submitted shorter and more succinct items to newspapers in various cities, such as the following item which appeared in the *Chicago Tribune*:

> RACINE COLLEGE—Racine College, with a larger number of Professors than heretofore, affording most efficient educational facilities, is now open for the reception of students. The Grammar School, where boys of eight years old and upwards are fitted for a College course, will be opened Nov. 1st. Address Rev. JAMES DeKOVEN, Racine College, Racine, Wisconsin.[20]

He wanted to assure the parents and guardians of potential students that the school had a new administration, with a new philosophy and a new spirit. It was with obvious enthusiasm that the first public event was held at the college campus. On the feast of Saint Andrew, November 30, 1859, Kemper Hall, the second building, named in honor of the bishop of Wisconsin, was formally opened and dedicated. DeKoven enthusiastically summarized the situation as it existed on the day of the formal dedication:

> Our hopes were very high. We hoped to have very many new scholars, and pay all our expenses. . . A few of Dr. Park's old students returned and we were waiting for new ones.[21]

DeKoven should probably have realized that there would be difficulties as he brought with him the organization and philosophy of the school that he had created in Delafield and imposed it on an already-existing

19. *Register of Racine College, 1859–1860*, 14.

20. *Chicago Tribune*, Nov. 8, 1859, 2.

21. DeKoven, *Journal*, Ga, 32.

institution. There were carryover students from the previous regime who balked at the new rules and regulations as well as the prayers and daily services. The situation seems to have continued peacefully enough, although the undercurrent of discontent existed, until a new student arrived from Chicago. "Who should gain the one new boy who represented the College that was to be? Should he be influenced by the new order of things, or not?"[22] DeKoven continued to move forward, and fortunately for him, the tension diminished in intensity when two of the "most influential Raciners" left the college.[23]

> The next year brought success. The school was the fashion in Milwaukee. Everybody wanted to send boys. We had about 60 lads, a marvelous increase. We engaged two new teachers—Mr. Ed. Spalding and Mr. Van Deusen. . . The Curator rejoiced, the Trustees began to take a more decided interest. Visitors flocked to see the establishment.[24]

In the years immediately following the move to Racine it becomes relatively difficult, if not impossible, to separate DeKoven's life from the life of this institution. Here he was able to put into operation his beliefs and understanding about Christian education and how it should be organized and effected. Here he was relatively free from the criticism and judgment of the older seminary students and faculty at Nashotah. Here he was not judged for his convictions in the same way that judgment had been passed on him for his work at Delafield and in the Nashotah seminary. At least such judgment was not apparent in the first years of his efforts.[25]

In reviewing the twenty years of his life that begin with this move to Racine in 1859, it is possible to see two distinct periods. The first period, covering the years 1859 through 1868, can best be described as the "private period." During these years the principal occupation of James DeKoven was the growth and success of Racine College. During that

22. DeKoven, *Journal*, Ge, 34.

23. DeKoven, *Journal*, Ge1, 34.

24. James De Koven made his first annual report to the board of trustees in July, 1860. In this report he was able to provide both positive as well as negative insights into the condition of the school.

25. The three primary sources of information about life at Racine College are the manuscript journal of James DeKoven called *The Story of a College*; the student publication called the *College Mercury*, first published in 1867; and the annual school catalogs called the *Racine College Register*.

time the enrollment grew from forty students (17 college/23 grammar school) to 208 (43 college/165 grammar school). In February of 1868, DeKoven took a leave of absence from his position at the school and traveled in Europe for several months. When he returned in the late summer of that year, he prepared for his first trip as an elected delegate to the General Convention of the Protestant Episcopal Church of America. This begins what can be considered the "public period" of his life. Through his speeches and his writings, his beliefs and principles became known to a wider audience. During both of these "periods" of his life, his role as a priest in the Episcopal Diocese of Wisconsin continued to develop and occupy more of his time.

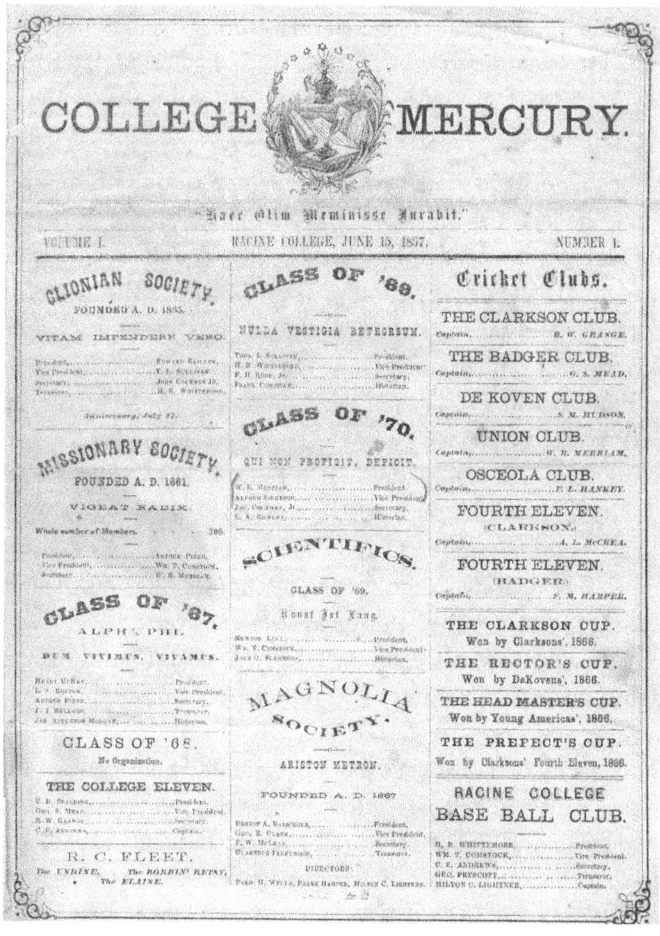

COLLEGE MERCURY.

"Haec Olim Meminisse Jurabit."

VOLUME I. RACINE COLLEGE, JUNE 15, 1867. NUMBER 1.

CLIONIAN SOCIETY.
FOUNDED A. D. 1865.
VITAM IMPENDERE VERO.

MISSIONARY SOCIETY.
FOUNDED A. D. 1861.
VIGEAT RADIX.
Whole number of Members. 306.

CLASS OF '67.
ALPHA PHI.
DUM VIVIMUS, VIVAMUS.

CLASS OF '68.
No Organization.

THE COLLEGE ELEVEN.

R. C. FLEET.
The UNDINE, The BOBBIN' BETSY, The ELAINE.

CLASS OF '69.
NULLA VESTIGIA RETRORSUM.

CLASS OF '70.
QUI NON PROFICIT, DEFICIT.

SCIENTIFICS.
CLASS OF '69.

MAGNOLIA SOCIETY.
ARISTON METRON.
FOUNDED A. D. 1867

DIRECTORS:

Cricket Clubs.

THE CLARKSON CLUB.
Captain, R. W. GRANGE.

THE BADGER CLUB.
Captain, G. S. MEAD.

DE KOVEN CLUB.
Captain, S. M. HUDSON.

UNION CLUB.
Captain, W. R. MERRIAM.

OSCEOLA CLUB.
Captain, F. L. HANKEY.

FOURTH ELEVEN.
(CLARKSON.)
Captain, A. L. McCREA.

FOURTH ELEVEN.
(BADGER.)
Captain, F. M. HARPER.

THE CLARKSON CUP.
Won by Clarksons', 1866.

THE RECTOR'S CUP.
Won by DeKovens', 1866.

THE HEAD MASTER'S CUP.
Won by Young Americas', 1866.

THE PREFECT'S CUP.
Won by Clarksons' Fourth Eleven, 1866.

RACINE COLLEGE BASE BALL CLUB.
H. B. WHITTEMORE, President.
WM. T. COMSTOCK, Vice President.
C. E. ANDREWS, Secretary.
GEO. PRESCOTT, Treasurer.
MILTON C. LIGHTNER, Captain.

Vol. I, page 1 of the first edition of the *College Mercury*, 1867.

With the publication of the *Register for Racine College for the Seventh Year* (1859–60), it is apparent that Rector James DeKoven is very much in charge of the institution and is moving forward with plans for the future. A calendar for the 1859–60 year is provided, and the beginning of the eighth year on September 29, 1860, is announced. There are significant statements and changes in this document that point out the direction that the school is taking.

The association of the school with the Protestant Episcopal Church and its ties to Nashotah House, and the preparation of students for continued studies in the seminary is detailed:

> The object of the College, as thus constituted, is to educate the youth placed in it, through the agency of the Church of the Living God, and in the principles of the Catholic Faith as held by the Protestant Episcopal Church in the United States, and with an especial view, moreover, to the preparing for the study of Theology those intending to become Clergymen.[26]

Following this explicit statement, a paragraph outlines living arrangements and the fact that the rector and clergy reside with the students as a family unit. Another sentence indicates that "definite religious instruction" is regularly given every Sunday. These are clear departures from the earlier standards of the institution where students were free to attend any church in the city. Under James DeKoven this religious affiliation became a stated requirement. Faculty and those on the board of trustees had to be members of the Episcopal Church.

Some very practical matters, such as expenses and payment deadlines, are included in the register. The Annual Session charge was raised with the new administration to $200. A $25 entrance fee was also added. These fees were definitely high for the period. In 1860, a skilled laborer made about $450 per year.[27] Tuition at a state university averaged $7 per term. The Racine College fee did include living costs (boarding, washing, fuel, lights, necessary furniture and tuition) but not clothing, books or medical fees.

Students in the grammar school lived in dormitories, in either Park or Kemper Halls and college students were assigned to private rooms in these two buildings. The use of tobacco was forbidden and students were warned against contracting any kind of debt. Although college students

26. *Register for Racine College for the Seventh Year, 1859–1860*, 14.
27. "Prices and Wages by Decade."

had more freedom to leave campus, with permission, the bounds were strictly limited for the younger pupils. Only the rector could grant time away from the college, and absence on Sunday was especially prohibited. Class days were Tuesday through Saturday, and Monday was a free day from schooling. Although no time schedule for the days is included in the first register, mornings came early—6 a.m. for everyone, and lights were out at regular times for both grammar and college students.

The number of students in the early years allowed for some innovation in instruction. DeKoven expressed his concern about the preparation of college-level students, especially in the classics including Latin. The following guidelines were provided to allow for differences in background:

> For the sake of convenience in instruction, students not prepared to enter the Freshman class are taught in Forms in the Grammar School according to their respective proficiency. A pupil, however, is not obliged to remain a certain period in one class, but is promoted according to his progress.[28]

This policy is remarkably advanced for the era. It allows demonstrated proficiency to be used for the determination of level and progress. DeKoven had witnessed good and poor teaching at both the college and seminary levels. He was not in favor of the rigid rote learning often practiced in educational institutions in this country. As teachers were hired for Racine College, new methods and new ideas were sometimes at odds with the philosophies of established professors. Often, as revealed in minutes of the faculty, James DeKoven was called upon to resolve potential conflicts. He did not hesitate to veto decisions made by the faculty. Flavel Luther was very accurate in his assessment of the nature of the institution; it was an autocracy, and James DeKoven was the autocrat.[29]

THE ACADEMIC STRUCTURE OF RACINE COLLEGE

The academic organization of Racine College under the leadership of James DeKoven was one of slow evolution. As established by Roswell Park, it was essentially a college program that involved two separate programs of study: the "full course" designed for those interested in pursuing

28. *Register for Racine College for the Seventh Year, 1859–1860*, 15.

29. Luther, "James de Koven, Teacher," 173.

a bachelor's degree, and the short course for those interested in the world of business.

With the arrival of DeKoven and company in 1859, Racine College became two schools under one name. The college program was designed primarily for those students who would go on to study at Nashotah House Seminary. The course of study for students in this program involved four areas: sacred studies, ancient languages, mathematics, general education in English, philosophy, and natural sciences. Enrollment in the college program was not automatic but involved passing an admissions test that covered areas in ancient languages, the New Testament, grammar, algebra, geography, and history.[30] The grammar school was created for younger students and involved three primary areas of knowledge: sacred studies, ancient languages, and English, which was a catch-all designation for work in history, philosophy, and mathematics, as well as composition, grammar, spelling, and penmanship. The grammar school consisted of six "forms" or grades under the guidance of the sub-rector. After completing these six years, students were eligible to enter the college department, whether or not they planned on continuing their work at Nashotah House.

During the years of Park's leadership, the academic year was similar to that of most institutions of higher education in the Midwest. The year had three sessions of fourteen weeks each. Classes started in late September or early October.

Once James DeKoven became the rector, the yearly schedules underwent several changes. The fact that most, if not all of the students lived on the Racine College campus and celebrated the two major Christian holidays, Christmas and Easter, with the college community required some adjustments.[31] Once the Christmas celebrations were finished, the students left for home and a winter vacation. The weekly schedule of the school also reflected the importance that was attached to practicing the Episcopal faith: classes met during the week from Tuesday through Saturday; Sunday involved several services in the chapel and concluded with

30. Such an admissions test was a requirement for Columbia College and undoubtedly influenced DeKoven's decision to implement the same type of testing at Racine College.

31. This practice of celebrating Christmas and Easter as a Racine College family continued until 1869, when students were allowed to leave before the holidays. It is of some interest that by this time there were so many students from so many different states, some of them at a great distance, that some students could not travel home.

different receptions hosted by the rector (later to be called the warden).[32] Monday was a day of rest and recreational activities.

DeKoven showed a willingness to make changes in the curriculum and adapt to student needs and popular trends. Aware of the increasing importance of scientific knowledge in mid-nineteenth century America, he accordingly championed the creation of a scientific school in 1867. In 1868, the study of modern languages was introduced into the curriculum. He expressed concern on several occasions about the weakness of some teachers and spoke out against the traditional methods of rote memorization and recitation as well as question-and-answer instruction. DeKoven was directly involved in the hiring of teachers, and many advertisements are found in local and national publications seeking instructors in particular disciplines. There are frequent published announcements concerning the school year and how information about the school can be obtained.

RECRUITMENT

Serious efforts were made at publicizing Racine College and its reorganization as soon as the decision for the merger became official. It is possible to follow the evolution and changes made through the various advertisements that were published in newspapers and publications throughout the country. The first advertisement with James DeKoven listed as rector of the college was this listing in the *Chicago Press & Tribune*, for Tuesday, November 8, 1859:

> Racine College with a larger number of Professors than heretofore, affording most efficient educational facilities, is now open for the reception of students. The Grammar School, where boys of eight years old and upwards are fitted for a College course, will be opened Nov. 1st.
> Address Rev. JAMES DEKOVEN. Racine College, Racine, Wisconsin.

By the time the following advertisement was published in the *Chicago Daily Tribune* on Tuesday, November 22, 1864, the information and the philosophy of the institution are more carefully spelled out:

32. In the course of his years in Wisconsin, James DeKoven had various titles in the different positions that he held. He came to Nashotah Mission as a tutor of ecclesiastical history. In 1857 with the establishment of St. John's Hall, he became warden of that institution. With the move to Racine College in 1859, he was given the title of rector and president. In 1867 he assumed the title of warden of the college.

RACINE COLLEGE,
A CHURCH SCHOOL FOR
BOYS AND YOUNG MEN,
RACINE, WISCONSIN.
Rev. JAMES DeKOVEN, D. D., Rector.

The Rector is assisted in the instruction of the scholars by eleven competent Professors and Masters.

The aim of the School is to give to the students: –

First. Sound religious instruction, according to the rules and discipline of the Church.

Second. Such intellectual training as will render a lad fit for business life, or thoroughly prepare him for any of the learned professions. The College course proper is in full operation.

Third. Careful physical training in all manly exercises. There is a large Gymnasium for the use of the scholars.

There are two large and very commodious buildings, giving accommodations for 110 scholars. There are 90 acres of land for playgrounds, &c. The scholars all live in the Buildings with the Rector and Masters, eat at a *common table, and form one family*. Vocal music and Elocution form part of the Regular studies of the school.

The Winter Term will begin December 1st, to continue until April 21st. For admission apply to the Rector. oc17-u294-5w

Ten years later, in 1874, an advertisement in the *Chicago Daily Tribune* provides a new source of information: it was now possible to obtain a catalog at three different locations in the city. (James DeKoven's brother, John, was head teller at Merchants' National Bank):

RACINE COLLEGE.

The twenty-second year of Racine College will begin Sept. 16. In the *Collegiate Department*, the School of Letters, the Scientific School, in the Preparatory Department, the Grammar School, the Mathematical School, will open on that day. The *system of houses* secures for the younger boys the personal care of a small school with the advantages of a large one. For admission, apply to the Rev. James DeKoven, *D. D.*, Racine. Wis. Catalogues can be obtained at the Merchants' National Bank, or at Mitchell & Hathaway's, No. 45 Clark-st., or at Jansen, McClurg & Co.'s.

An advertisement from August 4, 1875, indicates that Taylor Hall has been restored and improved:

RACINE COLLEGE.

The School of Letters, the Scientific School, and the Grammar School of Racine College will reopen Wednesday, Sept. 15.

The restoration of Taylor Hall, with many improvements, and a new Laboratory and Gymnasium which are to be finished before the term opens will add much to the advantages of the institution.

For admission apply to

REV. JAMES DE KOVEN, D. D.,
Racine College, Racine, Wis.

Catalogues can be had at Jansen, McClurg & Co.'s, Mitchell & Hathaway, 158 State-st., and at the Merchants' National Bank.

Newspaper advertisements were also used to recruit faculty members for the school. An ad which appeared in the *Church Journal* on July 13, 1864, listed membership in the Episcopal Church as a requirement.

WANTED—On or before Aug. 18th, an Assistant-Master for Racine College. His duties will be chiefly to teach Arithmetic and Writing, and to assist in the general care of the scholars. He must be a communicant of the Church. Apply to The Rev. JAMES DEKOVEN, D.D., Racine College, Racine, Wis.
598-4t

The attention that DeKoven gave to recruiting faculty members to the college is evident in the detailed letter he wrote on October 19, 1866, to Samuel Eliot of Boston, Massachusetts. In this letter he offers Eliot the "Professorship of History, English Literature, Etc. at Racine College" at a salary of $1,500.[33]

In true salesman style, DeKoven talks of the location of the college: "On Lake Michigan & has a most healthy and delightful climate . . . 2 ½ hours by sail from Chicago, one hour from Milwaukee and only about 40 hours from N.Y.; the duties of the position, to teach 4 hours a day, 5 days in the week"; possible housing, "a charming residence for sale just now close by the college," and the size of the student body, "between 150 & 160 scholars of whom 32 or there abouts [*sic*] will be in the four college classes." DeKoven points out what he thinks is most important for consideration: "We have begun on the right basis and the system is the true collegiate system of the Anglican Church unmixed with any shade of puritanism."

Professor Eliot did not accept the teaching position in Racine despite the sincerity and enthusiasm of the letter. DeKoven concludes with this heartfelt statement: "I am sure of one thing, that you could not bestow your labours & your powers, where with God's blessing they would be more sure of abundant fruits."[34]

This is the only example of a staff recruiting letter that has been located. However, it is a good example of the efforts James DeKoven made to attract qualified teachers to the college. He undoubtedly relied on suggestions and contacts from his network of friends and former classmates

33. Eliot had served as the president of Trinity College, Hartford, from 1860–64 and had returned to Boston where, at the time of the letter, he had no definitive position.

34. "Letter to Samuel Eliot from James DeKoven," Oct. 19, 1866, Boston Athenaeum Collections.

at Columbia and General in New York City. He had also established working relationships with the rectors of churches in Milwaukee and Chicago. DeKoven mentions the recommendation that brought Rev. Flavel Luther to his attention: "Dr. Tucker of Troy, who recommended him, thought that the name would be of special use to a college of ritualistic proclivities. . ."[35]

THE PREFECTORIAL SYSTEM

One of the innovations which DeKoven introduced at St. John's Hall and which he brought with him to the organization of student life at Racine College was the prefectorial system. In this "system," a great deal of the responsibility for maintaining order and for observing school rules and regulations is assigned to senior-level students who are chosen as prefects. It is difficult to determine exactly when DeKoven became acquainted with this idea, but it was championed by two of the educational pioneers who had influenced him.

For William Sewell, founder and warden of St. Peter's College, Radley, the prefectorial system was one of the three fundamental principles or ideals on which his institution was established. It is not claimed that Sewell invented the system but that he refined it. Its basis was the "government of boys partially by the boys themselves."[36] Prefects were chosen for their leadership qualities and their standing in the school.

A similar system for the organization of the student body was developed by Dr. Muhlenberg for his Flushing Institute. William Newton in his biography of Dr. Muhlenberg provided a description:

> For purposes of discipline, the whole number of boys was divided into sections of twelve. Each section was under the leadership of a prefect. These prefects were chosen from among the older pupils with reference to their character and qualifications for the work of influencing or restraining those whom they were appointed to lead and control.[37]

DeKoven was attracted to this idea for the maintenance of good order in a boarding school and worked on establishing it first at St. John's Hall in Delafield and then at Racine College. Although he did not divide the

35. DeKoven, *Journal*, Oi1, 107.

36. Bryans, *History of S. Peter's College*, 70.

37. Newton, *Dr. Muhlenberg*, 52.

student body into cohorts, he did choose prefects from among the natural leaders of the students. His efforts met with varying degrees of success, and his comments about the challenges he faced are found throughout his journal.

The first reference to this system of organization is found in the pages where he described the daily routine at St. John's Hall:

> In pursuance of the idea of governing the boys by boys the Rector appointed Pope, Whitney and Burton as Prefects. Their duty was to see that the boys attended Chapel and did their work and report to the Rector at the Prefects Meeting every Monday.[38]

DeKoven admits to the unpopularity of this "innovation," especially among the older students at Nashotah, those preparing for ordination. They viewed and criticized the system as "English & not American" and overstrict. In his commentary on these first efforts, he stresses the fact that he never asked the prefects to report on the other boys. Whether or not the students understood his ethical stance is not clear.

DeKoven brought the prefectorial system with him to Racine College. His refusal to abandon or seriously modify this method of governing the student body is probably the most clear-cut evidence of his stubbornness when faced with confrontation.[39] In his journal dated August 24, 1864, he provides this commentary:

> The College has 12 Prefects, the officers, I have labored for, who have charge of all discipline among the boys and punish without reporting. This has succeeded. The very dormitories are governed by Prefects who make no reports and are as well governed as by teachers.

The issue of the prefects and whether or not the boys and young men should be given such authority and responsibility never seems to

38. DeKoven, *Journal*, Di, 19.

39. At times DeKoven took misbehavior and disobedience very personally. He also saw it as an attempt to destroy the feeling of security that he wanted to permeate the culture of the college. In the following excerpt from his *Journal* dated September 18, 1870 (DeKoven, *Journal*, Ne1–Ne2, 95–96), note the repetition of the word "home." A student had surreptitiously been exploding fireworks inside Taylor Hall:

> We make such efforts to make Taylor Hall a true home, we spend so much time and thought and care to have it all it should be, that this was an offence far greater than the mere mention of it would indicate. It was really, as the event proved, an attempt to destroy this part of the collegiate work and make a barrack of the home we were seeking to build up.

have been completely settled in DeKoven's mind. Writing in his journal in June 1867, he makes this statement:

> The system of boy rule becomes every term more and more developed. Boys govern the dormitories, the dining room, the swimming, the going downtown, the gymnasium, etc., and now even the processions to Chapel.[40]

He admits that the responsibility caused difficulty for some boys and that others had suffered from poor and harassing treatment by their schoolmates. Over the years DeKoven continued to emphasize, through his sermons and weekly talks, the importance he attached to this system. He had even established a ceremony for the appointment of the prefects. In a journal entry in fall 1869, he described the assembly in the gymnasium at which the new prefects for the year were announced.[41] Under the leadership of the prefects, there evolved a guideline for behavior called "The Six Great Rules," approved by the rector in September 1862:

1. No tobacco shall be used.
2. Bounds shall not be broken.
3. Buildings shall not be defaced.
4. Debts shall not be contracted.
5. Bad language shall not be used.
6. Novels shall not be read without leave.

Although the prefecture system was part of the culture of Racine College and remained in effect throughout DeKoven's years as head of the school, it was not universally accepted by all faculty. The need for more serious types of discipline was regularly discussed at faculty meetings. On occasion there were votes to have students receive physical punishment. Drinking and smoking were offenses deemed worthy of whipping. DeKoven at times vetoed such a decision and always made it clear that it would be the responsibility of the headmaster, not his, to administer the sentence.

Thomas Gailor recounts in his memoir what discipline at the hands of James DeKoven felt like for the students:

40. DeKoven, *Journal*, Le2, 77.

41. DeKoven, *Journal*, Lu, 85. It is not difficult to imagine this gathering as being similar to that of Hogwarts in the *Harry Potter* series when the house membership is determined.

> Dr. James DeKoven we all regarded as our best friend. He made us feel that he was one of us. He took an active interest in all we did and shared in our pride when we won a game at baseball or cricket. Even when we endured punishment and had to be sent "up to the Doctor," we knew that it was like going to a big brother for a lecture; and we were ashamed of hurting him.[42]

James DeKoven played a dual role in the life of the boys, their families, and the college community. He was both priest and warden, although it was the title of rector that he chose when referring to himself. Diligent in watching after the spiritual life of the students, he kept track of academic progress of each boy. One very clever student used this duality to his advantage in discussing the dangerous topic of his smoking.[43]

> "D., have you been smoking?" D. replied, "Now, Doctor, do you ask this as a Priest, or as head of the school?" The Doctor smiled grimly, and said, "As the head of this school." D. replied, "No, sir." The Doctor said, "Now I ask you as a Priest, have you been smoking?" D. said, "Yes, Doctor; but you cannot punish me for saying so." The Doctor said, "No, but I can give you penance (twinkle in his eye). You may deny yourself of pie for six weeks."[44]

SPECIAL CELEBRATIONS

James DeKoven's insistence on creating a family group within the confines of the school is seen in the emphasis on eating meals, as well as participating in religious services together. Although some religious freedom had existed earlier in the history of Racine College, under the guidelines established by DeKoven it was the Episcopal faith that was practiced and expected of students as well as staff. The celebrations of Christmas and Easter are the most detailed examples of these ideas all coming together. These two holidays were part of the school year, and the Racine College students observed them at the school with their fellow students and teachers. Although the Dickensian idea of the Christmas holiday was not yet firmly established in American culture, it was slowly evolving from a

42. Gailor, *Some Memories*, 21.

43. The story is told by William Cox Pope in Chapter VII, "Reminiscences" of his biography *Life of the Reverend James DeKoven, D.D.*, 69–70.

44. Pope, *Life of the Reverend James DeKoven, D.D.*, 69–70.

purely religious feast to a more commercial and secular event.[45] DeKoven was able to keep the emphasis on the religious holiday, celebrated in the scholastic and spiritual family of the school, until 1869. After that year, students began their holiday vacation before Christmas Day.

The Christmas celebration of 1865 was described by James DeKoven in his journal.[46] Another version of the Christmas events was provided by the editor of the *College Mercury* in 1868.[47] According to the rector, there was much anticipation of the event during the weeks preceding the day. Part of this excitement was due to the arrival several times a day of the postal express wagon which was laden with packages and boxes: "The parents all send presents for their sons to be placed on the Christmas tree. The College provides a cornucopia for each boy and . . . I myself make a present to every boy and every member of the family."[48] The boys were undoubtedly aware of all the preparations, including the making of candy and cakes in the refectory kitchen. On Christmas Eve, after the younger boys had gone to bed, some of the teachers and older students went through the dormitories and filled the stockings that had been hung in each alcove with apples, oranges, nuts and candy. It is this scene that Mary Beach Johnson, DeKoven's niece, described in her letter of 1899, and of the delight that James DeKoven took in providing this holiday treat to his "family."[49]

Church attendance took up the greater part of Christmas morning. The first service was at 7 a.m. According to the student editor of the *College Mercury*:

> The Chapel heavily dressed with wreaths of evergreen and flooded with light, looked gloriously beautiful. The main body of the students entered first. The choir, in surplices, followed, singing as a processional the carol "Good Christian Men Rejoice." The clergy preceded by the College banner came last.

45. Charles Dickens published the novella *A Christmas Carol* in December 1843. It was an immediate success and has been credited with changing in many ways the celebration of the Christmas holiday throughout the English-speaking world, as well as in other cultures.

46. DeKoven, *Journal*, Ie1–Ja1, 51–58.

47. *College Mercury*, Vol. II, No, 3, Jan. 4, 1868.

48. DeKoven, *Journal*, Ie1, 51.

49. "That memorable visit to Racine will always be one of my most delightful reminiscences, and the Christmas festivities were of such a character that they made an indelible impression upon me." Letter from Mary Beach Johnson to William Cox Pope, dated May 2, 1899. Street Collection, Archives of the Episcopal Church.

Racine College Robed Choir

There followed a breakfast and then at 11 a.m. the communion service, with a sermon by the rector. DeKoven added this commentary: "Dinner at two. How splendid the turkeys, how glorious the mince pie, to say nothing of the more than usually good dessert."[50]

During the afternoon, the college Christmas tree and the accompanying gifts and treats were arranged in the gymnasium and the final decorations made for the evening celebration. This took place after the chapel service at 6 p.m., which was opened to the community and the chapel was filled to capacity. This description is in the *College Mercury*:

> From the Chapel all went to the Gymnasium, where was the Christmas tree, and where the presents were to be distributed. As we entered, we were almost blinded by the dazzling brightness. The tree seemed to be a pyramid of light, terminating in a glittering star surmounted by a brilliant cross. Suspended from the branches of the tree, arranged in piles at its base, covering tables in front and packed in baskets beneath, were the quantities of presents for the eager crowd around.

The Easter celebrations were quite a bit simpler than those surrounding the Christmas feast. There were, however, definite traditions

50. DeKoven, *Journal*, Iu2, 57.

that were followed. James DeKoven arranged for a series of sermons throughout the Lenten period, both for the regular Sunday service as well as for special services for the students throughout this penitential season. He often preached at these religious events and devoted a great deal of attention to the spiritual preparation of the students for the joy of Easter.

The 1865 Easter celebration at Racine College was a mixed event. In his journal DeKoven mentions that the Confederacy had fallen, Robert E. Lee had surrendered, and the boys had celebrated with an "extempore procession" using pans and kettles and old muskets as noisemakers.

> But Saturday in Holy Week what a day of horror it was when the news of Mr. Lincoln's assassination reached us. The Easter was a sad one for the land and us elders, but not even the assassination of the President could keep the boys from enjoying the breakfast, and the colored eggs and the Easter dinner.[51]

The *Chicago Daily Tribune* of Saturday, April 11, 1874, provided a very informative and descriptive article entitled "Easter at Racine College." The anonymous writer describes his visit to Racine for the Easter celebration one week earlier, on April 5, explaining the real reason for his visit: "To see and judge for myself whether there were practiced any of those forms, or ceremonies, or Romish rites, of which Dr. DeKoven has been accused, but which his masterly defense refutes so satisfactorily." What the inquiring visitor discovered was an impressively simple and solemn celebration of the Risen Christ. He describes the floral decorations, the hymns sung by the choir, the impressive manner in which Dr. DeKoven read the Gospel for Easter Day. He said that only one with a "heart of stone" would be unmoved by the beauty and reverential nature of the ceremony.

> As I looked with awe and the deepest solemnity upon this most touching and impressive scene, I remarked (as none can fail to do who have been present at the services in Racine Chapel) the entire absence of any form, or ritual, which ought to offend any sound Churchmen.

The author then described the Easter breakfast in the dining hall of the college. The ceremony of the day included a ritual with dyed Easter eggs. At the place of each of those at the breakfast was a plate with six colored eggs. The youngest boy in the school was called to come forward and attempt to crack the warden's egg with his own.

51. DeKoven, *Journal*, Ha2, 40.

> The egg is held so that the tip only projects, and is struck gently on the corresponding point of the competitor's egg. The egg which breaks is forfeited to the owner of the unbroken egg, and the contest continues until all the eggs except the specially tough ones are broken.[52]

DeKoven obviously took great delight in this traditional Easter egg game.[53] The author of the *Chicago Tribune* article details the enthusiasm with which Rev. Doctor participated in this egg cracking. "Herein, I think, lies one of his greatest charms, and one among many other reasons for his deserved success. It is in the perfectly-genial and even caressing manner toward his pupils."

The conclusion of the *Tribune* article, in a section entitled "The Rev. Dr. DeKoven and His Boys" centers around a description of the Sunday evening reception in the library of Taylor Hall. The author describes the almost ceremonial greeting and hand-shaking exchange DeKoven had with each of the participants. The mutual confidence displayed in these greetings as DeKoven spoke with the students was evident. "Here I again remarked the close intimacy and confidence existing between them. No fear, no awkwardness; but affectionate and kind inquiries from one, and gentleness and manly politeness from the other."

These scenes of James DeKoven among the students in celebration at Racine College provide a vivid insight into his dedication to the idea of the school as family. He obviously found special energy from participating in the rituals that came to be associated with the holidays. His role as the head of this spiritual family, because it was indeed a family centered on the religious nature of the events, was one that filled him with joy and obviously a sense of accomplishment.

There were other rituals and ceremonies that filled the year and life of the students at Racine College. Different clubs and organizations encouraged school spirit. Each student was assigned to one of the two major clubs: the Badger Club or the Clarkson Club. Several societies were formed, including the Addison Society for philosophical discussion and the Missionary Society for religious works. Different teams were organized for different age groups and sports including football, baseball, and cricket. Five different awards in each of these sports were given each year.

52. Student, "Racine and Dr. DeKoven VI." *Church Scholiast*, Vol. IV, No. 6, Mar. 1887, 99.

53. The egg-cracking game is a traditional Greek celebration at Easter called *tsougrisma*. Where or how it became established at Racine College is unknown. "Student" indicates that he had heard that this was an Easter custom common in Louisiana.

The commencement events were carefully planned and centered around the recognition of the accomplishments of students, as well as friends and supporters of the college. DeKoven chose the speakers at the graduation events with great care: he was interested in providing inspiration for the future based on solid religious beliefs. Over the years various prizes, all with a monetary award, had been established by friends and alumni of the college. These included the Larrabee Prize for Elocution ($30 in books); the Woolworth Philosophical Essay ($50); the Edwards Greek Prize ($50); and the Latin Composition Prize ($50).

There was one other ceremony that James DeKoven found emotionally difficult yet nevertheless an important part of the school year. This was the formal leave-taking of the boys as they gathered at the front door and sang their farewell song, "Dulce, Dulce Donum." In his journal he commented on this ceremony in a brief paragraph with reference to one student in particular but with application to many:

> I was very sorry to bid good bye to Merriam, dear fellow, he has been here for six years or more. That indeed is the trial of this kind of life. One learns to love the boys and young men as though they were one's children and then they go away and come back but rarely and other ties grow up with them, and then too, other boys come to me and so things change.[54]

SPECIAL EVENTS

One other special event, inaugurated in 1869, was an annual reunion of former students at Racine College. James DeKoven had a remarkable memory for the history of each boy. He was well-known among his colleagues in the Episcopal Church for the way he kept track of the old boys of Racine College. He described this inaugural reunion:

> During the summer term we established a new feature. We invited the 660 boys who had been at the college back to the college for a certain day early in August. Between 60 and 70 came besides, of course those who were here as scholars. We had letters too from many I had not heard from for a long time.[55]

The weather was particularly pleasant and cooperative, and the returning alumni were treated to special activities that were designed to remind

54. DeKoven, *Journal*, Ni2, 99.

55. DeKoven, *Journal*, Mi1, 87–88.

them of their years of study in Racine. There was a choral service in the Chapel of St. John, and a special dinner, with greetings and speeches, was served in the gymnasium.[56] After the dinner there was a cricket match with alumni of the two houses, Clarkson and Badger, competing again. As DeKoven summarized his feelings, "It was so pleasant to see the old faces; old, yet new, with beards and additional height and new duties, all so glad to come back."[57]

The reunions of "old boys" continued throughout the years of DeKoven's time and beyond. There are various photos and memorabilia of these gatherings as well as some from the years after his death and the continuation of the school. One of the most celebrated photos is the one taken of the 1870 and 1871 class reunion in 1906.[58]

56. DeKoven adds this comment in his journal: "Mrs. Franklin outdid herself with her admirable arrangements." He was amazingly consistent in giving credit to the women who played such an important role in the life of the institution. Here he credits Mrs. C. H. Franklin, the Matron of Taylor Hall, for her work in organizing the meal for the reunion attendees. DeKoven, *Journal*, Mi1, 88.

57. DeKoven, *Journal*, Mi1, 88.

58. These are the individuals from the classes of 1870 and 1871 who were present in the photo: Rev. Dr. Piper of Racine, Rev. Luther Pardee of Chicago, Rev. John Coleman of New York, Mr. John Slemmons of California, Judge Winslow of the Wisconsin Supreme Court, Alfred Sorenson of Omaha, Fred O. Osborne of St. Paul, Rev. Dr. Maclean of Joliet, Former Governor Merriam of Minnesota.

THE POPULATION OF RACINE COLLEGE

Student Enrollment—Racine College, James DeKoven Era, 1859–1880

Academic Year	College Students	Grammar School Students	Total Enrollment [Graduates in brackets]
1859–1860	17	23	40 [0]
1860–1861	23	39	62 [6]
1861–1862	18	51	69 [6]
1862–1863	10	86	96 [4]
1863–1864	13	110	123 [4]
1864–1865	17	134	151 [6]
1865–1866	17	150	167 [8]
1866–1867	36	141	177 [4]
1867–1868	43	165	208 [4]
1868–1869	43	167	210 [8]
1869–1870	53	135	188 [9]
1870–1871	54	131	185 [7]
1871–1872	69	135	204 [6]
1872–1873	64	157	221 [18]
1873–1874	57	139	196 [27]
1874–1875	42	141	183 [26]
1875–1876	31	119	150 [16]
1876–1877	35	111	146 [20]
1877–1878	38	97	135 [11]
1878–1879	44	125	169 [13]
1879–1880	36	114	150 [14]

When one walks through the peaceful setting of the DeKoven Center campus today, it is difficult to imagine the high level of activity that filled the place when the school was in full operation. One way to get an idea of what life was like at Racine College during its years of prosperity under the leadership of James DeKoven is to review some statistics about the population at various times. As can be seen in the accompanying chart, the number of students enrolled reached an all-time high in 1872–73. In addition to the students, there were also adults who lived on the campus for whom the college grounds and buildings were "home," and others who only came to work there.

According to the 1870 Federal Census, there were 180 young men identified as "At School" by the census taker. These students ranged in ages from eight years old (one person) to twenty-three years of age (one person). The greatest number fell in the range of fourteen to eighteen years; 144 of the 180 were in this age group. Those older than eighteen numbered twenty. Those over the age of seventeen were most generally enrolled in the college-level courses.

The college registers provide information about the students' permanent place of residence. There are two states with the largest number of students: Illinois, 58, and Wisconsin, 38. Ohio, Indiana, Michigan, and Missouri had relatively large number of students at the school. The 53 college students who lived in Taylor Hall came from fourteen states and Canada. The 135 grammar school students, who lived in Park and Kemper Halls, came from seventeen states and Cuba. This information depicts widespread knowledge of the school and its growing reputation, although students from states west of the Mississippi had not yet begun to enroll at the institution.

The energy associated with this number of nineteenth-century teenagers might have been different in its effects than what we would see today, but there were creative outlets, and sometimes pranks got the better of common sense. The "boys" were aware of the latest developments in science and technology: they created a telegraph line between the East Building and Taylor Hall. They inaugurated a student newspaper. Some of the boys brought their firearms with them so that they could go hunting; fishing was also a favorite pastime.

There were reports of fireworks and other explosives, and tricks being played on friends and "enemies" alike in the student body. Local farmers and vegetable growers were sometimes victims of petty thefts. Reports came to the warden of apples and other fruit being stolen in late summer and fall. The melons from James DeKoven's private garden one year were the produce selected for pilfering.

Daily living also required a great deal more energy and effort from the students: wood had to be chopped for stoves and fire places. Central heating was installed only with the reconstruction of Taylor Hall in 1876. Water for personal hygiene had to be sought, warmed, and distributed. Chamber pots and interior basement earth closets had also to be cared for. Although servants performed most of these duties, some were the responsibility of the students.

A significant change in the number of workers housed on campus can be seen when comparing the 1860 census with that of 1870. In 1860, one "laborer," a young man from Ireland (age twenty-four) and one "servant," a young woman from Denmark (age twenty-two) lived in college buildings. A decade later in 1870, there were twelve resident male laborers living in campus buildings: ten were in their twenties; two in their thirties. Of these twelve men working at the college, ten had been born in other countries, and two were born in the United States. They were responsible for the "heavy lifting" work of the institution, with several working as farm laborers.

In 1870, the number of female servants was indeed significant: thirty-four. Twenty-two of these young women (twenty were aged twenty or younger) had been born in other countries.[59] The two youngest servants were the only workers listed as "Black" in the group of employees. They had been born before emancipation in their states. Clara Davis, thirteen, was from Missouri and Laura Wells, eight, was from Tennessee. Their presence and their work as "servants" makes one wonder about their personal stories, along with the stories of the other workers. No specific mention of these two young girls has been found in other records or listings.

Racine was seeing an influx of immigrants from several countries including Denmark, Bohemia, and Prussia, as well as Ireland and England, as listed in the federal census. Although Racine College was essentially a white, Protestant, middle- to upper-class institution, it is impossible to ignore the diversity that students saw in their daily lives on the campus. With the presence of so many workers, speaking a variety of languages and representing a variety of cultures, there had to be some awareness of changes that were taking place in the life of the country.

DEKOVEN'S FINAL FOUR YEARS AT RACINE COLLEGE

It is a rare happening in a person's life that one day and date can provide a demarcation point for changes that impact the remaining years. Such, however, is the significance of the events that occurred early in February

59. The male laborers were from Denmark, England, Ireland and Prussia. The servants represented individuals from Prussia, Ireland, Denmark, Bohemia and England.

1875 in the life of James DeKoven. In Chicago, on the evening of February 4, at a convention of the Episcopal Diocese of Illinois, DeKoven was elected bishop of the diocese. Early on the following morning, a fire broke out and destroyed Taylor Hall on the campus of Racine College. This was DeKoven's home.

DeKoven faced many concerns and decisions as he sought to rebuild the Taylor Hall and reorganize the school. Frequently in his diary, he mentions his efforts to guide the institution toward a successful future. In addition, he had to deal with the death of his mother two months earlier, in December 1874, and the loss of his home as a result of the fire. On September 5 of 1875, he wrote, "The past has been the saddest and most distressing year of my life, full of sorrow and care, but God's will is, I hope, my will in such matters."[60]

A major problem was the significant decline in enrollment. The decrease in student numbers meant a decline in income for running the institution. In his typical logical approach to problem-solving, DeKoven outlined possible explanations for this decrease in numbers. He provides six possible causes: among them, the hard economic times in the country, rumors that he might leave the college, and the destruction of Taylor Hall by fire. Two of the concerns were ones he felt he could address through action.

DeKoven mentions the lack of an endowment frequently in his journal. He also is critical of the lack of support from the organized Episcopal Church. He mentions time and again his firm belief that it is the duty and responsibility of the church to educate. In an attempt to change the status quo, he created a plan which he called "A Church University for the West and Northwest." He convinced the nine regional bishops of the Episcopal Church to adopt Racine College "as the Collegiate Institution of their respective Dioceses."[61] It was his hope that the bishops would help by encouraging enrollment and providing additional financial support for the school.

The personnel issues that DeKoven faced were also personal issues. Several of the instructors who were weak in their respective disciplines had been at Racine for many years and reacted negatively to the efforts

60. DeKoven, *Journal*, Re2, 124.

61. The details of this plan are published in the *Register of Racine College 1876–77*. The bishops of the following dioceses agreed to the plan: Michigan, Indiana, Nebraska, Missouri, Colorado, Wisconsin, Western Michigan, Illinois and Fond du Lac. They attend a meeting of the board of trustees in the summer 1876.

to impose new standards. More recently hired teachers were rewarded by the board for their positive contributions to the changes while those with more seniority, and less involvement, were passed over. A disgruntled few saw in these decisions a betrayal by their "friend." Several resigned their positions and left with hard feelings. DeKoven summarized the situation:

> What a term it has been. Following the fire, the reduction in students, and consequent lessening of revenue. The endeavor to reorganize the college. The attempt to make the teaching what it ought to be, which has really been the sacrifice of private friendship to the interests of Christian education—all these have been full of great trial.[62]

It can be assumed that James DeKoven shared his difficulties with his family members. In the fall of 1875, he made the following entry in his diary: "My sister is coming out to keep my rooms for me instead of a matron as heretofore. This is a comfort, I trust."[63] The sister was Margaret, the widow of Dr. William Casey, the caregiver of the family. She had looked after her mother until her death. Later she was joined in Racine by their eldest sister, Elizabeth, who had lived in Chicago and whose eldest son and family still lived there. It is apparent that the family was concerned about their brother in Racine, and the support and help of these two older sisters brought him some peace.

James DeKoven was generally able to see the positive aspects of his life, even in the midst of the turmoil and problems of administering a school and dealing with the religious controversies that swirled about him. In the last pages of his journal, while dealing with financial and enrollment difficulties, he also mentions some of the good he experienced. He is excited about the beginning of construction for the new St. Luke's Hospital in Racine. He talks about the sons of four of his old classmates enrolled in Racine College in 1877. They had proved to be outstanding students. The celebration of the twenty-fifth anniversary of the school in the same year was a fitting time to reflect on the past. DeKoven delivered a powerful and positive sermon on the occasion of this celebration. And as always, the beauty of the natural world that surrounded him on the Racine College campus brought him comfort and peace.

But it was not enough. He turned to the board of trustees for help in resolving some particular problems. As he summarized the situation,

62. DeKoven, *Journal*, Se2, 129.

63. DeKoven, *Journal*, Re2, 124.

"They passed resolutions, appointed committees to raise the money, etc. and did nothing."[64] His friends were concerned about his health and suggested a major change in his life. An offer for a position at Trinity Church was made to him, and he thought seriously about accepting it. He wrote in his journal:

> I am weary with all the care. My nerves are not as strong as they were. I bear less easily the manifold anxieties of the work here. A change of life and work might be of great service. My friends all urged it. Even many friends of the college did the same, though some were more earnest the other way.[65]

But his dedication to duty made him hesitate and eventually decide against such a change.

The last entries in his journal contain some positive news: there was a large increase in number of students at the school in 1878. He was able to pay off $5,000 of the floating debt that had concerned him for years. And another of his goals had been achieved with the arrival of the two sisters of the Community of Saint Mary to take charge of Kemper Hall. He had been assigned by Bishop Welles to be their spiritual director. The final three sentences relate to another development that DeKoven sees as a positive omen for the future:

> Steps have been begun to make the Board of Trustees at Nashotah the same as that at Racine. Should this be accomplished, a union will be accomplished at last. How strange if this were to take place at the end of my 25th year of work in the West.[66]

THE RACINE COLLEGE CAMPUS

The quality of education provided by Racine College was just as important to DeKoven as the physical environment in which the students and faculty lived and worked. When DeKoven and his "pilgrims" arrived at Racine College on September 30, 1859, the campus consisted of one completed building and a twin to the first that was still under construction. The school had been granted a charter by the state legislature on March

64. DeKoven, *Journal*, Ti2, 140.
65. DeKoven, *Journal*, Ti1, 139.
66. DeKoven, *Journal*, Ua, 144.

3, 1852, and the cornerstone for the first building, called Park Hall[67] from its inception, was laid on May 5 of that year. There is some question about who designed and built these first two buildings, but it is generally accepted that J. F. Miller of New York was the architect/designer and Lucas Bradley, of Racine, was the builder.[68] Park Hall, completed in September 1853, served as administrative offices, residence hall, classroom building, library, laboratory, chapel, and dining hall. As the enrollment grew, by 1857 a second companion building, Kemper Hall, was begun 240 feet to the south of the original structure. Both buildings were built using cream brick with some imported red-brick trim. There is no indication in any of the earliest documents about a "master plan" that included the other buildings eventually constructed which joined these two early structures. However, the placement of Kemper Hall is so obviously parallel to Park Hall that it is logical to assume that there was an early plan.

The citizens of Racine, who had raised more than $10,000 for the construction of Park Hall, were called upon again to help fund the second needed building. Although $12,000 was donated, it was not sufficient to complete the structure, which remained unfinished and unused when DeKoven and students arrived. As part of the negotiations for the closing of St. John's Hall, the $2,000 that James DeKoven had raised for the construction of a school building in Delafield was given to him to use on the Racine College site. The first official ceremony involving the new rector and student body was the formal dedication of Kemper Hall on November 30, 1859. This completed building had a new and larger dining hall, additional dormitories, some private rooms, as well as several classrooms. One other addition to the campus was a wooden gymnasium constructed in 1861, at DeKoven's request. In his appeal to the board of trustees during their fall meeting, he made this plea:

> It is extremely difficult during the winter months, to find amusement for the students. Amusement is as necessary almost as prayer for boys . . . without it they assuredly become discontented and often fall into very terrible sins. I speak from

67. Roswell Park was named president before the college was organized. He came to Wisconsin from Connecticut where he had established a school in Pomfret. No explanation was ever given as to why the first building was named in his honor. Was this done to attract him to this "frontier" community?

68. The most recent discussion of the buildings and their history was written by Dorothy Osborne in 2002 for Preservation Racine's newsletter. She provides information about all the existing buildings on the campus, including references to Miller and Bradley. See "A History of Racine College," especially page 3.

> full knowledge of the subject when I say that it is impossible to carry on a Christian College without sufficient amusement for the Scholars.[69]

He also requested authorization to provide a pond for skating, a hill for coasting and inclusion of a bowling alley and billiard table in the gymnasium. He added that he was certain the parents would approve of these additions to the recreational opportunities for the students.[70]

Life at Racine College continued without major changes or interruptions until January 15, 1864. On that evening, during a snowstorm, a fire broke out in Park Hall. January 20, the *Racine Advocate* described the catastrophe:

> The Fire at the College.—The alarms of "fire" rang through our streets, on Friday evening last . . . The scene of the conflagration proved to be the north building of the Racine College. It was some time after the breaking out of the fire before aid could reach there, the distance being so great, and the snow so impeded the progress of the first apparatus that the main and north portion of the building was completely enveloped in flames before any water could be got on the fire. Engine No. 3 got onto the ground with the assistance of a team, furnished from the stable of Mr. Chas. Smith, and it was mainly through the efforts of this company, aided by citizens, and directed by Chief Engineer, Mr. Osborn, that the south portion of the building was saved from much damage . . .[71]

The article reported that most of the possessions of the students were saved, although the contents of the classrooms, library, and chapel were destroyed. Students who could not be housed in Kemper Hall that night were temporarily housed by residents in different parts of the city. Plans to replace and/or restore the building were already in progress by the time this article was published five days later.[72]

69. Racine College Board of Trustees Minutes for Fall Meeting, 1860.

70. DeKoven indicates that the billiard table caused talk "among the righteous—overmuch," and added, "If they knew as much as I do about boys, they would correspond with any amusement, however innocent, to save the poor children from the dreadful temptations which beset them, if unamused and unemployed." DeKoven, *Journal*, 42, He2.

71. "Local News," *Racine Advocate*, Jan. 20, 1864, 3.

72. On January 18, 1864, James DeKoven as rector sent a letter to all parents with children at the college. In this letter he stresses that the school continues with some changes: "The Rector of Racine College desires to relieve the natural anxiety which the

The fire also served as an introduction for DeKoven to his role as a fundraiser for Racine College. DeKoven sent out two of his colleagues on solicitation trips to Milwaukee, Philadelphia, and Boston. He himself made several visits to raise funds in Chicago. He wrote many letters to potential donors, as well as explanations of the need to different newspapers. These efforts resulted in a Racine College fund of $14,049.45, not counting seven donations from England in pounds sterling.

With this money, DeKoven paid for the restoration of Park Hall. There remained some funds that could be used to begin planning for the construction of a new chapel, separate from the other buildings. In a letter of appreciation published in the *Church Journal* in May 1864, DeKoven explains very succinctly the necessity for this project:

> The great need still remains of a chapel for us to worship in. Every congregation needs its House of God, but most of all a congregation of Christian boys in a Christian College. We feel it more and more to be the centre of all our work. It is the heart of the College, and from it flows the life blood of the Institution . . .[73]

In the same letter, DeKoven points out that the students are currently worshipping in a part of the gymnasium that has been rearranged temporarily to provide a place for religious services. He emphasizes the unique nature of Racine College, the only church college operating in the region, and the fact that the enrollment of the school is increasing.

DeKoven's appeals for additional support were obviously successful, and the cornerstone for the Chapel of Saint John was laid on August 17, 1864; the building was ready for use during the winter term of 1865.[74] It is remarkable how quickly the restoration of Park Hall and building of the chapel progressed. Students had returned to the use of this northernmost building for the fall term in 1864. The chapel was officially opened for

parents of the scholars must feel in regard to their children and the arrangements which are made for them for the future." DeKoven Center Archives.

73. *Church Journal*, Vol. XII, No. 88, May 4, 1864, 4. DeKoven wrote this letter to thank the support of the editors for their aid in making the situation of the college known. This comment was included in the letter: "With the avails of the insurance there is enough to place the building in better order than it was before the fire, to restore to use some of the other losses, and to leave a little more than $3,000 for a chapel."

74. In his report for Racine College as part of the *Journal of the Proceedings of the Nineteenth Annual Convention of the Protestant Episcopal Church*, June 14–15, 1865, DeKoven provided this information, "The corner stone of St. John's Chapel was laid August 18th, 1864 by the Bishop of the Diocese. It is now so far completed that we are able to use it for service. Several thousand dollars more will be needed to finish it, and furnish it as it should be." 79.

services on December 25, 1865, although interior improvements continued throughout the next two years. The whole cost of the chapel, including stained glass windows and organ, was nearly $18,000.

Chapel of St. John built in 1865, modeled after the chapel at Radley, Oxford.

Almost as interesting as the relatively low cost of the completed Chapel of Saint John is the origin of its design. There can be little doubt that it was modeled on, if not copied from, the plans for the original chapel at St. Peter's College, in Radley, England. James DeKoven visited this school during his summer trip of 1858 and apparently returned with an idea to replicate this traditional-style chapel in Racine.

Two long-time members of the board of trustees played significant roles in the development of the Racine College campus. Marshall M. Strong from Massachusetts, the first lawyer to practice in Racine, was one of the incorporators of Racine College.[75] He died in Racine on March 4, 1864. One of the stipulations in his will provided for the sale of eighty acres of land to Racine College at a very low price. He had purchased this land for the specific purpose of donating it to the college. These acres, adjacent to the campus to the west, became the college farm.[76] James DeKoven took a personal interest in the products of the farm and mentions successful garden harvests in his journal.

75. Leach, "Marshall Mason Strong," 335.

76. Sydney Hugh Croft, "Life of James DeKoven," 76.

> The grounds have never looked so charming as they do this spring. We have built a new barn and the old sheds are gone—brick walks have been laid, the garden is in capital order, the flower garden looks pretty and it is all beautiful.[77]

> This year [1867] our garden prospers, we have already picked more than five bushels of strawberries and shall pick more. We hope someday to have everything there should be on a gentleman's place. We have seven cows, a yoke of oxen, etc.[78]

The funding and construction of the college building, Taylor Hall, resulted from the generosity of local businessman Isaac Taylor and his wife Emerline.[79] Born in England and raised in an orphanage, Taylor eventually moved to Racine, where he achieved prominence in the lumber business. He served on the board of trustees of the college from the beginning and became a trusted friend and advisor for James DeKoven. He supported DeKoven's plans for a separate college building but died before he could put into action his many philanthropic ideas. It fell to his widow to carry out his plans. She provided a gift of $65,000 to the college, with the stipulation that $30,000 be put toward an endowment, the rest going toward the construction of Taylor Hall. The building, as eventually constructed, was smaller than the original plan, but it did fulfill DeKoven's desire of having a separate facility for the living and learning quarters of the college students. The completed building included rooms for fifty students, a library and classrooms, separate quarters for the rector and sub-rector, and "parlors" and recreational spaces for the students.[80] Taylor Hall, which DeKoven called "a noble building,"[81] was formally opened with great ceremony on Wednesday, January 29, 1868.

In a period of two years 1870–72, DeKoven oversaw the construction of two architecturally striking and utilitarian buildings that are still

77. DeKoven, *Journal*, Le1, 77.

78. DeKoven, *Journal*, Le2, 78.

79. Both Taylor and Strong had contributed $1,000 each in 1852 to purchase an additional acre of land to add to the nine acres that the Wright brothers had given for the location of the college.

80. In true student fashion, the editors of the *College Mercury* complained about the failure of the builder to meet deadlines and finish the building: "The contract for the building of Taylor Hall has in no wise been lived up to, or at the beginning of the College year the students would have taken possession of both the wings, and today the main building would be rapidly approaching completion." *College Mercury*, Vol. II, No. 1, Dec. 1, 1867.

81. DeKoven, *Journal*, Lu2, 82.

impressive today. The 240 feet of space between Park and Kemper Halls were filled first with a dining hall. James DeKoven insisted on the importance of the school eating together and ranked a refectory as next in importance to a chapel. By the fall of 1871 there was an imposing great room where the college could have its meals together. The kitchens were in the basement of the building, and the equipment and furnishings of the dining room were of the highest quality.

Racine College Dining Hall, completed 1871.

In a direct statement about the dining hall, the financial role that DeKoven's personal wealth played in the life of Racine College is made evident:

> The beautiful dining hall which was built by contributions of people in Chicago chiefly was finished in the autumn of 1871, and in the spring of 1872, we determined to build a new school room making the front of the quadrangle complete. We went into debt for it hoping to pay for it out of our earnings. I myself advanced the money for it . . . It was finished in time for

> the fall term in September, 1872, and added greatly to our accommodations.[82]

The School Room, a large single-story space, could accommodate at least one hundred student desks. The two-story section, which linked this new building to the dining hall, contained small classrooms on both levels that were used for recitation and course meetings. Now called the East Building, these four connected buildings are a witness to James DeKoven's ideas for a Christian school for boys and young men. They are a lasting testimony of his determination and dedication to the institution he created.

As shown in this chapter, fire devastated both Park Hall and Taylor Hall. After the Park Hall fire, fire safety was a major worry for the conscientious warden. He mentions this several times in his journal, and the staff and students were well aware of his fear. Alexis duPont Parker wrote:

> The nervousness of Dr. deKoven in regard to fire was a well-known fact . . . One was liable to meet the Doctor out on the grounds at almost any hour of the night, he having seen an unexpected light somewhere in the buildings and unable to rest until its cause was ascertained. During my Sixth Form year (1874–75) I had charge of a dormitory heated by a large coal stove with the usual mica doors. Several times that winter the Doctor came across from Taylor Hall late at night and climbed the flights of stairs to assure himself that my fire was not dangerously high.[83]

The winter of 1875 was a very cold and blustery one. The temperature fell below negative twenty degrees on a regular basis. Early in the morning of February 5, a serious blaze destroyed Taylor Hall. The experience from a student viewpoint is found in a "Racine Diary" kept by Thomas Frank Gailor, who had entered the school in September of 1873.[84] He started writing his account a few days after the fire.

82. DeKoven, *Journal*, Oa, 104–5.

83. Student, "Racine and Dr. DeKoven V," *Church Scholiast*, Jan. 1887, 54. This statement has allowed the identification of the student who authored these articles as Alexis duPont Parker, whose father, Stevens Parker, eventually succeeded DeKoven as warden of Racine College.

84. Gailor graduated from Racine College as valedictorian in 1876. He studied at the General Theological Seminary in New York City, was ordained a priest in 1880 and taught at the University of the South where he eventually became vice-chancellor of that institution. He was consecrated Assistant Bishop of Tennessee in 1893 and third Bishop of the state in 1898. In 1919 he was elected president of the National Council of the Episcopal Church. He died in Sewanee in 1935.

> About six o'clock roused by the cry of fire I rushed from my bedroom only to see the roof above me on fire and hear the shouts of the frightened students in the halls below. Put on hurriedly in the dark the *worst* pair of pants I had, two undercoats, and hat and threw my two large Lexicons out of the window and some clothes. Then rushed frantically into Smythe's room and after throwing my *boots* and overcoat out the window exclaim in a very tragic manner that I have nothing on my feet. After putting on Smythe's shoes I descended by the rope which hung from the window generally called a "fire escape" and so reached the ground in safety.[85]

Gailor described his feeling as one of awe about having survived the fire and having witnessed it.

There was obviously never any doubt about the decision to rebuild Taylor Hall. Even though the interior of the building was completely gutted, most of the exterior was intact. Only the east façade had to be torn down and redesigned.[86] The decision was made to install a central steam heating system and more or less modern plumbing throughout the building.[87] The restoration and reconstruction of the building proceeded quite rapidly, using both insurance payments and additional donations. In a letter to parents and patrons on June 19 of that year, the warden of Racine College was able to write, "I am happy to inform you that Taylor Hall, will, God willing, be ready for occupation on September 1st. A new Gymnasium and a very excellent Laboratory will also be completed and ready for use at the same time."[88] This was the final major building project that DeKoven oversaw for the College campus.[89]

85. Gailor, *Some Memories*, 23.

86. One of the greatest losses for DeKoven was the destruction of the "College Clock." This clock had been installed in 1871 and had three dials on the tower, and another dial three stories below in the entry hallway. These three separate dials on the tower were connected with the inside dial and by an ingenious arrangement, the hands of each dial moved simultaneously. The funds for the clock were raised by the Ladies Aid Society. *College Mercury*, Vol. VIII, No. 4, Feb. 1, 1871.

87. On January 12, 1876, DeKoven made the following comment in his journal: "We now have been comfortably fixed in Taylor Hall since the latter part of September and except great distress from sewers badly constructed have been quite comfortable. The sewers, however, reserved the crises of bad smells and gases until the students had left. We have been able to fix them during their absence." DeKoven, *Journal*, Ri2, 126.

88. DeKoven, "Letter to the Patrons and Friends of Racine College," June 19, 1875. Racine College Object File, Racine Heritage Museum Archives.

89. Additions were made when needed. The following appeared in the *College Mercury* on June 12, 1876: "The carpenters are rapidly completing the gallery in the

Taylor Hall front entrance and clock tower, originally built 1867, reconstructed 1875.

James DeKoven's practicality and his awareness of all the needs and concerns on the school's campus is evidenced by a few final decisions he made and causes he championed. The final building project he oversaw was the construction of an up-to date "earth closet" brick building located outside and close to the East Building and the Chapel. He also sought a means of providing a more reliable source of fresh water on the campus by digging an "artesian" well, but this was not accomplished during his lifetime.

James DeKoven loved the Racine College campus and was proud of the buildings that were built under his leadership. He was also very proud and interested in the upkeep of the grounds and location of the campus

Gymnasium. It is calculated [to] hold a hundred people, and will be a great addition to the comfort and conveniences of Commencement Day, as the band and part of the Grammar School will be seated there." *College Mercury*, Vol. XIX, No. 6, Jun. 12, 1876.

along the shores of Lake Michigan. He dedicated the last twenty years of his life to the creation of a place of beauty and peace for the students who studied and lived there. This place now attests to his ideas, saintliness and influence. In many ways, the buildings that make up the DeKoven Center campus and the landscaping that surrounds them are a fitting and lasting memorial to the man who oversaw their planning, construction and maintenance.

THE PRESENT BUILDINGS OF RACINE COLLEGE.

Published in the Racine College Register of 1875–76

6

James DeKoven in Images, Words and Deeds

On June 30, 1867, Mary Todd Lincoln wrote from Racine, Wisconsin, to her friend Elizabeth Atwater of Chicago, describing her visit to the city located on Lake Michigan. She had come to investigate the possibility of sending her son Tad, age twelve, to the grammar school associated with Racine College. Mrs. Lincoln was escorted on a visit to the college by the wife of Senator James Rood Doolittle. As she describes their visit, "We were of course most graciously received by the head professor, Dr. DeKoven—attired very much like a *Jesuit* Priest, with an air of great suavity he conducted us throughout the building . . ."[1] The somewhat critical tone of this brief description of James DeKoven is apparent by the use of the words "Jesuit" and "priest." There can be no doubt that Mrs. Lincoln held definite ideas about the high church and even "romish" nature of the religion as practiced at Racine College.[2] Her description of his manner as "suave" contains an implied comparison of this man with the society in which he operated. East Coast suavity is found in this educational

1. Letter to Elizabeth Emerson Atwater, June 30, 1867. In Turner and Turner, *Mary Todd Lincoln*, 426.

2. Justin Turner, editor of the Mary Todd Lincoln letters, provides this observation: "Her letters from Racine provide evidence that she was prejudiced against the school—against any boarding school—almost before she saw it. This one seemed a bit too 'high church.' The tuition was prohibitive. An 'air of restraint' about the place put her off." 421–22.

outpost of the great northwest. For some reason this made Mrs. Lincoln uncomfortable.[3]

IMAGES

The brief description by Mary Todd Lincoln can be compared to the earliest portrait of James DeKoven that has been found.[4] It was obviously a formal photo setting and probably taken early in his public life. The quality of the portrait is such that it can be roughly dated as the late 1850s/early 1860s. The seated DeKoven is wearing a black cassock with what appears to be an over-the-shoulder cowl or caplet and a full neck-band white clerical collar. This is the photo of a young man in his prime, an individual who has achieved some of his goals and is ready to face the accomplishment of others. A definite feeling of pride emanates from this portrait. Due to the clerical garb, it seems appropriate to conjecture that this photo was made to memorialize his ordination to the diaconate (1854) in Middletown, Connecticut or to the priesthood (1855) in Delafield, Wisconsin. There is no indication of the photographer or studio location on the copy in the DeKoven Center Archives. This is definitely a younger James DeKoven, since he is not wearing the frameless glasses that are seen in almost all other photos taken later in his life. His deep-set, piercing eyes attract one's attention: they are described as "grey" in the passport "Description of James DeKoven" from 1868.[5] His well-trimmed beard and mustache are full and appear darker than his hair, which is neatly combed and described as brown. According to the passport description he has a "medium" mouth, his nose "Grecian" and his complexion is "light." The description of his chin as oval can cause wonderment since all of the existing photos show him as bearded with no clear view of a chin. James DeKoven, five feet nine and one half inches, was slightly taller than the average American male during the Civil War period. The average soldier was five feet, seven inches tall.

3. In many ways the word "Jesuit" was, at the time, a not-too-subtle way of expressing anti-Catholic sentiments.

4. The photos of James DeKoven used in this chapter are all from the archival collections of the DeKoven Center. No sources are listed with these photos. Rev. Sydney H. Croft, who served as a part-time chaplain of the Community of Saint Mary in the 1950s, is credited with collecting photos and documents related to the history of Racine College and the DeKoven Foundation.

5. There is no photograph accompanying this passport application. Photos did not become a regular part of the passport application until after World War I.

The DeKoven of this early portrait is a handsome young man who would definitely attract attention with his demeanor and suavity. It was not enough, however, to convince Mary Lincoln to send her son Tad to Racine College for the continuation of his education. She visited the college and its grounds several times during her more than two-week stay in the city. She was particularly distressed by the idea that Tad would be required to board at the school, "My feelings were especially moved by seeing the little white cots of the boys, where they are wont to repose so far away from the[ir] loving Mothers."[6] Although she conceded that "it must be a most excellent school," she returned to Chicago and enrolled Tad at a day school there. This visit of Mrs. Lincoln to Racine with her son is the source of the local legend that Tad Lincoln had been a student at Racine College.

6. Turner and Turner, *Mary Todd Lincoln*, 421.

It is of some interest that James DeKoven did not write about this visit of Mary Todd Lincoln in his journal. Her visit came at a very busy period in the history of Racine College, and he did write about several other events that had taken place around the time of her stay in Racine. Various other visitors had come to the college in late June and early July. The school had its largest enrollment since its founding in 1852, with 167 students, and many improvements were being made to the building and grounds. A student newspaper, the *College Mercury*, published its first issue (June 15, 1867).[7] But the visit of Mary Todd Lincoln was not mentioned in DeKoven's diary nor the student newspaper.

We are fortunate that James DeKoven lived in the early days of the photographic era. There are several photos of DeKoven either alone or with others. His association with students insured that he would be introduced to new developments in technology and communication. Students then, as now, were fascinated by the latest inventions. Although no descriptions are attached or joined to the group photos that exist, it is easy to deduce that it is he who is pictured in them with students or colleagues. The photographs do allow us to see the aging of James DeKoven and, unfortunately, his physical deterioration as his heart disease progressed.

The second portrait of James DeKoven in the archival collection is the only portrait with a full facial straightforward view. It is also the only photo where the subject is identified, "Rev. Dr. de Koven." The DeKoven in this photo is dressed in everyday attire, somewhat belying the general impression that he wore the cassock as his regular garb. He is thinner in this picture and has a more formal bearing. As noted in the earlier photograph he is not wearing his customary glasses. It is in his eyes that we can see the spirit of the man: they are clear and could be piercing with the right moment.

7. DeKoven, *Journal*, Li1, 78.

This group photo was probably taken in a local studio in Racine; the backdrop is typical of studio settings of the era.[8] The nine young men who surround James DeKoven are of different ages, although all appear relatively young. The two seated men on either side of the warden could well be teachers or administrators at the college. The ages of students pursuing the college curriculum varied greatly; sometimes they were as old as the instructors. James DeKoven is definitely at his heaviest in this photo, perhaps an indication of the healthiest period in his life.[9] Racine College experienced an uptick in its numbers toward the end of the Civil War; due to the increase in revenue, the expansion and maintenance of buildings was possible. His worries were fewer and his success with the

8. The original photo has the studio mark "Billings photo" (E. T. Billings, Studio).

9. The food served in the refectory at Racine College varied somewhat depending upon the matron who was in charge. However, DeKoven insisted on good food and the same quality of food for everyone in the dining hall. Many of the vegetables that were served were grown in the college farm after it was established in 1864.

school was recognized. It was a period of relative contentment. We see James DeKoven as the confident and confirmed leader of an educational institution of higher learning.

The most widely known photo of James DeKoven is one that was taken in Racine probably around 1868. On the back of the photograph in the DeKoven Center archives is the name "Thomas Photographer."[10] A copy was used as the model for the oil painting that currently hangs in the Taylor Hall library at the DeKoven Center. It was purchased by the board of trustees in 1884 for display in the refectory. A recent restoration of the portrait confirmed that it is the work of Henry Eric Christopher Peterson (1841–1918).[11]

10. This information is found on the reverse side of many photos in the DeKoven Archival Collections: *Thomas Photographer, College Avenue between Twelfth and Thirteenth Street.*

11. The minutes of the board of trustees provide information about the purchase of the portrait. In 1884, a payment of $295 ("paid for portrait") is listed in the expenditures for that year. The portrait was first hung in the Refectory. Sometime later, the portrait itself was reduced in size and place in a new, smaller frame. Re-stretching and remounting the canvas resulted in the artist's signature being hidden.

An engraving based on this photograph, called the "Paris Crayon," was used by Morgan Dix for the frontispiece of the publication *Sermons Preached on Various Occasions* published in 1880. The copy that Dix used was signed by DeKoven, "Ever affect. yours." It was also used by William Cox Pope for the publication of his 1889 biography *Life of the Reverend James De Koven, D.D., Sometime Warden of Racine College.*

A final photographic image in the DeKoven collection reveals a more mature image of the Racine College warden. He is not as carefully groomed as in the other settings: his beard is longer, greyer, and not as neatly trimmed. There is, however, a softness in his regard and warmth in the slight smile on his lips. The physical and emotional stress of the 1870s has contributed to a more mature outlook on life in general. The copy in the archives is a hand-tinted photo in relatively poor condition. This photo was taken at the Thomas Photography studio in Racine.[12]

12. A copy of this portrait was published in a two-volume collection of photographic

WORDS

The brief written description of DeKoven by Mrs. Lincoln is the unique example we have of his encounter with a "famous person." There are other sketches written by students, colleagues, and friends, as well as relatively impartial observers that supplement the photographic images in the archival collection. We can turn to them in an attempt to come to a better understanding of James DeKoven as a human being in a particular time and place.

One of the more interesting, and seemingly unbiased, descriptions of DeKoven was published in the *Chicago Daily Tribune* on Sunday, February 15, 1874. The unidentified author recounts the appearance and

portraits of prominent nineteenth century figures in politics, education, and the arts. These albums are part of the collection of the Philadelphia Library Company.

presentation that DeKoven made before the Special Council of the Episcopal Convention in Milwaukee. This was DeKoven's attempt to provide a thorough explanation of his theological ideas that were being challenged by members of his church. The language of this description is evocative of the journalistic style common in newspapers of the era and the written portraits of prominent people provided in published articles.

> First in order, as first in attainments, gentlemanly bearing, and magnetic eloquence, combined with an overwhelming Logic, comes the Rev. James DeKoven, D.D. and Director of Racine College. This eminent cleric is still in the vigor of manhood,—he appears to be no more than 40,—although his acquaintances assert that he is nearer to the confines of half a century. He is, evidently, of Teutonic descent—perhaps some of the Knickerbocker blood may course through his veins. In person, he is over the medium height, squarely built, but rather inclined to flesh, but graceful withal. He wears a short all-round beard, which is, like his hair, of a very light-brown color and rigidly straight. His eyes, like those of most distinguished men, are gray, approaching blue. He has a straight, handsome nose, a well-formed mouth, and very fine teeth. The face, taken as a whole, indicates strong intellectuality and latent power. He looks like a man capable of tremendous work, and his general physical appearance, when the man is not excited, is suggestive of a lion at rest.[13]

There are probably few writers today who could provide such a thorough word-portrait of a famous individual. The image of the "lion at rest" combined with the sentence referring to his facial features is memorable.

The *Nashotah Scholiast* was published by individuals associated with Nashotah House Seminary and provided a forum for several articles that dealt with James DeKoven. Letters and documents relating to other prominent figures and events in the early history of the Episcopal Church in Wisconsin were also published. Two series of articles written about the life of DeKoven were published in 1885 through 1887. The first set of remembrances was written by John Henry Hopkins Jr. who was acquainted with DeKoven's years at the General Theological Seminary in New York City. He had graduated four years before DeKoven.

Soon after the unexpected death of James DeKoven, Hopkins announced that he would undertake the writing of a biography of his colleague and friend. In preparation for this project, he solicited personal

13. *Chicago Daily Tribune*, Sunday, Feb. 15, 1874.

papers and documents from family and friends that could be used in preparing such a life story. This biography was never was realized, but in 1885, he did write a series of articles entitled "A Few Recollections of James deKoven." The seven recollections are devoted to DeKoven as churchman and participant in the general conventions and church congresses. In the introduction to the first recollection, Hopkins indicates that there are others who had more personal knowledge of DeKoven than he and were thus better qualified to write biographical reminiscences: "The gleanings, then from my field of memory cannot but be meagre and disappointing. But I will do my best."[14]

A common theme repeated in his recollections is what he describes as DeKoven's "singular combination of sweetness and strength."[15] Hopkins says that this personality trait was apparent from his first days at the General Theological Seminary (1851) and was accompanied by what he called "his power of initiative." Later in his life, when DeKoven was a delegate to the General Convention in 1868 in New York City, Hopkins observed these qualities again. DeKoven began to play a role in the deliberations on the question of ritualism. He spoke twice in reply to reports from the Committee on Canons. Both his speeches were brief, but they clearly demonstrated what would be his talent in all future remarks he would make at such assemblies. James DeKoven had an ability to read documents with an unusual clarity and find explanations, contradictions, and problems others did not see. Hopkins comments on DeKoven's second speech at this General Convention: "Brief as it was, [it] made its mark. Not one word was thrown away. Every point told; and the winsome sweetness of manner gave a subtle insinuating power which the mere force of correct reasoning would never have produced."[16] Perhaps DeKoven's most important speech at a general convention came in 1874,

14. Hopkins, "Few Recollections of James DeKoven No. 1," *Nashotah Scholiast*, Vol. II, No. 4, Feb. 1885, 64.

15. Hopkins realized that not everyone viewed James DeKoven with the same positive acceptance. In Recollection 4, he provides this quotation from Dr. Adam of Nashotah House, in which Adams warns participants at the General Convention about being taken in by DeKoven's mild manner: "I do not want members of this House to get under an excitement and imagine that they are persecuting him and putting him down . . . But at the same time, if this House imagine that my colleague [DeKoven] is a meet lamb to be martyred here, they make a great mistake. My colleague is simply one of the shrewdest and ablest party leaders that has ever been on the floor of this House." Cited in Recollection No. 4, May 1885, 118.

16. Hopkins, "Few Recollections of James DeKoven, No. 2," *Nashotah Scholiast*, Vol. II, No. 5, March 1885, 83.

at the New York meeting. His presentation against the restrictive Canon on Ritual is described by Hopkins, who once again uses the word "sweet" in reference to his voice and disposition. DeKoven spoke for almost two hours on this occasion:

> Throughout the whole of this remarkable speech, with its great variety of subjects and points, its arguments, its wit, its humor, its pathos, its transcendent power, with the marvelous flexibility of his sweet and sympathetic voice, the speaker held the whole House spell-bound.[17]

One of the most thorough of these written portrayals of James DeKoven is found in another series of articles that appeared in the *Church Scholiast* in 1886. The author of these eight articles is identified only with the word "Student." He deals with DeKoven as head of Racine College. The writer provides some wonderful insights into the personality of James DeKoven and indicates that he has written these articles with the hope that others, former students and clergy friends, would likewise share their reminiscences of life at Racine College with the warden.

"Student" points out that his preconceived ideas of what he would find at the college and with James DeKoven were essentially the result of his own background, growing up in a very "low church diocese."

> I had been led to regard Racine College as a hotbed of ritualism (which was a synonym of all that was wrong in Church affairs), and Dr. deKoven as the incarnation of Jesuitism within the church . . . I thought Dr. deKoven would be a tall, dark-featured man, who habitually appeared in a cassock and wore a crucifix.[18]

"Student" came to Racine in the fall of 1875 and spent the next four years studying at the college, during which time he became devoted to DeKoven and learned to respect and admire him for his genuine love of the students under his care. "Student" describes his first encounter with the warden on the day of his arrival at the school.

> Suffice it to say that in the genial, somewhat portly, bearded man, who met me with a warm grasp of the hand, a winning smile and a few earnest words of welcome, I failed to find the slightest trace of the reported "Jesuit in disguise." There was, to

17. Hopkins, "Few Recollections of James DeKoven No. VI," *Nashotah Scholiast*, Vol II, No. 4, Jun. 1885, 132.

18. Student, "Racine and Dr. DeKoven II," *Church Scholiast*, Vol. IV, No. 1, October 1886, 2.

> be sure, a single keen glance through the clear rimless spectacles he always wore, which made one feel that one's character had been read and the result laid away for future reference; but one could not but feel that here was a man he could trust. This wonderful faculty of inspiring confidence and respect was eminently a characteristic of James deKoven.[19]

It is apparent from the observations made throughout these eight articles that "Student" grew in his respect for the doctor and came to admire his calm and positive interaction with people. He talks of the pleasant meals he had with DeKoven and his sisters and the love the former had for anecdotes and the droll way in which he told them. Even when he had to deal with a disciplinary issue the result was positive, "Here, as at all other times, in some way I cannot describe, one was made to know that the fault and the culprit were not identical in Dr. deKoven's mind, and however strongly he might censure the former, his affection for the latter was not altered."[20]

The four years that "Student" attended Racine College were some of the most active and stressful in DeKoven's life. His role in the Episcopal Church in America was becoming more and more visible not only because of the success of Racine College but also due to his ability to express clearly and forcefully his ideas on ritual and the Eucharist. DeKoven always maintained a forgiving attitude toward those who criticized him: "Amid all the misrepresentation and calumny to which Dr. deKoven was subjected, he ever forbore to refer to it in any way. He would not even allow it spoken of in his presence."[21] If someone did mention a criticism, DeKoven would answer, "There, my boy, be still. Remember they think they are right in what they say."[22]

One interesting and intriguing comment made by "Student" in his first article concerns the biography of DeKoven as planned by Hopkins:

> It is probably not a matter of general knowledge that it is reported that shortly after the Doctor's death, the Rev. J.H. Hopkins,

19. Student, "Racine and Dr. DeKoven, III," *Church Scholiast*, Vol. IV, No. 2, Nov. 1886, 20.

20. Student, "Racine and Dr. DeKoven I," *Church Scholiast,* Vol. III, No. 12, Sep. 1886, 202.

21. Letter of Mary Beach Johnson to William Cox Pope, dated Mary 2, 1899. William Cox Pope Papers, Record Group 137, National Episcopal Archives, Austin, Texas.

22. Student, "Racine and Dr. DeKoven III," *Church Scholiast,* Vol. IV, No. 2, Nov. 1886, 20.

> D.D., stood ready to write a life of Dr. deKoven, but unexpected obstacles prevented the accomplishment of such an undertaking. This unlooked-for termination of the plan was most unfortunate, for there is probably no one better fitted for such a task, or one whose work would be received with more respect and favor by the Church than Dr. deKoven's fast friend, Dr. Hopkins. The lack of such an account of James deKoven's life is a great loss.[23]

Not only did Hopkins abandon his project of a biography because "of unexpected obstacles," but the supporting documentation he had collected from family and friends also disappeared. This disappearance was substantiated in a letter written in 1921 by DeKoven's niece, Mary Beach Johnson.

Another moving description of DeKoven by a colleague was published in 1921 in *The Living Church* with the title "James de Koven—Teacher." This article was a transcription of a speech given by Flavel S. Luther at Christ Church in Redondo Beach, California. Luther taught at Racine College from 1872 through 1879 and went on to serve as President of Trinity College in Hartford, Connecticut. He describes his first encounter with DeKoven:

> In 1872 I found myself engaged as a teacher in the Racine Grammar School and went there in August of that year, accompanied by the young bride who for nearly half a century since has been my co-laborer and my inspiration. We went to what was then the far West, Wisconsin, from Connecticut, and on an August evening in what was called the Visitors' Parlor in Racine College I first met James de Koven. We arrived there early in the evening and he came over from his own quarters to greet us; a rather tall man, stout but not broad-shouldered and not of athletic physique. His hair was nearer brown than yellow and he had bright blue eyes usually partially concealed by glasses. He wore a full brown beard. At that time he was 41 years old.[24]

It is obvious that DeKoven had a life-long impact on Rev. Luther because this speech was given some forty years after the warden's death.

Luther served as head of the grammar school at Racine College and taught mathematics. He is very frank in his assessment of some of DeKoven's ideas about the organization of the school. He admits that only James DeKoven could have controlled both a grammar school and

23. Student, "Racine and Dr. DeKoven I," *Church Scholiast,* Vol. III, No. 12, Sep. 1886, 202.

24. Luther, "James de Koven, Teacher," 172–74.

college on the same campus. Luther is blunt in his analysis of the situation as it existed at Racine College under the leadership of James DeKoven:

> Racine College was an autocracy and James de Koven was the autocrat—sweet, beautiful, lovable, but nevertheless with an iron will and strong personality which maintained discipline by pure force of that sweetness and power of character. Racine in those days had fully its fair share of boys and young men who needed very strong handling. They required severe discipline at times. Dr. de Koven could quiet the worst row you have ever heard in a school room by simply looking in at the door. He dominated his faculty, his trustees. Everything went as he, the Doctor, said; and he generally said that which was just about right; and the result was a loyalty on the part of his teachers, students, and boys, very seldom excelled. I have never loved any place beyond my birthplace as I have loved Racine.[25]

Flavel Luther also comments on DeKoven's manner of dealing with the criticism and antagonism directed at him: "He loved mankind; he was the friend of all the world and had no condemning words for those who differed with him. In his wide toleration he had no bitter words for those who had very, very bitter words for him."[26]

The question of the objectivity of these observations and descriptions of James De Koven is one that cannot be answered fully. Some of the writers even admit their subjectivity and base it on their knowledge of the man; what they share is truth as they know it.

Dr. Samuel Johnson, renowned biographer, made the following statement about finding information for a biography, "more knowledge may be gained of a man's real character by a short conversation with one of his servants, than from a formal and studied narrative begun with his pedigree, and ended with his funeral."[27]

It is unfortunate that we cannot travel back in time in order to interview those associated with James DeKoven at various points in his life. His position was such that he lived constantly among others, students as well as other priests and educators. Interviews with his numerous family members would also have added to our deeper understanding of his character. But if Dr. Johnson's analysis is to be accepted, it would be great to talk to those who served him throughout his life and public career.

25. Luther, "James de Koven, Teacher," 173.

26. Luther, "James de Koven, Teacher," 172.

27. Johnson, *Rambler*, 60.

As the size of Racine College grew, so did James DeKoven's responsibilities as a manager of an increasing work force. Not only was he responsible for teaching and administrative employees but also cooks and launderers and domestic servants. During his first year in Racine, 44 students lived on campus along with two domestic employees. Ten years later, in 1870, there were 174 students, 5 matrons, and over 40 domestic workers living in the five buildings.

Although we cannot interview any of these individuals, one document in the DeKoven Center archives provides insight into DeKoven's character, as observed by one who served him at the end of his life. This item is a prayer book that DeKoven had given to Charles Olson on February 7, 1879. Olson, who was with DeKoven when he died, had written the following on the inside cover of the book: "I was at the time pushing the wheel chair when he failed & passed away . . ." "[I] . . . had been living with him 16 months as a butler. He was a wonderful, good man to all and was loved by all." Charles Olson visited the tomb of James DeKoven annually until his own death in 1937. This devotion to an employer speaks volumes through the simple inscription inside a prayer book.[28]

In order to gain some insight into the inner thoughts and feelings of James DeKoven, we must look in the pages of his journal since there are so few personal letters that have come down to us. In many ways these entries are more reliable as an expression of what he was honestly thinking and feeling because he was not writing for someone else, but rather for himself.[29] On occasion he does turn to the entries he makes to share his thoughts and reactions. He very seldom expresses self-doubt or a lack of hope. One rare example is found early in his journal when discussing his work with the boys and their education: "I suppose I do wrong in ten thousand ways."[30]

Sometimes he does express feelings of loneliness and sadness. On September 19, 1864, he indicates that he is writing on his birthday and shares that he had spent the previous day in Beloit, Wisconsin. He went there most likely to visit his aunt, Elizabeth Isaacs Smedes, half-sister of his father. She lived in Beloit with her daughter, Mary Smedes Sherwood.

28. Chester Olson, the son of Charles, donated his father's prayer book to the collection in 1967, and told of his father's devotion and annual visit to DeKoven's tomb.

29. Twice in his journal, DeKoven does address an unidentified "reader." This reference seems to be more a literary device than an actual statement communicating to someone who would read this diary entry.

30. DeKoven, *Journal*, Gu, 38.

DeKoven was obviously feeling lonely and somewhat sorry for himself. The Sherwood household was filled with family, several boy and girl cousins, and lots of activity. It had been a good visit.

> Sept. 19th, my birthday. I spent yesterday at Beloit and came home this morning. I felt not very well, and was forlorn, thinking if one had a family more would be made of the occasion. Ungrateful—after dinner all the Prefects came to congratulate me, the boys cheered me outside and lo and behold, a very nice set of Shakespeare as a birthday present from "my family." I was very pleased and very thankful. I had to give an evening holiday. . . All the boys were greatly gratified at their own loyalty and it did me good and them also.[31]

It did not take much for DeKoven to abandon a mood and realize the positive situation of the life he led at Racine College.

This relatively swift recovery is symptomatic of the sweetness that has been described by several of those who wrote about him. Examples of his "sweet" disposition can be found in his own writings, too. DeKoven definitely had a soft spot for animals and nature in general. One such passage is found in his journal for January 11, 1875. He is giving a summary of the past school year (fall term 1874) and explains why his penmanship is less than perfect: "(if the writing is bad, it is because of a cat who is purring and rubbing her head against my hand as I write. The creature jumps at my pen even)."[32] He finds pleasure in this feline interaction; it represents his general attitude toward animals. He would not tolerate wanton acts of cruelty to animals on the campus. In one lecture to the assembled school, he explained the concept of the "Peace of God" that existed during the medieval period when certain people were protected from the harm of warfare. DeKoven declared the "Peace of God" for the Racine campus which meant that the boys were not to disturb animals and birds in any way. Every moment was a teaching moment and had an impact on the youngsters in his care.

His sensitivity to nature and the beauty that surrounds one is also evident in his written words. James DeKoven loved the Racine College campus and was proud of the buildings that were built here under his leadership. He was also very proud and interested in the grounds and location of the campus along the shores of Lake Michigan. During his trip

31. DeKoven, *Journal*, Gu, 38–39.

32. DeKoven, *Journal*, Pi1, 112.

to Europe in 1868, he noticed beautiful window boxes on many buildings in different countries. Upon his return, he established a competition among the students to create window boxes for the buildings of the college. It was a successful beautification project. He also wrote about the vegetable and fruit production of the farm that was part of the school. In his journal (August 1874) he reveals the eye of a poet as he writes about the beauty of the place.

> Today . . . I left my study and walked about the college grounds. There had been a storm and now the clouds had vanished and the sun was shining brightly. The grass which the drought had nearly withered looked fresh and green again. The flowers in the window boxes were very bright. The pleasant wind played in the woodbine which covers one side of the chapel and a part of Taylor Hall. Never did the chapel garden with its foliage bed and the tryst Geraniums and verbena seem more lovely. The buildings now all fresh and clean and ready for the term which is soon to open were very noble to look upon. I thank God for it all.[33]

DEEDS

There is a natural progression from a discussion of James DeKoven's appreciation of nature and the joy he took in his work at Racine College to the actions of his life. In many ways his dedication to Racine College and his role in the Episcopal Church in Wisconsin is the great "deed" of his life. Although the exact reasons for his decision to reject possible church positions in the East when he graduated from General are unknown, it is apparent from his own writings that his motivation was to be an educator through whatever means he could find. His friend and colleague, Rev. Flavel Luther, commented on the incongruity of DeKoven becoming a missionary in the Wild West:

> One can almost smile and yet it is a pity to think of this young James de Koven, 24 years old, whom I have been trying to describe, with his delicately nurtured habits, with his perhaps ultra refinement, plunged down there in the wilderness among some doctors of divinity indeed, who nevertheless had acquired something of the wilderness.[34]

33. DeKoven, *Journal,* Pe1, 110.

34. Luther, "James de Koven, Teacher," 172.

For twenty-five years he labored in the "wilderness," and, according to Mrs. Lincoln, he maintained an air of refinement that was in some ways out of place. In the last two years of his life, when his health was failing and he had to deal with continued criticism of his ideas, he could not abandon his work in Wisconsin. Various positions were offered him, including that of a senior assistant at Trinity in New York City, but he chose to stay: "I could not accept it. It did not seem to be right."[35]

We know from records left by DeKoven's friends and students[36] that he was generous with his wealth. For the period he was indeed a wealthy man. He made significant contributions to various building projects and provided emergency funds when needed. But he was not content with the work he set for himself at the school and reflected on this desire for additional challenges in his journal. On August 24, 1864 he wrote the following:

> I feel greatly anxious, if God will, to start some other work besides the College. Old Mrs. Christie, who walks 12 miles from Raymond Town to receive the Holy Communion here, presents herself as a desirable candidate for a house for aged women. We also desire a Sisterhood and an Orphanage.[37]

It is important to note that DeKoven did eventually fulfill all these goals. The last one was accomplished in 1878, with the arrival of two sisters of the Community of Saint Mary to take over the direction of Kemper Hall in Kenosha.[38]

In the paragraph above, not only do we see outlined his objectives for charitable work, but we also are introduced to Mrs. Christie. This needy lady becomes a project whose story appears with some regularity in the pages of his journal. DeKoven was an organizer and turned to the women of the city for their help with his works. He sent two women to visit Mrs. Christie, and not long after this first entry he is able to report, "We moved Mrs. Christie down to a little house near the college, and

35. DeKoven, *Journal,* Ti2, 139.

36. Clinton Locke in his memorial sermon, "The Upright Man," speaks of DeKoven's generosity: "Before his death he had reduced by one-half the fortune he inherited by the money he was continually given away." "Student" mentions that he knew of almost daily letters that DeKoven sent out which contained donations for individuals and charities. Student, "Racine and Dr. DeKoven V," *Church Scholiast,* Vol. IV, No. 4, Jan. 1887, 55.

37. DeKoven, *Journal,* Go, 36.

38. DeKoven, *Journal,* To2, 141.

called her our aged and infirm asylum."[39] In 1865, a separate building was built to house some of the workers employed by the college and a room was set aside for Mrs. Christie. Over the years we learn of her health and its deterioration. In 1871 he wrote:

> Before I forget it, I must record that old Mrs. Christie grows feeble. She said on Thanksgiving Day that it was the quietest 4th of July she had ever passed and that Dr. would not let the boys have any fireworks because of the dried leaves on the ground.[40]

There were others who received the hospitality of Racine College. DeKoven often tied this charity with make-work projects on the campus. For example, when able, Mrs. Christie helped in the kitchen. James DeKoven was a realist when it came to working with the poor and the downtrodden. In his journal, after discussing the goals he hoped to achieve and some of the people he encountered, he commented, "It is well, however, to remember that there is nothing romantic about charities when you come to do them."[41] One man who became a "fixture" on the campus was referred to by DeKoven as "Old Uncle Rowe." According to the story that came with him, he had been a bookkeeper to the cook at Trinity College in Cambridge, England. He arrived at Racine College "utterly destitute." He soon assumed duties that included sweeping the chapel and blacking boots.

> He was very deaf and wore a wig. As he swept the chapel, he sang old songs which I fear were not very pious—as no one could ever distinguish anything that he sang, we were fain to believe that they were of a religious character. . . We cared for him well and he died peacefully.[42]

DeKoven's involvement with the community was not limited to the religious sphere. Working with Dr. John G. Meachem, he helped organize the sponsoring board for the first hospital in Racine, St. Luke's. This hospital opened in a rented two-story house on Park Avenue and 10th Street in 1872. The need for the hospital and the role that it played in the health of the community is reflected in the fact that a new and permanent building was started just four years later in 1876. DeKoven noted in his journal, "The new St. Luke's Hospital was begun on Monday, August 27.

39. DeKoven, *Journal*, He2, 41.
40. DeKoven, *Journal*, No2, 101.
41. DeKoven, *Journal*, Ha2, 41.
42. DeKoven, *Journal*, Nu1, 102.

We have gotten about $5,000 for it and Mr. Porter gave the land."[43] The twenty-bed hospital was opened in February 1877.

Many of the good deeds that illuminate and illustrate the life of James DeKoven result from the profound sense of pastoral care that he had for the students of Racine College. This sense of charitable obligation extended to the members of the Racine community as well. In many ways being an educator, for him, was synonymous with being a priest. He watched over and guided the boys and young men while they were students at the institution, but his care did not end there. Several times in the pages of his journal he writes about encounters with former students and how he played a role in their post-Racine College life.

One story in particular, that of Charles W. Oakes, is striking for the depth of concern and love that it portrays. It is the longest continuous narrative in DeKoven's journal.[44] Charles was brought to the college in 1860 by his mother, a woman of mixed race, half Chippewa. As DeKoven describes Charles, he was . . .

> tall, lithe, handsome, of rich olive complexion, with just enough marks of the Indian blood in him to make him more attractive and pleasing. Strong, capable of fatigue, grand at games, who so likely as he to be all that one could wish. Affectionate and irrepressible, one could not but love him, even though one could not always approve or fail to be anxious.[45]

Charles left Racine in 1863 and returned to Minnesota, where according to DeKoven he was "wild and dissipated." Charles revisited Racine on at least one occasion, being "drawn to the college and drawn away from it." The story reaches its climax when Charles became seriously ill at Vermillion in northern Minnesota, where he was supervising a quartz mill. He struggled to return to his family home via canoe, and his liver disease progressed. One of his sisters wrote to DeKoven, asking him to come to the bedside to comfort her brother. James was in Middletown visiting his mother who was also ill; he cut short his visit, returned to Racine and the next day took another train to Minnesota. DeKoven describes the final days and how Charles suffered: "He expected to die and was trying to be ready for it." DeKoven's role was that of comforter and priest; he prayed

43. DeKoven, *Journal*, Si1, 131.

44. DeKoven, *Journal*, Miu2–Na1, 88–94. Richard J. Mammana Jr. includes this story in his excerpts selected from "The Journal of James DeKoven," 19–21.

45. DeKoven, *Journal*, Mo1, 89.

with him, read hymns to him, and celebrated the "Holy Sacrifice" for him and his family. Charles was comforted by DeKoven's presence and revealed to him how his care for him led him to reform his life. DeKoven describes his feelings at this death bed, "Who would not have journeyed weeks for such a welcome, and for such love all undeserved." DeKoven gives a moving description of the night he spends in the room next to the room where Charles's body lies. The next day, before the funeral, he had to leave for Racine and the beginning of the next term:

> I went into the room to take one last look at him. There he lay so still and calm. The room was cleaned of all the various things which sickness gathers together for the relief or comfort of the sufferer. The bed on which he had suffered so long was empty. There was a certain ghostly tidiness about everything. The dim and dreary light of the dull snowy morning swept in through the half-closed blinds and I left him there—all that was mortal and physical and earthly of him—for his soul was at rest.[46]

DeKoven's good deeds were not all tied up with sorrow and suffering. He frequently officiated at weddings for "old boys," baptisms for their children, and often spoke at the ordinations of those who had gone on to study at seminary. He served as godfather for some of the children of alumni, and several former students named sons in his honor. He comments on several occasions in his journal about visits from "old boys" with their wives: "This year has seen a new feature of kind remembrance on the part of old boys. Several of them have brought their newly married wives to see me. It was very pleasant to have them do so."[47] He was known by his fellow priests for keeping in touch with graduates and former students of the college and often called on individuals when his travels took him to their place of residence.

James DeKoven had a remarkable memory about the boys who had attended Racine College. They were obviously an important part of his life, and he was concerned about them as individuals as well as members of his extended Christian family; their faith practices were his obligation. He recounts in his journal an encounter he had in Knoxville which brought him information about a former student who had "disappeared" from his mental "file":

46. DeKoven, *Journal,* Na1, 93.

47. DeKoven, *Journal,* No1, 102.

> On a visit to Knoxville, which I made this year, the week after Easter, I met a young girl, one of the pupils from Salt Lake City. I asked her about a boy who left the college some eight or nine years ago, and whom I had not seen since, and only heard of as at Salt Lake City. To my surprise, she knew all about him; he had been in her father's office (a government office), had married, and one year after having returned to Illinois took the yellow fever at Cairo and died. I had but one question to ask, and I asked it trembling. He had been confirmed and indeed baptized at the college, coming, I fancy, from a very irreligious family. She said he had been at one time "fast," but had received the communion with his wife the Easter before he died. James Clifford Arich. May he rest in peace![48]

And DeKoven could rest in peace now that he had found one more of the sheep from his flock who had strayed away from the sight of the shepherd. This ability to remember and associate former students with locations and evidently unrelated individuals demonstrates a deeply caring attitude.

DeKoven speaks often of the affection he has for the students in the school and the attachment he feels for them. This was evident earlier in the comments he made about the end of the school year closing ceremony and song. There one sees his emotional attachment and also his realism: he knows that this is simply the process of what happens in a school, especially a boarding school. This growing close to students and then sensing a loss when they move on was doubly a result of the type of "family" he created with the organization of the school year and the organization of the life of the institution.

One of the most complete summations of DeKoven's personality and character was preached at a Memorial Service on Tuesday, March 25, 1879, at Grace Church in Chicago. It was the work of Rev. James Dewitt Clinton Locke, friend and colleague of DeKoven. He entitled this eulogy "The Upright Man," and it was reprinted by newspapers, both religious and secular, throughout this country.

Locke summarizes his friend's life in the different roles DeKoven played. There were seven that he outlines: orator/preacher, theologian, educator, man of the world, realist, priest, and Christian. Locke emphasizes the earnestness and deep conviction as the forces that made DeKoven's preaching so effective. He sets the record straight about DeKoven's

48. DeKoven, *Journal*, Ra1, 120–21.

practice of liturgical ritual and his willingness to submit to ecclesiastical authority. Locke mentions that he trusted DeKoven totally as a head of school and had enrolled his eldest son, Robert Locke, in Racine College. He shares this episode as illustrative of the depth of DeKoven's care for his boys: "Many a time has the watcher by some sick boy been surprised in the middle of the night by the appearance of the warden, too full of anxiety to allow himself to sleep when even one of his boys, perhaps the very one who tried him the most, was sick."[49]

There was a calm dignity about DeKoven that made it possible for him to function as an effective administrator guided by common sense and good humor. He was described by someone once as "an iron pillar cased in velvet."[50] According to Locke this was a happy illustration, for no man ever combined more beautifully a firm, unbending devotion to principle and to his own sense of right, with the most confiding, dependent, trusting devotion to those whom he held dear. He was a humble priest, aware of his unworthiness and remarkable in his efforts to submit every act of his life to the will of God.

49. Locke, "Upright Man."

50. Cited in Locke, "Upright Man."

7

James DeKoven: Storyteller, Preacher, Orator

STORYTELLER

On August 2, 1858, James DeKoven wrote a letter from London to the students of St. John's Hall, Delafield. This was the fourth of at least eight letters that he wrote to them in the late summer and early fall of that year during a trip he made to Europe.[1]

> My dear children,
>
> I must write you one more letter from the great city of London & tell you of some of the wonderful things I have seen. First of all, I often write you about churches. I will describe for you something very different from a church and that is the great Bank of England. Imagine a great building covering 3 acres of land that is to say a piece of ground as large again as the land at Delafield, full of rooms of every size & shape and stairs & passages until a stranger would certainly get lost in them . . .

What is remarkable about this and the other letters that DeKoven wrote to the boys in Wisconsin is his ability to grab the attention of his readers and make comparisons about the information he is presenting with

1. On this trip, DeKoven traveled with this good friend George F. Seymour. Together they visited England, France, Belgium, Germany, Scotland, and Ireland. The original letters are in the "Street Papers" at the National Episcopal Archives in Austin, Texas: documents numbers 3 to 11 (MS:68, 70.82, Street).

what they know. He does this time and again in these letters. In this particular epistle, he makes a reference to the size of the land where their school and church are located in Delafield, as well as to two of the St. John's students. He makes these references in order to heighten their appreciation of his story:

> We saw the printing presses where the bank notes are printed & which were taken care of by boys about as large as Robert Hill & Cassius Hoys although perhaps they may have been a little older. It seems like hard work for they could not stop for a moment & there was a curious mechanical register which showed how hard they worked by registering the number of bank notes they printed.

The rector doesn't need to draw a moral to his story, he just makes an observation that helps summarize the experience: "It almost makes one tired to see how quick they had to be in putting the blank paper in the presses to be printed." The life of school boys in Delafield is certainly different and not as hard as that experienced by boys of about the same age in England. DeKoven goes on to describe other intriguing machines in the bank before turning his attention to other sites that he visited, including Windsor Castle.

During the four months of his trip, DeKoven wrote letters from Chester, Leeds, Oxford, and London in England. He also wrote from Heidelberg in the Grand Duchy of Baden and Cologne in Prussia, as well as Edinburgh in Scotland. He described visits to Paris and Strasburg in France and a trip via a steamer to Ireland. Each of the letters is written on a single sheet of paper that is completely covered front and back in small script. DeKoven's handwriting is generally difficult to read, but he obviously made a special effort to write carefully, if not clearly, so that the letters were legible for many readers.[2] The amount of information contained in these letters is amazing. DeKoven the teacher and storyteller is truly alive on each and every page that he sent back to the school in Delafield.[3]

2. Many years later, as George Seymour wrote about this trip, he remembered the amount of time DeKoven devoted to these letters. He said that DeKoven described each and every boy at the school and how much they meant to him. (Letter of George Seymour to William Cox Pope, dated Nov. 5, 1884, Eckels-Cox-Pope Papers, National Episcopal Archives.)

3. Photographs were not included in passports until the early twentieth century. James DeKoven and his traveling companion George Seymour obviously learned about the importance of having a passport after they had planned their trip and left for England without having one.

He instructs the boys about what it means to travel in another country and to be surrounded by people who speak a different language. He recalls his reaction to this "isolation" and how it felt "odd" at first. He provides comfort for the traveler and states that "at almost every hotel there is someone who speaks English" (Letter of August 14, 1858). He describes a passport, what it does, and the information it contains:

> In order to travel on the continent each traveler is obliged by the laws to carry with him a paper called a *Passport.* This passport tells how each traveler looks, what is the color of his eyes, the shape of his nose, the color of his hair, and so on, so that each traveler carries a description of himself in his pocket and should he be so unfortunate as to lose it, it would put him in a great deal of trouble. (August 14, 1858)

He also recounts the challenges that the traveler faces with the different currencies used in different countries. He provides the names of florins and kreugers, francs and centimes, thalers and grochen (August 22, 1858). Fortunately for the traveler, there are guidebooks that provide all types of information. James DeKoven mentions using *Murray's Guidebook for Travelers* as a source of knowledge about what to do and see in different cities and countries while in Europe.[4]

In addition to the visit to the Bank of England, DeKoven gives descriptions of what were and continue to be tourist highlights for the visitor to Europe. He means to impress his schoolboy readers with the size of London, saying that it has two million inhabitants with 2,800 streets. To make this number more impressive, he gives statistics about the number of sheep, cattle and pigs consumed every year by this city's population. He goes to the Tower of London, visits the British Museum, and describes churches and cathedrals in many cities. He is especially moved by the choral service at Litchfield Cathedral, where he saw boys clad in surplices singing most beautifully, and he thinks fondly of the young men at Nashotah also engaged in the divine service.

Perhaps the most typically "modern" tourist excursion that DeKoven made was a trip by small steamboat with other travelers down the Rhine River. The descriptions that he provides can in many instances be seen today, but those of us reading these letters are reminded that it is

4. Written by John Murray and first published in London in 1836. It is curious that DeKoven did not mention, nor did he use the work published by Putnam in 1853 entitled *A Handbook for American Travelers in Europe* and written by his predecessor at Racine College, Roswell Park.

1858 and a lot of history has yet to happen. When they sail past Bonn, he remembers and writes in his letter that it was at the famous university in the city that Prince Albert, the husband of Queen Victoria, studied. The queen and the prince are both alive when DeKoven writes and the world is a much different place than ours in the twenty-first century.

But what has not changed are the subjects which capture the attention of young readers and DeKoven's innate understanding of them. He tells many stories that are wonderfully gory and frightening. We read of the "martyrdom" of King Charles I of England, the beheading of Marie Antoinette and her husband Louis XVI in the French Revolution of 1789, and the assassination of the archbishop of Paris during the Revolution of 1848. DeKoven gives great detail about the selfishness of the wicked Bishop Hatto, whose barns were full of grain and the people around him starving. He gathered the peasants in a granary and set it on fire and then fled to his tower on an island in the Rhine River. There he felt safe from whatever might happen, even from the huge army of rats that he heard was attacking his grain stores. "But as he looked out of the window, swimming through the water and climbing up the sides of the tower & gnawing through the walls came the army of rats. And that was the last of the wicked Hatto." He paid for his sins "and he was punished" (Letter of August 1858).

One more story was provided by a side trip to a monastery along the Rhine. There, DeKoven went on a visit to an underground cemetery:

> Down into the vault we went and there in open coffins lay the bodies of the monks all turned into mummies. It was a strange & a horrible sight & I was glad to climb up again and into the bright fresh air & to see far away in the distance as we looked from the top of the tower the great dome of the church of Cologne.

James DeKoven traveled to Europe again in 1868 and once again he wrote letters to the students he left behind. Only two of these letters have survived because they were printed in the *College Mercury.*[5] Unlike the earlier letters addressed to "Dear Children," he begins these letters with the greeting, "My Dear Boys." As in the earlier letters, he uses this opportunity to inform and educate as well as to inspire. In the letter dated

5. In his Journal on September 30, 1868, DeKoven made the following entry: "Six months of travel all over Europe. I wrote regularly to the boys and in those letters I described all that I saw. I prayed for the college in almost every church I went to and at many a holy shrine. How sorry I was to go away—how glad to get back again." DeKoven, *Journal*, Lu, 83.

February 26, 1868, he describes in great detail a visit to the Tower of London, emphasizing its dark and sad history:

> They showed us, too, the very ax with which Charles I was slain, and the block on which the Scotch Lords, who rebelled in 1745, for the Pretender, were beheaded. You could see the very dents in the oaken block which the sharp ax made. There, too was the black mask the executioner wore, with which to hide from all his execrated countenance.[6]

At the close of this letter, DeKoven expressed his regret at not finding any letters waiting for him from the college.

The next letter was written from the Grand Hotel in Paris. DeKoven describes several historical monuments and churches, as well as the Louvre, that he and his traveling companions visited.[7] Their most significant encounter was seeing Napoleon III and his wife, the Empress, as they drove along the Champs Élysées from the Bois de Boulogne. From Paris, DeKoven and friends traveled to the south of France and on to Italy. He concludes this letter with a most endearing comment: "Meanwhile each day, I think no sea prospect as beautiful as Lake Michigan—no town as fair, in my eyes, as Racine—no cathedral as noble as the Chapel—no person so dear as my own dear boys."[8]

James DeKoven's talent as a storyteller played a significant part in the regular activities at Racine College during the school year. Just as the daily meals and religious services emphasized the "family" spirit of the institution he led, on Sunday evenings there were regularly scheduled gatherings of the boys and members of the staff called the Doctor's Receptions. Several former students have left a record of these receptions, but the most complete account of them is found in the articles entitled "Racine and Dr. DeKoven" published in *The Church Scholiast* in 1886. The author begins his commentary with this opening remark: "Among the pleasant memories which linger in the mind of a student at Racine under Dr. DeKoven must be the Doctor's Sunday evening 'receptions.'"[9] There were three categories of these weekly gatherings: one for the

6. *College Mercury*, Mar. 21, 1868.

7. He was traveling with Dr. Ashley of Milwaukee and LeGrand Burton, a student who had just graduated.

8. Letter dated March 2, 1868, written from Paris, France, published in the *College Mercury*, April 11, 1868.

9. Student, "Racine and Dr. DeKoven II," *Church Scholiast*, Vol. IV, No. 1, October 1886, 1.

students of the grammar school, one for the students in the college, and one that was opened for all students and faculty and called the General Reception. James DeKoven's emphasis on ritual and form can be seen in the organization of these events.

The grammar school reception began at 8 p.m. in the library of Taylor Hall after Sunday's evening meal. The students came over to the college building from their rooms in Park and Kemper Halls.[10] DeKoven always wore the collegiate gown and entered from his quarters after the students were present. Everyone stood when he came in. He usually began the evening with a commentary on events from the previous week and concerns about problems that had arisen. He would also give an idea of special happenings or visitors coming to the college. He would sometimes read from a recent publication or recite a poem. The main attraction, and one that the students looked forward to, was his telling of a story that usually continued from one week to the other and stopped at a "cliffhanger" close to 9 p.m. The author of the *Church Scholiast* article provides this information:

> The stories were all given *extempore,* and the Doctor generally had to be told what had gone before in order to take up the thread where he had left off. They were usually about boys in school, their trials, their work, and their sports. With his power of mimicry he imitated the voices of the different characters, and as he became absorbed in the narrative, he would rise from his chair and assume their manner and walk, and act out the story as he went along.[11]

The College Reception took place immediately after the grammar school event and would be held in DeKoven's private library when the number of participants was smaller. The format was essentially the same, although the nature was a little more religious and included a prayer at the beginning and a hymn at the conclusion of the evening.[12] James

10. As would be expected in any school setting, there was not unanimous enthusiasm about the required receptions. Thomas Gailor, who was a relatively new student at Racine College in 1875 and who kept a journal at the time of the fire, provided this entry on Sunday, February 7: "Went to reception at 8 o'clock, which was monotonous as usual." Gailor eventually became Bishop of Tennessee and his appreciation of James DeKoven grew during his time at the school: "Had a talk with the Rector this afternoon . . . He is very kind and I like him more and more."

11. Student, "Racine and Dr. DeKoven II," *Church Scholiast,* Oct. 1886, Vol. IV, No. 1, 2.

12. Although James DeKoven possessed many talents and abilities, singing was

DeKoven insisted that the students in the school have the ability to carry on a conversation with their peers as well as adults. Polite and informed discussion was the rule for the college reception. The rector also insisted that the students be able to execute the necessities of social interaction: the shaking of hands and accompanying greetings was required at each reception for all participants.[13] These weekly rituals were an essential part of the education that James DeKoven advocated in preparing "his boys" for their future lives. He wanted them to be comfortable in social situations and respectable in their interactions with others. Some of his stories emphasized these abilities.

There was a third type of reception hosted by the rector. Once a month, on the first Sunday, there was a general reception that occupied the entire evening and involved all students plus faculty and families. On Easter Sunday, there was a general reception that also included guests from the Racine community. Poems were read, short stories were told, and hymns were sung. One special feature of this Easter reception was the possible granting of amnesty for all punishments incurred by the students. The nature of these receptions and the stories that DeKoven told became part of the general knowledge about Racine College. The author of the *Scholiast* articles summarizes their importance to the students:

> The fame of these narrations is known to many who never listened to them, but a Racine boy can never forget them. To describe them as we used to hear them is impossible. It is a great loss that only one of them has been preserved.[14]

The one in-depth story that has been preserved is entitled *Dorchester Polytechnic Academy; Dr. Neverasole, Principal.* Although some of the former students who had heard his stories believe this isn't the most

---

apparently was not one of them. On one occasion when the choral director was absent for a service, DeKoven decided to perform the duty and the result was not successful. He never volunteered for that task again.

13. DeKoven seemed to feel that the manners of the great Northwest were somewhat lacking. I have not found any direct comment on this in his writings. However, when he compared the students at Racine College with those at St. Paul's School in Concord, New Hampshire, he made this reference regarding behavior and discipline, "They have a better class of boys to begin with. The homes they come from are better . . ." DeKoven, *Journal*, Gu, 39.

14. Student, "Racine and Dr. DeKoven II," *Church* Scholiast, Oct. 1886, Vol. IV, No. 1, 2.

interesting or the best example of his storytelling skill, it is the most extensive story that has come down to us.[15]

This story is an example of a minor genre of literature, British school novels. The most famous example of this type of fiction is the series of three stories called *Tom Brown's School Days* by Thomas Hughes and published in 1857. This novel is set in the 1830s at Rugby School in England. Another English author who wrote in this genre, and whose life was very similar to that of DeKoven, was Edward Monro (1815–66). Monro was an Anglican priest, influenced by the Oxford movement and devoted to the education of boys through his College of St. Andrew. He was well-known for his stories and allegories that he delivered "impromptu." He wrote several novels in the school boy genre, including *Eustace or The Lost Inheritance: A Tale of School Life*, published in 1863.[16] DeKoven's copy of this novel is listed in the inventory of his personal library.

The serialized publication of *Dorchester Polytechnic Academy; Dr. Neverasole, Principal* began in *The Church Register* in August 1869.[17] Chapters of the work appeared in issues of this publication of the Milwaukee Church Union from August 1869 through November 1870, skipping the May and July 1870 numbers. This text that was used for the book published posthumously in 1879, by L. H. Morehouse of The Young Churchman Company in Milwaukee, Wisconsin. In a short preface, Morehouse wrote, "The Publisher undertakes this work as a labor of love, and in the interest of one of the departments of Church work, very dear to the heart of his sainted friend" (3). The book is relatively long and has thirteen chapters and 226 pages.[18]

15. "Student" comments on *Dorchester Polytechnic Academy*: "This is not a fair specimen of what the stories were; indeed, it was greatly surpassed by others of which no record remains." Student, "Racine and Dr. DeKoven II," *Church Scholiast*, Oct. 1886, Vol. IV. No. 1, 2.

16. Monro, Edward (1815–66), *Dictionary of National Biography, 1885–1900*, Vol. 38, 183.

17. There is no known complete manuscript of this story set in the fictitious world of Dorchester and its school called the Polytechnic Academy. A partial manuscript has been located in the Wadsworth Collection of the archives of the Middlesex County Historical Society in Middletown, Connecticut (2015.009. Box 7, DeKoven Books).

18. James DeKoven, *Dorchester Polytechnic Academy, Dr. Neverasole, Principal*. Milwaukee, Morehouse Publisher, 1879. Mabel Benson DuPriest published a study of James DeKoven as fiction writer in *To Hear Celestial Harmonies*. The essay was titled "James DeKoven, Novelist: A Review of Dorchester Polytechnic Academy." DuPriest points out that evaluating the novel as a period piece, or of interest because of its author, is relatively straightforward. Analyzing it on its literary merit is "more challenging."

DORCHESTER

Polytechnic Academy;

DR. NEVERASOLE, PRINCIPAL.

By the late Warden of Racine College,

THE REV. JAMES DE KOVEN, D. D.

MILWAUKEE, WIS:
L. H. MOREHOUSE, PUBLISHER.
1879.

Dorchester Polytechnic Academy title page

Many of the topics that occupied DeKoven as rector of Racine College find their way into the lives of the characters and events portrayed in his novel. He deals with issues of discipline, religious beliefs and practices, honesty and duplicity. DeKoven does create some enjoyable characters, such as the school matron, Mrs. Jollipop. He describes amusing scenes and tells funny stories that reveal the personal flaws of several characters. He uses sarcasm effectively in his depiction of Dr. Neverasole, as well as in his description of some members of the Episcopal clergy and faculty members of the school. He presents these characters with their nicknames as created by the students. When reading the novel, one has the feeling that DeKoven enjoyed finding ways of including ideas and episodes from his school life in it.

DeKoven had a deep disgust for the use of tobacco in any form. The main character of the novel, Robert Graham, who is often the port-parole for DeKoven, expresses this dislike when describing an incident in a churchyard: "Robert was doubtful whether it was right to smoke at any time; but to sit on a tombstone and smoke, seemed to him almost a sacrilege" (22). Another of DeKoven's pet topics for criticism was what he called popular religion and pseudoscience. One of the characters, Mrs. Stebbins, was devoted to phrenology. Early in the story, she analyzes the bumps on Robert's head and is shocked: "Here's combativeness, very large; philoprogenitiveness, enormous! Mercy!" (31). By this time in the novel, we've already concluded that Robert is not combative or disruptive.

One of the themes found in DeKoven's sermons and interactions with the students in Racine College is the importance of confirmation in their Christian life. This topic appears early in the story as Robert is preparing to leave for enrollment at Dorchester Academy. His grandmother, who has been responsible for him up to this point in his life, is concerned: "There was one thing about which she had been very anxious—he had never been confirmed, and had not received the Holy Communion" (27).

DeKoven's love of language and wordplay is evident throughout the novel. One minor character refers to the sick ward as the "infummary." A well-motivated wife of a pastor much influenced by the Tractarians and Oxford Movement as a sign of her religious commitment provides this evidence: "Had she not named her three eldest boys, respectively, Pusey, Keble and Newman,[19] and when John Henry Newman went over to Rome, had she not ceased to call the last Newman, and reverted to Johnny?" (183). DeKoven's knowledge of human relationships can be seen in the portrayal of the interaction of married couples. He describes the ability of two loving and devoted wives to have their way in dealing with their priestly husbands:

> So, Mrs. Gooby and Mrs. Perkins prevailed, as they always did; for fully acknowledging the apostolic precept, that wives should be subject to their own husbands, in all things, they first made their husbands command the thing they wanted to do, and then, like obedient wives, they always did it. (182)

Dorchester Polytechnic Academy does not resemble the DeKoven model of a good school in any way. It is not Christian-oriented, and boys are allowed to decide for themselves about religion and religious

19. The three great English leaders of the Oxford Movement.

practices. The principal, Dr. Neverasole, is not a spiritual man at all, but in fact he is an amazing hypocrite. For him, appearances are more important than truth. Discipline is singularly lacking in the institution. The buildings are marked with names carved everywhere; the outhouses are full of inscriptions.[20] The boys prepare and eat meals in their rooms, where they also have alcohol.

The impact of this lack of discipline and order is reflected in the life of one of the faculty members, who is victim of the theft that serves as the focal point of the novel. Mr. Whooney has been saving his salary for ten years with the eventual goal of returning to England for his fiancée, who waits for him there. DeKoven provides a very sensitive description of this schoolmaster:

> Gentle and quiet by nature, unaccustomed to rude and untrained boys, conscientiously trying to do his duty, yet unable to do it properly, he was just in that weak and unprotected condition, which would have excited compassion in any other community than the Dorchester Polytechnic Academy. (54)

But Whooney does not receive compassion or understanding from anyone in the establishment except Mrs. Jollipop.

The same is true of the sad story of the fatal illness, diphtheria, that takes the life of one of the students, young Hubbers. Mrs. Jollipop is the one who tells the principal that the boy is dying and who insists that Mr. Neverasole visit and comfort him. She is seconded in this request by Mrs. Neverasole. His reaction is symptomatic of what seems to be his way of handling all difficult situations:

> "Oh, dear!" Said the Doctor, "It is too bad!" The Doctor seemed to feel as if Hubbers was really injuring him, and dying, as it were, on purpose. He was not a hard-hearted man, at all; it was only that he was not prepared for the emergency. Into his calculations, and his mode of instruction, and his care of his scholars, death did not enter. (102)

Mrs. Jollipop in many ways is the voice of reason. She summarizes the main problem with the school as it currently exists:

> "The truth is, boys are a mixture, made up of original sin and something good besides. And education," continued Mrs. Jollipop, smoothing down her apron, "is bringing out the goodness

20. There were "Six Great Rules" that governed the discipline of students at Racine College. Number three was that buildings shall not be defaced.

> and keeping down the original sin. And you can't do that without religion, and that's what's the matter with the Dorchester Polytechnic Academy." (131)

Especially pertinent is DeKoven's portrayal of several challenging issues that faced the Episcopal Church of his day and in which he would eventually play a significant role. One of these questions is that of the creation of a cathedral in Milwaukee and establishing that city as the see of the diocese. This development was strongly opposed by the rectors of several of the churches in Milwaukee. James DeKoven worked with Bishop Armitage on writing a "canon" for the cathedral. The whole question is reflected in the portrayal of the church issue in the fictional city of Dorchester. There is a bishop of Dorchester whose residence is a small house located not far from the large church of St. Bridget, which has a stately parsonage:

> Meanwhile there were, at least, three or four Bishops, besides himself, in the city of Dorchester. We do not mean the Roman Catholic Bishop, or the Methodist Bishop, or the excellent Pastor of the First Presbyterian Society; but the four Episcopal rectors, who were really the Bishop of Dorchester. (153)

DeKoven obviously takes delight in poking fun of imaginary characters who represent very real and difficult situations.

This book provides positive insight into the workings of DeKoven's mind, reveals his sense of humor, emphasizes his primary role as teacher, and underlines his efforts to create for the enjoyment of those around him. He was a master storyteller. His creation of a fictional world is filled with sympathetic and unpleasant characters, interesting descriptions, and amusing situations. Although the style is more melodramatic than suits the modern reader, it is a remarkable effort by a writer whose main occupations were definitely in other pursuits.

PREACHER

SERMONS

PREACHED ON VARIOUS OCCASIONS

BY

JAMES DE KOVEN, D.D.,
LATE WARDEN OF RACINE COLLEGE.

WITH AN INTRODUCTION BY
MORGAN DIX, S.T.D.,
RECTOR OF TRINITY CHURCH, NEW YORK.

NEW YORK:
D. APPLETON AND COMPANY,
549 AND 551 BROADWAY.
1880.

Title page of *Sermons* and James DeKoven's portrait.

On July 8, 1879, Rev. Morgan Dix, rector of Trinity Church in New York City, signed the introduction he had written for the publication of *Sermons Preached on Various Occasions.* He wrote this introduction four months after DeKoven's death and with this publication demonstrated his desire to continue the tribute he felt due the late warden of Racine College. Dix states that in writing this introduction about DeKoven he would "dwell on two points only—his zeal in the work of Christian education, and the sanctity of his life as priest and pastor."[21] Dix had known DeKoven since their years at the General Theological Seminary and respected him as a leader in the American Episcopal Church. During the last months of DeKoven's life, Dix had tried valiantly to have him move to New York City. He wrote several long letters encouraging the move, not only for the benefit of Trinity Church, where he would be considered a "Special Preacher,"[22] but also for the improvement of DeKoven's health.[23]

21. Dix, "Preface," v.

22. Flavel Luther makes an allusion to this title and role offered to DeKoven ("DeKoven Teacher").

23. Letters from Dix to DeKoven, dated April 24, April 26, May 2, May 24, 1878,

Ultimately, DeKoven turned down this offer out of a sense of obligation to the college.

In describing DeKoven the preacher, Dix emphasizes the fact that he preached without notes and without a written manuscript.[24] However, he did not preach without extensive preparation. After he had preached a sermon, he would write down complete notes of what he had said with the intention of writing out the full sermon as he had preached it. Dix indicates that "of these notes of sermons already preached there remain some six volumes—mere skeletons of discourses, with remarks and observations thrown in here and there to show the train of thought."[25] These six volumes of notes have disappeared. The sermons published in the 1880 volume were ones that James DeKoven had developed more thoroughly with the ultimate goal of publication. He had often been encouraged to publish his sermons but had never found time in his short, hectic life to do so. Dix stressed that the sermons had not been edited or changed in any way for their publication. But he also emphasized the idea that the printed sermons were passive documents, and although providing them for publication was a major task in honoring James DeKoven, it really was not enough:

> Who can convey an idea, to one who never saw or heard him, of the effect produced by that impassioned manner, and that wonderful voice, which, now ringing like a clarion, and anon sinking to the lowest, gentlest tones, thrilled the soul and sounded depths within men which perhaps in their case may never be touched again by mortal speech? . . . Yet, surely we shall all be the better for communing with that spirit even under these imperfect forms.[26]

James DeKoven obviously felt his sermons were an important part of his religious and scholarly production. He took great care to collect and keep them. We know from an entry in DeKoven's journal that these

---

Nos. 186, 174, 174 and 179 of the Street Collection.

24. The "Student" author of the eight articles on "Racine and Dr. DeKoven" also stresses this fact: "His sermons were almost always delivered without notes. Although not only his ideas, but his words were prepared in his study, merely a brief skeleton of the discourse entered into the volumes of sermon notes which he kept." Student, "Racine and Dr. DeKoven VIII," *Nashotah Scholiast,* May 1887, Vol. IV, No. 8, 122.

25. Dix, "Preface," xvi.

26. Dix, "Preface," xvii.

volumes were saved from the disastrous fire in Taylor Hall on February 5, 1875.

The "Student" author of the series of articles published in *Nashotah Scholiast* commented on the manner in which the rector preached his sermons when he officiated at the weekly Sunday service for the students:[27]

> In the College Chapel he almost invariably spoke from the centre of the chancel steps. He would come from his seat with head bowed and hands clasped before him, and after the invocation would give the text and begin the sermon in a low, quiet voice, only glancing now and then at the congregation. But as he proceeded the air of quiet meditation would disappear, his face would light up, and in accord with the thought, his voice would take on the modulation of which he was so perfect a master.[28]

Included in this commentary are remarks about James DeKoven's voice. These observations are echoed by several writers. It is more than likely that today we would find his vocal qualities unusual for a public speaker. "Student" gives a brief summary of his impression of DeKoven's oratorical delivery. He talks about his power as a preacher and public speaker:

> But this power did not lie in the things which some great orators use. His voice was not especially powerful and his gestures were few and simple, and even these but rarely made. His pronunciation of the sibilant letters was unusually clear and gave to a stranger what seemed, for the first moment or two, an undue hissing sound to his speech.[29]

A similar description of DeKoven, both his physical appearance and his speech characteristics is given by Flavel S. Luther in a lecture entitled "James deKoven—Teacher" first referenced in chapter 6. Luther continues his description with what he thought one of the most striking things about DeKoven: his voice. In what might seem like a contradiction, Luther refers to the high-pitched quality and the "thrilling" impact it had on the listener:

27. I am convinced, after much searching and analyzing of writing styles and historical context, that the anonymous student who wrote the eight articles that appears in the *Church Scholiast* was Alexis duPont Parker.

28. Student, "Racine and Dr. DeKoven, VIII," *Church Scholiast*, May 1887, Vol. IV, No. 8, 122.

29. Student, "Racine and Dr. DeKoven VIII," *Church Scholiast*, May 1887, Vol. IV, No. 8, 122.

> A musician would say it was a tenor voice, but de Koven could not sing. His voice was high, a falsetto, and at first sound you would say it was a feminine voice, but in his oratorical efforts it rang with the clang of a silver bell and then at times it would vibrate with the deeper note of a trumpet. No more thrilling voice ever sounded from a pulpit in this country.[30]

E. W. Leach, an author known for his many articles and books that dealt with the early history of Racine, recounts an incident from his youth. He, too, mentions the unusual qualities of DeKoven's voice and emphasizes the intensity of the delivery of his message:

> The writer was a boy, not yet in his teens, in the middle sixties, when he was taken one evening by his mother to Belle City Hall, where Dr. DeKoven delivered a formal address. The subject is not now recalled, but three things he does remember about it:—the breathless attention of the large audience;—the speaker's frequent allusion to Louis Philippe (pronounced Louie Filleep);—and the way he hissed his s's; particularly in the case of words ending in that letter. Whatever the subject of the address, it was beyond my understanding, but I can visualize on the instant, today, the picture he made, as with intense earnestness and emphatic utterance, he seemed determined to make the most of his opportunity to deliver a vital message to that large audience.[31]

The sermons of James DeKoven have come down to us in the volume published by Morgan Dix in 1880. The volume contains the complete text of thirty sermons and is introduced by a preface.[32] The first sermon listed was preached in 1859, when James DeKoven had moved from Delafield to Racine, Wisconsin. The last sermon included in the publication was the one he delivered on January 26, 1879, in Fond du Lac.

James DeKoven was invited frequently to preach sermons at churches and events throughout the country. He notes many of these events in his journal, and quite frequently articles in local newspapers record

30. Luther, "James de Koven, Teacher," 172.

31. Leach, "History of Racine County, James DeKoven." One can't help but notice the difference between Leach's description of DeKoven's voice and the one cited earlier by Morgan Dix. The commentary by the "Student" writer is also more in keeping with the description by Leach. It might simply be that, just as beauty is in the "eye of the beholder," vocal power and impressive oratory might reside in the "ear of the listener."

32. De Koven, *Sermons Preached on Various Occasions.*

his visits and sermons.[33] Of the thirty sermons included in the volume, fifteen were preached at Racine College. Five of the sermons were given in Milwaukee at different events in different churches. Two sermons were given at the Berkeley Divinity School Chapel while he was visiting family in Middletown, Connecticut. His association with this institution came through family connections, especially the work of his older brother, Rev. Henry Louis DeKoven, who was professor of homiletics at Berkeley from 1861 through 1873. James DeKoven was a frequent guest celebrant and preacher at various churches in Chicago, where several of his closest clerical friends were rectors. One of the sermons in this collection was given during his trip to Europe in 1868 at St. Augustine's Church in Canterbury before the archbishop of that historic place.

It is essential to keep in mind the fact that the sermons were not created for the reader but rather for the listener. The description of the delivery of these messages, as given by Flavel Luther and "Student," joined with a study of the rhetorical devices DeKoven used enable a better understanding of the power of the words. James DeKoven loved words. Plays on words, puns and malapropisms, especially religious ones, were his favorite forms of humor.[34] To the extensive vocabulary can be added an impressive arsenal of rhetorical devices that he employed with remarkable ease.

A few examples illustrate the richness of words and themes that can be found in his sermons. One of DeKoven's strengths was using repetition to catch the attention of his auditors. In the following example, the word "amid" is used first with positive ideas and then with negative ones. He describes the condition of the "demoniac" mentioned in Mark 5:5:

> No longer amid the walks of men, amid the joys of home or the sounds of the busy world, had he his dwelling. . . It was in these tombs . . . that he had his abode. Amid the silence of the dead, amid bones and skeletons and pallid faces, amid winding-sheets and the damp of death, he dwelt (Sermon I, "Spiritual Blindness," 1859).

33. *Gospel Messenger and Church Record of Western New York*, 1870. "On Sunday evening a sermon was preached before the Brotherhood [of theological students] by James DeKoven, D.D. at Trinity Chapel." *Lowell Daily Citizen and News*, Oct. 30, 1873. A separate entry for another event: "The sermon is to be preached by Rev. James DeKoven, D.D." St. Anne's Church, Lawrence, Massachusetts.

34. He loved telling the story of a worker who told someone looking for DeKoven, that "the Warden had gone to the Purgatory (instead of laboratory); or of the concern expressed by a parishioner, fearful of Roman Catholic practices who had heard that the priest would "elevate the ghost" (instead of host)

In the same sermon, repetition of a supposition verges on anaphora, as the preacher builds to the climactic idea:

> If it be true that man is made in the image of God, though that image be marred,
> If it be true that 'the light of God lighteneth every man that comes into the world,'
> If it be true that God wills all men should be saved,
> We must know that God speaks to the soul of every man . . .

DeKoven was a master of painting images with words. In the sermon "Tempting Christ," he compares the willing victim of sin with the struggling victims of a serpent, as seen in a famous statue in the Vatican Museum:[35]

> In the gallery of the Vatican stands a wondrous statue. It represents one struggling in the embrace of a serpent. Each nerve is strained, each muscle is bent; each limb, each feature reveals the agonizing but unavailing effort. It is one intense struggle to be free. But here there is no struggle, no effort. Around the willing captive the serpent of sin winds its coils, nearer and nearer, closer and closer, tighter and tighter, with its clammy touch and slimy folds, enfolding, binding, and crushing the unresisting victim (Sermon II, "Tempting Christ," Berkeley Chapel, 1861).

One theme that is frequently seen in his journal, when he writes about the passage off time as well as in his sermons, is the idea of change. In the following passage, he emphasizes the antithesis that can be seen in our lives:

> Even if there were no external changes, the changes within us are still harder to bear. We are not what we were. Time more surely alters our inner selves than even it does what is without us. We do not love what we loved, we do not seek what we sought, we do not fear what we feared, we do not hate what we hated. We are not true to ourselves. . . we are compelled to acknowledge our own inconsistencies (Sermon IV, "Christian Hope," Berkeley Chapel, 1864).

James DeKoven was a fervent defender of the historic Christian church and not at all hesitant in his criticism of what he called the popular religion of the day. In this stunning image, he equates the ineffective benefits of such newly created religions with the inadequate care given by a kind-hearted but ignorant nurse

35. DeKoven was undoubtedly referring to the statue *Laocoön and His Sons.*

> who watches by the beside of one ill of some mortal disease. She tries to relieve this or that symptom: she bathes the aching head; she kindly moves the pillow for the uneasy sufferer; she gives now a morsel of food, now a drop of some cooling drink; she moves around the room on tiptoe, spares neither time, nor pains, nor talk; but, all the while, the unknown disorder gnaws at the vitals, and Death, with hurrying footsteps, mounts the creaking stairs, and breathes his icy breath in the passageway, and pauses on the threshold, and waits a moment longer before he enters in and takes the watcher's place at the bedside and stills the throbbing heart forever (Sermon V, "The Church of the Living God," St. Paul's Milwaukee, 1865).

At times, the power of his repeated structures lends an ascending rhythm to the words that is essentially a combination of music and poetry and seems to dispense with the necessity of understanding the entire meaning. The medium is the message in this almost Whitmanesque hymn.[36] In the following excerpt, DeKoven compares the role of the Church, the "her" in the passage, with that of the Church's Divine Lord:

> now in the midst of the doctors,
> now in the carpenter's shop
> now in the crowded city,
> now on the lonely mountain-top
> now casting a pitying glance on Magdalen,
> now denouncing woe on the scribe and Pharisee,
> now bending in agony,
> now in the midst of innumerable host of angels; yet ever,
> from the glance of her eye,
> from the touch of her hand,
> from the intercession of her prayers,
> from the sternness of her wrath,
> from the majesty of her triumph,
> from the wail of her humiliation, nay, even
> from the hem of her garment, and
> her very shadow as she passes, sending forth strength, and healing, and peace.
> (Sermon XXII, "Men of Understanding, 1874)

DeKoven's knowledge of the Bible and ease in using references to different books and stories in the sacred Scriptures is truly amazing. The church fathers were like his friends. There are several multi-volume

36. Walt Whitman's *Leaves of Grass* was published in 1855.

collections of these patristic writers in his library. His ability to relate concepts from one source to another demonstrates a profound acquaintance with not only the original texts but also an extensive study of scriptural scholars and commentators. His references were not limited to religious writings and commentators but also included the great thinkers and writers of Greek and Roman literature. His ability to provide quotations in Latin and Greek emphasized the depth of his classical training.

DeKoven was very much aware of the writings of contemporary authors both in the United States as well as those in other countries. He refers to writers such as Alfred Lord Tennyson, Henry Wadsworth Longfellow, and Nathaniel Hawthorne. He includes quotations from religious leaders and spiritual writers such as John Kebel, Thomas Moore and Jean-Baptiste Henri Lacordaire.

He recognizes the immense changes that are taking place in the world because of new technologies associated with the developments in electricity and steam power. In one sermon he comments on the effects of these technologies on culture and people:

> No thoughtful traveler can fail to notice how the increased facilities of travel and intercourse are destroying peculiarities of dress and manner and custom, and changing the very aspect of cities. And thus, in some measure making countries far apart less unlike one another. . . (Sermon XI, "The Unity of Christendom, Canterbury, England 1868).

Yet in all the changes that are going on in this world, where the "miracles of yesterday" become the science of today, he sees lessons for the faithful. He firmly believes in the spiritual world that surrounds us at all times and sees in some developments an illustration of the power of love and prayer. He talks about the laying of the transatlantic cable that joined two continents and provided the "marvelous conquest of time and space which electricity produces." While there is movement and action on the surface of the sea,

> far below, in the calm, untroubled depths, the electric current flows to and fro. So, between the living and the dead, though they hear one another no more, though they feel or perceive one another no more, because they are one in Christ, flows to and fro the electric current of love and prayer (Sermon VII, "The Dead in Christ," St. Stephen's College, 1866).

Although DeKoven commented rarely about current events in his sermons, he was obviously very aware of political and cultural developments that were impacting his life and the lives of those around him. The Civil War was a very real event for the inhabitants of Racine College. There was an army camp established in the close vicinity of the campus, and the ongoing campaigns and battles were items of daily discussion. DeKoven himself, as well as other teachers, were directly concerned with the military draft: "The Draft worries us. 6 here are liable, and I have been to Milwaukee to get exempt on account of near-sightedness—in vain."[37] He was happy to record the end of the war: "The Confederacy has fallen! Thank God! Lee has surrendered and Richmond is taken."[38]

He was perceptive about the consequences of the war and what he referred to as the question of the Black race in the United States. He understood the complications that would result from the emancipation of the enslaved people. He knew that this was a problem and a troubling question: "That difficulty will not be remedied even by universal freedom, though that will be a step toward it. The problem will still lie at our door, and rest like a heavy weight on heart and conscience through ages yet to come" (Sermon V, "The Church of the Living God," 1865).

ORATOR

It was as an orator that James DeKoven came to prominence in the Protestant Episcopal Church in America. During the years from 1859 to 1868, as DeKoven succeeded in his role as Rector of Racine College and as this success became known beyond Wisconsin, he also began to play more of a role in the life of the Wisconsin diocese. He spoke frequently at the annual conventions of the church and served on numerous committees, especially those dealing with Christian education. It was in these different settings that his power as a speaker came to be recognized. His friend, Rev. Clinton Locke of Chicago, spoke of DeKoven's style in his memorial sermon "The Upright Man":

> He was not a graceful orator. But there was that power, with pathos, that resistless energy of love burning and breathing through all his words, which went like an arrow to the hearts of his hearers. Earnestness, deep conviction, reality—these were

37. DeKoven, *Journal*, Go, 37.

38. DeKoven, *Journal*, Ha2, 40.

> the forces which made his preaching so effective; and these soared on the wings of a cultivated style, a full acquaintance with all the treasures of literature, a glowing imagination, and a tact, which never failed to gauge the wants of his hearers.

It was at the triennial general conventions of the church that the largest and most important audiences were treated to his ability as a speaker. In the same sermon, Dr. Locke comments on the impact of DeKoven's words and style on those who were in attendance at the conventions. He stresses the deputies' relatively stoic and nonchalant attitude about speeches in general and how they were not impressed by "flights of oratory or bursts of rhetoric,"

> but to this man it listened spell-bound. When he began to speak, a hush came over the scene; the reading, the note-writing, the whispering, the coming and going, all ceased; and everyone, no matter whether friend or foe, gave mute attention. The gavel of the president would fall again and again, to mark the expiration of the time allotted to each speaker; but the cry would go up "Let him go on." And on in the resistless tide of burning eloquence he went.

The General Convention of 1871, held in Baltimore, was dominated by the question of the ritual of the church. This was an issue that had started to take on importance several years before and resulted in a committee report from the bishops. Questions of clerical clothing were again brought forth for discussion. DeKoven's ability to use humor to redirect attention away from the relatively absurd to more serious matters is seen in his speech against a proposed canon based on rules in use in the American provinces before 1789. DeKoven commented on a much earlier canon on "Decency of Apparel Enjoined to Ministers." According to Henry Hopkins, DeKoven "convulsed the House with laughter by reading that Canon aloud, very impressively, with all its minute injunctions concerning long buttons, light colored stockings and nightcaps!"[39] He used this humor to introduce a conclusion which was a powerful exhortation to his colleagues. According to DeKoven, by focusing on issues of ceremonies, incense, candles, and reverencing, the convention was ignoring relevant concerns such as Christian education and the organization of women's work. He spoke out powerfully against any more prohibitory legislation:

39. Hopkins, "Few Recollections of James DeKoven No. III," *Nashotah Scholiast*, Vol. II, No. 6, April 1885, 99.

> We are doing absolutely nothing to meet the great wants, the terrible wants, the cries of anguish, which are going up to Almighty God in this our land. I ask gentlemen of this House to *let us work*—work not in the spirit of prohibitory resolutions, but in the honest confidence in the Church of God, which is mighty, and powerful, and glorious, and great, and will accomplish its work, if *canonists will only let it!* Our Lord seems to me to be standing before the grave and saying to the Church bound with grave-clothes and cerements, 'Come forth!' And I hear His Voice saying, too, "loose it, and let it go!' And I beseech this Convention not to bind it with any *more* grave-clothes and cerements in the shape of prohibitory legislation."[40]

The year 1874 proved to be the great oratorical year in the life of James DeKoven. It was also the beginning of a period of great sadness for him. It started with the death of his friend and colleague, Bishop W. E. Armitage, in December, 1873. His sermon on February 10, 1874, "In Loving Memory" of Armitage, was followed the next day by the much-discussed Wisconsin Episcopal election. DeKoven defended his theological ideas in a powerful speech that was later published as a pamphlet, *A Theological Defense for the Rev. James De Koven, D.D.*

A review of this speech was published in the *Chicago Daily Tribune* on the following Sunday, February 15, 1874. The anonymous author provided this analysis:

> Dr. DeKoven, when he made that thrilling speech to the Council, explanatory of his theological position, on the afternoon of Thursday, literally astonished and even appalled his hearers. So grand an outburst of ecclesiastical oratory was never heard in Milwaukee before, and it is to be doubted whether Dr. DeKoven in all his future days can ever equal that glorious effort. . . The peroration swelled beyond the bounds of theology, left ordinary rhetoric at an infinite distance, and appealed to a principle of religious toleration that other ages could not comprehend, and the even the enlightened intellectual progress of this boasted century might find it difficult to entertain. In any case, the effect was magical. . . The conclusion of the effort was marked, for a full minute, by an awed silence, and then, forgetting dome and sanctuary, high-priest and temple, the audience, friends and foes joined in a crash of applause that might be heard at the gates of Paradise.

40. DeKoven, *Journal*, Ha2, 40.

Other writers and witnesses have spoken on the minute-long silence at the end and the thunderous applause that followed. Although the author of the *Chicago Daily Tribune* article doubted that DeKoven would ever be able to "equal that glorious effort" that had been heard in Milwaukee, the meeting of the General Convention in New York City in October of 1874 did present the occasion for another example of his ability to command the attention of the House of Deputies as he explained his position on the Canon on the Ritual.

An indication of the importance now attached to DeKoven's reputation is the fact that before he began to speak, a vote of the house gave him a full hour for his presentation. There were three main topics at issue: the use of incense, the placing or carrying of a crucifix, and the elevation of the elements of holy communion. The presentation of his ideas in this defense is amazingly straightforward. He slowly creates a framework that can result in only one conclusion for each topic. Of course, he does not hesitate to use religious history or humor in proving his points. About the use of incense, he provides this anecdote:

> I remember upon one occasion having a gentleman call to see me at my own chapel, and when he arrived in the chapel a very singular thing came over him. He commenced making a sort of snuffing as if he were smelling something; and finally, he said to me, "My dear brother, is that incense that I smell?" [Laughter.] I was compelled to say to him that I never had used incense, and that I thought the smell was nothing but the smell of oakwood; and he was perfectly satisfied. [Laughter.][41]

In response to the prohibition of certain ceremonies related to the Eucharist, he made one of his most moving and impassioned statements:

> You may take away from us, if you will, every external ceremony; you may take away altars, and super-altars, and lights, and incense, and vestments; you may take away, if you will, the eastward position; you may take away every possible ceremony; and you may command us to celebrate at the altar of God without any external symbolism whatsoever; you may give us the most barren of all observances, and we will submit to you. If this Church commands us to have no ceremonies, we will obey. But, gentlemen, the very moment any one says we shall not adore our Lord present in the Eucharist, then from a thousand hearts will come the answer, as of those bidden to go into exile, "Let me

41. DeKoven, *Theological Defense*, 33.

> die in my own country and be buried by the grave of my father and my mother!" To adore Christ's person in His Sacrament, is the inalienable privilege of every Christian and Catholic heart; the thing itself is what we plead for, and I know I should not plead to unkind or unfeeling hearts.[42]

The effects of his presentation were apparent in the fact that a call for order had to be made several times by the president of the House. However, he was allowed a second hour and ended with a plea to his fellow churchmen:

> And I call you brethren, in a time like this, not to narrow-hearted legislation, but to broad, Catholic, tolerant charity, and to work, as men never worked before, for the souls of those for whom the Savior died.[43]

Hopkins described the spell-bound attention of those present in the assembly. He also pointed out that several of the bishops had come to hear DeKoven speak. When they returned to the House of Bishops, after more than an hour's absence, and were asked where they had been, one of them replied about being at the House of Deputies where they learned how to give a speech.

With the two speeches given in 1874, James DeKoven had earned the title as one of the greatest orators of the day. He continued to attend conventions and councils and to speak on issues that impacted the church to which he had dedicated his life. He was still a controversial presence, and his name continued to elicit reactions that he found troubling and unwarranted. He believed he was misunderstood and unjustly persecuted, as did many of his friends and followers.

There are many ways in which the words and ideas of James DeKoven have come down to us. To see him as a storyteller is to gain special insight into his character as consummate teacher. He told these stories with joyful delight in his ability to captivate an audience and educate at the same time. Just as teaching was the guiding principle of his stories, it was also the basis of his efforts as a sermonizer. In his role as a preacher, he demonstrated a profound understanding of human beings. He was not shy in his analysis of both the good and the bad in the human condition. The thorough grounding of his beliefs in biblical scholarship contributed greatly to his tolerant compassion. His ability to capture an audience with

42. Quoted in Hopkins, "Recollection No. 5," *Nashotah Scholiast*, Vol. II, No. 8, 135.

43. Quoted in Hopkins, "Recollection No. 5," *Nashotah Scholiast*, Vol. II, No. 8, 136.

his words was what made him a powerful figure, if not a universally popular one, in the church of his day. Although one can read the transcripts of his sermons and speeches, the power of his delivery is understandably missing. What was it about his ability as an orator that allowed him to command such attention? E. W. Leach refers to the "intense earnestness" of DeKoven. His whole demeanor conveyed the sincerity and conviction of his beliefs and his lifelong dedication to these beliefs.

8

James DeKoven in the Public Eye

The importance of James DeKoven to the Racine College community is emphasized by the many articles that were published in the *College Mercury* during his absence, beginning with the announcement of his departure for Europe on February 8, 1868. During the ensuing months of his travels, regular updates were given along with letters addressed to the students of the school. In writing these informative and heartfelt letters, DeKoven was continuing a task he had begun during his first trip to Europe in 1858. Once again these letters demonstrate DeKoven's devotion to the students and staff of the school. Though he was far away, they were often on his mind, and he missed them greatly. They felt the same way and expressed their joy on his return. The final article in the series relating to his return was published in the *College Mercury* on August 18:

> As was expected, the Warden of the College returned on Thursday, the 6th inst. A number of the student officers went as far as Kenosha by the morning train, and there awaited his coming. The entire body of the students, and members of the faculty were at the Junction, and gave him such a welcome as we are sure he must have been proud of... On his arrival at the College, he met in the parlor of Kemper Hall, the ladies of the institution, and members of the Faculty who had not gone to the Junction. As soon as the first greetings were over here, the bell rang, and all

> repaired to the chapel, where the *Te Deum* was sung and thanks returned for his safety.[1]

Six weeks later, on September 30, 1868, DeKoven wrote this version of his happy return to Racine. He was somewhat apprehensive about how his travels might have changed him.

> I was suffering with a fear lest after all the noble buildings I had seen, the college might suffer, but when I saw the pleasant grounds and Lake Michigan smiling in the sunshine and heard the bell ringing for service and saw the truly noble proportions of Taylor Hall, my misgivings passed away. It was as beautiful as ever with a beauty all its own. They had made an arch over the gateway and put over my mantelpiece "Welcome Home" in beautiful flowers and we went at once to the chapel for a thanksgiving service. Afterwards all the professors and their families dined here and we were together again.[2]

The events and celebrations associated with this homecoming in 1868 are in sharp contrast to the relative lukewarm reception he had received in 1858 when he returned to Delafield. Much had changed and was continuing to change, not only in his living and working conditions, but also in the country, in the state of Wisconsin, and in the Episcopal Church. The next ten years of his life are filled with his efforts to deal with these changes and to be a positive part of what was taking place around him.

In 1868, Wisconsin had been a state for twenty years. Its population was growing at an incredible rate. In 1850, the state had 305,391 inhabitants. With the Federal Census in 1870, the population had grown to 1,054,670.[3] Although still primarily an agricultural economy, cities were beginning to develop. The student population at Racine College had also experienced a rapid growth. There were forty students enrolled in 1859; for the 1868–69 academic year, there were 188 students enrolled. Almost as significant as the increase in numbers was the increase in states of origin for the students. Racine College was no longer a parochial school but welcomed students from throughout the country. The student body in 1868 represented twenty-two of the thirty-seven states in the union.

1. *College Mercury,* August 18, 1868.
2. DeKoven, *Journal,* Lu, 83–84.
3. "Population of Wisconsin."

Racine College was definitely a national school and was developing a national reputation.[4]

Upon DeKoven's arrival in 1854, the total number of Episcopal priests in Wisconsin was thirty-five, with thirty-two organized parishes. By 1868, the list of clergy had grown to sixty-eight, with sixty-one parishes and fourteen missions.[5] In addition, the diocese had been allowed to choose an assistant bishop to aid in the administration of this large territory. William E. Armitage was chosen for this position in 1866 and established his residence in the city of Milwaukee, thus indicating a major reorientation of the structure of the diocese. Bishop Kemper continued to live near Nashotah, and this decision to locate the assistant bishop in the major metropolitan area of the state emphasized the evolution of the church from a rural missionary faith to a more urban and centralized religion.

James DeKoven had also seen major changes in his life: he was the head of a successful educational institution. His abilities as an administrator and educator were being recognized in Wisconsin, and his reputation was growing throughout the United States. Evidence of his growing involvement in the life of the Episcopal Church in Wisconsin is found in the published journals of the annual convention of the Diocese of Wisconsin. These publications were used by both Bishop Kemper and Bishop Armitage to praise the work of and encourage the diocese in its support of the college. A quotation from Bishop Kemper's address at the sixteenth annual convention in 1862 illustrates the efforts made by the bishop to support the mission of the college and work of its staff:

> Racine College is flourishing. Most richly does it deserve the encouragement of every person who anxiously desires the future prosperity of our country. The teachings of that institution, the untiring energy of its President and Professors, and their Christian walk and conversation, must make the deepest impression for good upon the affections and study of the pupils.[6]

4. Enrollment data for 1859 is found in the *Register of Racine College for 1859–60*, 11. Enrollment for 1868–69 is found in the *Register of Racine College for the Academical Year, 1868–69*, 20. State of origin for students is listed on 12–19.

5. Eighth Annual Convention, June 14, 1854, 3–4; Twenty-second Annual Convention, June 11, 1868, 6–8.

6. Sixteenth Annual Convention, June 11 and 12, 1862, Trinity Church, Janesville. 35–36.

James DeKoven and William E. Armitage were seminarian friends in New York City and developed a close working relationship with Armitage's election as assistant bishop in 1866.

Armitage was a strong advocate for the work that DeKoven was doing at Racine College. In 1867, with a very public and direct statement, he defended his colleague and asked for understanding as DeKoven dealt with the unusual combination of a grammar school and college:

> I beg all who take exception to anything in its management, first, to assure themselves that they are rightly informed,—which seems to be seldom the case,—and secondly, to consider that in such a work the Rector's individuality and experience have a right to assert themselves . . . While I might order some things differently, perhaps, if I were the Rector, I am not the Rector, nor could I do his work as well.[7]

During his relatively short time as bishop (1870–73), Armitage turned to DeKoven for his help in creating guidelines and policies for the growing diocese. Under the leadership of Bishop Armitage, DeKoven participated in almost every committee and special assignment in the diocese.

DeKoven's role in the life of the national church began in 1859 with his appointment as a member from Wisconsin to the board of trustees of the General Theological Seminary in New York City. For the next twenty years, he very faithfully participated in the annual meetings of this board. Even more significant for his national exposure was his election as a deputy from Wisconsin to the tri-annual general conventions of the Protestant Episcopal Church. His appointment as a deputy came at the twenty-second diocesan convention in June 1868.[8] It was at this diocesan convention that his title as warden of Racine College was recognized and the completion of Taylor Hall on college campus announced.

JAMES DEKOVEN AT THE GENERAL CONVENTIONS

New York City, October 7–29, 1868

With his election as a deputy from Wisconsin to the General Convention in New York City in 1868, James DeKoven entered upon the broader stage

7. Twenty-first Annual Convention, June 12–13, 1867, St. Paul's Church, Milwaukee, 61.

8. Twenty-second Annual Convention, June 1868, 4.

of the Protestant Episcopal Church in the United States.[9] His work with Racine College was becoming recognized. His reputation as a ritualist was becoming better known throughout the country as he was called upon to preach at churches in different locations. The high church character of the diocese of Wisconsin was a comfortable fit for James DeKoven.

Many of the contentious issues that were discussed in 1868, and at subsequent general conventions where DeKoven was a delegate, have long since been resolved. The issue of ritualism had become an important topic of discussion prior to this convention, primarily because of the publication by John Henry Hopkins, bishop of Vermont, of a work entitled *The Law of Ritualism*. Bishop Hopkins had great foresight about the direction the Episcopal Church would take:

> I incline then to regard it as most probable that this Ritualism will grow into favor, by degrees, until it becomes the prevailing system. The old, the fixed, and the fearful will resist it. But the young, the ardent and the impressionable will follow it more and more. The spirit of the age will favor it because it is an age of sensation and excitement. The lovers of glory and of beauty will favor it because it appeals with far more effect to the natural tastes and feelings of humanity. The rising generation of clergy will favor it because it adds so much to the solemn character of their Office, and the interest of their service in the House of God.[10]

In his chapter on DeKoven, Frederick Cook Morehouse, writing about this issue and the debates surrounding it, provided this frank observation:

> Just what was meant by "Ritualism," as the term was used by its opponents, was never distinctly defined. The influence of the Oxford Movement in the Church of England had permeated the whole Church, and was now bearing fruit in a deeper spirituality and a closer approach to the devotional standards of the primitive Church."[11]

Questions about clerical clothing and the use of liturgical candles and incense were vigorously debated. Some opponents of these questions

9. The General Convention is the governing body of the Episcopal Church. Every three years it meets as a bicameral legislature that includes the House of Deputies and the House of Bishops, composed of deputies and bishops from each diocese. The first meeting of this assembly took place in 1785 in Philadelphia.

10. Hopkins, *Law of Ritualism*, 94. Cited by Chorley in *Men and Movements in the American Episcopal Church*, "Ritual Movement," 373–74.

11. Morehouse, "James DeKoven, Warden of Racine College," 163.

and proposed changes, especially because of their identification with Roman Catholicism, were even prepared to separate from the organized Episcopal Church.

John Henry Hopkins, Jr., son of Bishop Hopkins and DeKoven's friend, was an observer during the conference and wrote that DeKoven displayed the natural modesty of a new member and didn't speak much during most of the meeting.[12] DeKoven did, however, play a significant role as chairman of the Committee on Christian Education. This committee was charged with reviewing the state of the educational institutions under the supervision of the church and was especially concerned with the status of those schools and colleges in the recently reunited southern states. James DeKoven was most earnest in his leadership, and the committee eventually forwarded a series of resolutions to both houses of the convention. The one, somewhat weakened resolution that was eventually agreed upon, recommended the "establishment of Christian schools in every Parish where possible."[13]

In the course of the meetings, DeKoven first spoke on behalf of the Oneida Indians and in support of Bishop Kemper who championed their cause. The chiefs of the Oneida Tribe in Wisconsin were seeking the help of the leaders of the Episcopal Church in keeping their lands and having access to the support promised them by the federal government. The House of Bishops approved a letter of support for the Oneida chiefs that was rejected by the House of Deputies, who invoked the policy of separation of church and state in their resolution.

It was during this convention that the first serious attempt to legislate against ritualism was made. There were proponents on both sides of the issue, those who wanted to increase the rules against more rituals in the church, and those who wanted to relax those rules that did exist. On the eighteenth and penultimate day of the session, minority and majority reports from the Committee on Canons were presented for debate. James DeKoven spoke twice during the debate. In the first instance he displayed what was to become a signature technique in his arguments: a close and careful reading and knowledge of significant historical documents. Those who were against an increase in rituals stated that the General Convention of 1814 described those ecclesiastical vestments accepted by the

12. Hopkins, "Few Recollections of James DeKoven, No. II, *Nashotah Scholiast,* Vol. 2, No. 5, 83.

13. *Journal of the General Convention, 1868,* Thirteenth Day of Proceedings, Oct. 21, 1868, 95.

Episcopal Church as "bands, gowns and surplices." DeKoven pointed out, correctly, that what was referred to in the cited document was not what clergy should wear but what lay readers should not wear. DeKoven disproved the foundation of the argument by fact-finding.[14] He also reminded the opponents of increased ritual that this same General Convention of 1814 declared that the Protestant Episcopal Church in the United States was the same church that earlier was known as the Church of England.[15] This was a chief claim the ritualist faction used in supporting a more traditional liturgy. The Episcopal Church of the United States was an heir of the Anglican Communion. He argued on behalf of peaceful cooperation and emphasized that ritualism was not a development toward Romanism but rather a "drawing away from rationalism and a gathering round the personality of our Lord Jesus Christ."[16]

John Henry Hopkins believed that almost as important as what DeKoven said was the way in which he said it. Hopkins refers to the "winsome sweetness of manner" that gave DeKoven's words a subtle power. He felt that those present at this first display of James DeKoven's ability as a speaker were aware that here was an individual, young and relatively unknown though he might be, who would have a major role to play in the American church.[17]

James DeKoven's support of ritualism and a return to earlier practices and ceremonies, valued and valuable, are expressed clearly in an unpublished sermon circa 1858. He used a striking metaphor to argue his concept of the catholic nature of the Episcopal religion:

> Just as a sick man when he gets well from his disease is not another man because he is cured of his malady, so is the Protestant Episcopal Church the same Church which existed before the Reformation with the sicknesses and corruptions which the Church of Rome had engrafted on it, healed and taken away.[18]

In DeKoven's conception of worship, the rituals, vestments, incense, candles and accompanying objects of esthetic beauty, were not part of

14. *Debates of the House of Clerical and Lay Delegates*, 1868, Seventeenth Day, 142.

15. *Debates of the House of Clerical and Lay Delegates*, 1868, Seventeenth Day, 143.

16. *Debates of the House of Clerical and Lay Delegates*, 1868, Eighteenth Day, 154.

17. Hopkins, "Few Recollections of James DeKoven No. II," *Nashotah Scholiast*, Vol. 2 No. 5, 83.

18. DeKoven, Unpublished Sermon, Document No. 11, Street Papers, MS:60,70.82 Street, National Episcopal Archives.

the corruption and false doctrines of the Roman Catholic Church of the Renaissance but rather symbols of a traditional Catholic faith.

There were two reports related to ritualism issued by the Committee on Canons on the seventeenth day of the convention. The majority report stated simply, "It is the sense of this Convention, therefore, that the enactment of any canon of the subject of ritual would be unwise and inexpedient at the present time."[19]

Baltimore, October 4–24, 1871

These reports of the Committee on Canons provided the fuel for discussion and debate during the next three years before the thirtieth General Convention in Baltimore. As a final action, the House of Bishops did appoint a five-member committee "to consider whether any additional provision for uniformity by canon or otherwise, was practicable and expedient."[20] This committee was to report to the next General Convention in 1871. Those concerned with this issue, which meant the large majority of the convention attendees, especially those who wanted to legislate on ritual, came well prepared. In many ways this convention was another turning point in the life of James DeKoven. When all the debates were finished and all the speeches made, it became apparent that he had been the one who caused most discussion, and raised the most issues. In the years following this convention, almost everything he said or wrote was analyzed and criticized, praised, or condemned. Often his words were taken out of context and misinterpreted and used to accuse him of ideas or beliefs that he did not espouse. DeKoven's ability to deal with this constant criticism and misrepresentation demonstrates great patience and a spirit of Christian charity that was exceptional.

The report of the special committee from 1868 indicated that it did not seek to make ritual identical in all areas. However, the report did recognize that there were some corrections and adjustments needed to be made. Prohibitions of incense, crucifixes, processional crosses, liturgical candles, mixed chalices, ablutions, bowings and other ritual practices were recommended. Appropriate clerical dress was also discussed. The report caused quite a reaction, and the debate surrounding it lasted

19. *Journal of the General Convention,* 1868, Seventeenth Day, 140.
20. *Journal of the General Convention,* 1868, Twentieth Day, 167.

for several days.[21] A decision was made to set up a joint committee "to examine the Canons of the Church of England of 1603 and report to the next General Convention what portions were in use in the American provinces in the year 1789.[22] James DeKoven spoke frequently on the different topics involved in these discussions. He demonstrated the absurdity of some of the recommendations and pointed out how in some instances there could be no "winners" because everyone would be negatively impacted. DeKoven's use of humor was not always appreciated or understood. It was part of his normal way of communicating and was part of his life as a teacher. He lived with and taught young men and boys who all appreciated a good joke. His humor is reflected in comments he made when speaking to the delegates:

> Now, Mr. President, I want to make a little joke, and I tell you that it is a joke, for the reason that I tried to make one the other day, and it was taken in such seriousness and earnestness that two days afterward I heard a very solemn speech about it, which quite overcame me and made it appear that I had never better make any more.[23]

He argued consistently against any legislation which would narrow the scope of worship in any manner. Some of his most inspiring and insightful comments come from speeches he made at this time in the convention and in the discussion of the ritual canon.

He called for tolerance of beliefs with the understanding that all who are believers, whether high churchmen and ritualists or low churchmen and evangelicals, are seeking to come closer to Christ:

> I desire to say that between Evangelical men and men who hold the views of the sacraments that I do, there is no chasm. They seek the Lord Jesus Christ, independently, they think, of sacraments and ordinances, and have a kind of idea that sacraments and ordinances come between Him and them. We seek Him in and through the sacraments and ordinances; but there is this union between us, that we both alike seek Him, and if we have the same object and the same end it is only a question of time as to when and how we shall come together.[24]

21. *Debates of the House of Deputies in the General Convention*, 1871, 157.
22. *Debates of the House of Deputies in the General Convention*, 1871, 323.
23. *Debates of the House of Deputies in the General Convention*, 1871, 342
24. *Debates of the House of Deputies in the General Convention*, 1871, 342.

One of DeKoven's most famous and often repeated comments followed this statement. He pleaded with the convention to stop worrying about preventing things and to turn to more positive work, such as efforts to improve Christian education in the country. In a reference to the raising of Lazarus, he said:

> Our Lord seems to me to be standing before the grave and saying to the Church bound in grave clothes and cerements, 'Come forth.' And I hear His voice saying too, 'Loose it and let it go,' and I beseech this Convention not to bind it with any more grave clothes and cerements in the shape of prohibitory legislation.[25]

A fellow delegate from Wisconsin, Rev. William Adams, cautioned the delegates in the House to pay careful attention to the arguments presented by DeKoven. He stressed that James DeKoven was a very competent and faithful priest, that he was not a heretic, and that his doctrines were ones tolerated by the church.

> I do not want the members of this House to get under an excitement, and imagine that they are persecuting him and putting him down. . . But at the same time, if this House imagine that my colleague is a meek lamb to be martyred here, they make a great mistake. My colleague is simply one of the shrewdest and ablest party leaders that has ever been on the floor of this House. . ."[26]

James DeKoven again served as a member of the Committee on Christian Education for the General Convention in 1871. The two resolutions that were forwarded to the houses are essentially ones asking for continuance of the committee until more complete statistics can be obtained.[27] Many of the arguments and issues raised in the relatively brief report that was presented echo the ideas that James DeKoven repeated frequently. Especially familiar is this statement regarding the status of Episcopal colleges and their lack of endowments: "Until we strengthen our colleges with liberal endowments, and place them on broad and deep foundations, and then cause our sons to throng their halls we will

25. *Debates of the House of Deputies in the General Convention*, 1871, 343.

26. Cited by Hopkins in "Few Recollections of James DeKoven No. IV," *Nashotah Scholiast*, Vol. II, No 6, April 1885, 99.

27. "Report of the Joint Committee on Christian Education," Appendix VII, *Journal of the General Convention, 1871*, 586.

continue weak and dependent in one of the most important means of growth and influence."[28]

The General Convention of 1871 did not end on a peaceful note. On the last day of this three-week long meeting, a canon was passed unexpectedly by the House of Bishops and sent to the House of Deputies. In essence, the canon as proposed would forbid those reverential acts in the celebration of holy communion which imply a belief in the real presence of Christ in the Holy Eucharist.[29] An attempt to delay consideration of this last-minute item until the next convention was not successful. It passed the House of Bishops by a vote of twenty-two to fifteen and was sent to the deputies, who were surprised by its seriousness and unanticipated arrival.

Protests against consideration of this canon by the deputies with so many delegates already absent were not successful. It was in this tense atmosphere of unfairness that James DeKoven rose to the occasion and gave one of his most powerful speeches. He secured his reputation as an outstanding speaker by this spur-of-the-moment eloquence and sincerity. It was during this speech that his fellow delegates voted to allow him to exceed the ten-minute time limit of the session several times and continue to a conclusion. In essence, DeKoven answered the doctrinal questions raised about adoration of the Eucharist by referring to historical facts. He pointed out that eucharistic adoration, that is the reverential acts made to the holy communion species, had existed in the rituals of the church long before the doctrine of transubstantiation had ever been promulgated. He also emphasized the difference between the Catholic doctrine of the real presence and the Roman doctrine of transubstantiation. This statement about his own belief was widely quoted and later used against him:

> I believe in the Real, Actual Presence of our Lord, under the form of bread and wine, upon the altars of our churches. I myself adore, and would, if it were necessary or my duty, teach my people to adore, CHRIST present in the elements under the form of bread and wine.[30]

28. "Report of the Joint Committee on Christian Education," Appendix VII, *Journal of the General Convention, 1871*, 588.

29. *Journal of the General Convention of the Episcopal Church, House of Deputies*, Eighteenth Day, 193.

30. *Debates of the General Convention of the Episcopal Church, House of Deputies*, 506.

He brought the argument back to the issue of ritualism or anti-ritualism. In his mind the question was one dealing with the essential role of what he called the American Catholic Church in the future of this country. Although he did not deny the importance of the Protestant Revolution in the history of the religion known as the Episcopal Church, he saw that in the future the Catholic beliefs of this Christian denomination would play a more important role in its mission.

THE CRAIK/DEKOVEN CORRESPONDENCE (1871–72)

Although the General Convention ended in October, discussion of issues raised during the meeting continued in the religious press, where James DeKoven was frequently quoted and often criticized. The first of the press assaults came early in November 1871 when an editorial appeared in the *Church Journal* which attacked DeKoven for comparing the church to a sleeping Lazarus. The editor summarized his criticism of DeKoven with a slightly indirect accusation of idolatry:

> According to him the Church is asleep, like Lazarus; and such is his mastery of the arts of sentimental rhetoric that he carried the feelings of the Deputies with him to so large an extent as to defeat all legislation having as its object the repression of Eucharist Idolatry.[31]

On Sunday, November 12, in the same week that this article appeared, Rev. James Craik, who had served as the presiding officer of the House of Deputies at the last two General Conventions, preached a sermon at Christ Church in Louisville, Kentucky. Although the stated objective of the sermon was a review of the General Convention just completed, Craik actually devoted most of his words to a criticism of the ritualists and their spokesperson. Craik never mentioned DeKoven by name in his sermon. Excerpts of this sermon were published in the November 29 issue of the *Church Journal*. It repeats the earlier accusation of idolatry:

> There is a ritualism which expresses, and is avowedly intended to express and teach, this unworthy fiction, this gross idolatry . . . But one man in all that assembly—a man of mark and of great force and beauty of character—professed to hold this false doctrine.[32]

31. "Lazarus," Church Journal, November 18, 1871. 356.

32. Craik, "Sermon," *Church Journal*, Vol. XIX, No. 984, Nov. 29, 1871.

There were those who came to DeKoven's defense. One writer in a letter to the *Church Journal* accused the editor of distorting DeKoven's words and pointed out that DeKoven's wit kept the convention from dying a dull death.[33] The editor obviously printed the letter not to be fair but to use it as a chance to continue his condemnation of DeKoven's ideas. The editor called DeKoven "romish" and "popish" and condemned him for profaning the house of God with his humor.

In general, DeKoven did not provide replies to the criticism that was directed at him in these publications. When he did, he never descended to the level of his critics but demonstrated remarkable restraint and calm in his answers. His first concern in this exchange with the rector from Louisville was to confirm that he was the "one man in all that assembly" being referred to by Craik. Although DeKoven was outraged that Craik labeled him an idolater, he was also bothered that the Louisville pastor never used his name.

In July of 1872, after the correspondence between DeKoven and Craik had come to an end and their letters had been published, DeKoven provided an explanation of why he had made an exception to his policy of not replying to published criticism:

> I made no reply to other attacks made upon me and would not have done so even to this, but an accusation of so terrible a character—for who that knows what the Holy Scriptures say of idolatry can deem it otherwise, made by the President of the House of Clerical and Lay Deputies seemed to demand it. Placed as I am by God's Providence in the care of the young, I felt that perhaps I ought to show, what I knew to be the case, that the doctrines I held were, to say the least, doctrines a loyal Priest of the church could hold and teach. I have made no attack upon others who might think differently.[34]

The exchange of letters began in earnest in December of 1871 and continued for the next six months. The essential question that guided the written discussion of these two scholars was DeKoven's doctrine of real presence in the Eucharist. His statement at the General Convention was repeated by Rev. Craik. DeKoven's main point was to let it be known that he did not hold the doctrine of transubstantiation or any other doctrine like it and that his critics' attacks were a misrepresentation of his beliefs.[35]

33. Craik, "Sermon," *Church Journal*, Vol. XIX, No. 984, November 29, 1981.

34. DeKoven, letter dated Dec. 19, 1871, in *Holy Eucharist, A Correspondence*, 4.

35. DeKoven, letter dated Dec. 19, 1871, in *Holy Eucharist, A Correspondence*, 3.

For each explanation or example that DeKoven produced, Craik replied with a vengeance and detailed refutations. The letters became longer and more theological as the exchange progressed, and on Craik's part, somewhat nastier. DeKoven patiently explained what doctrine he held, and Craik would insist consistently that DeKoven meant the opposite of what he said. Early in the correspondence DeKoven set forth his belief in the real presence:

1. That no physical change of the natural substance of bread and wine is produced in the consecration.
2. That there is in the Eucharist, no corporal presence of Christ's natural flesh and blood . . . but after consecration the very Body and Blood of our Saviour Christ are really, truly, but spiritually and ineffably present under form of bread and wine.
3. That while no adoration is due to the Sacramental bread and wine, which would be idolatry, they are to be regarded with reverence.[36]

Craik replied to this statement of belief in his letter of December 23:

> There is all the difference between the presence of Christ in the Sacrament and the presence of Christ in the material elements of the Sacrament, as between a blessed truth and a pernicious error.[37]

The erudition of both Craik and DeKoven is evident throughout their letters. They both were thoroughly versed in the writings of many other eucharistic scholars and theologians. They are both amazingly able to produce relevant quotations and examples to support their beliefs and statements.

There is a part of this story that has never been published and is revealed in the additional unpublished letters that are part of the Street Collection at the Archives of the Episcopal Church. James DeKoven believed in the power of personal contact. At some point in the exchange of their letters, he had apparently invited James Craik to visit Racine College. This visit is disclosed in a letter of appreciation from Craik to DeKoven dated June 20, 1872: "My Dear Dr. I have been wanting to write you ever since our most enjoyable day or two at Racine."

36. Craik, letter dated Dec. 23, 1871, in *Holy Eucharist, A Correspondence*, 6.
37. Craik, letter dated Dec. 23, 1871, in *Holy Eucharist, A Correspondence*, 7.

Dr. Craik eventually explained he was uncomfortable with the correspondence. In his decision to not write any more, he portrayed DeKoven as a victim of the turmoil that was pervasive in the Anglican communion. His condescending attitude toward DeKoven was not lessened by the praise he wrote about him and his work at Racine College. Craik obviously saw himself as a wiser, older scholar dealing with a young, reckless religious maverick. This correspondence occupied a great deal of DeKoven's time; he made no entries in his journal during the year 1872. It was also a busy time in the college, with several building projects to complete. In January of 1873 he wrote about the year that had passed:

> All that winter I was engaged in a controversy on the holy eucharist with Dr. Craik of Louisville, who accused me of idolatry; this was the result of the General Convention and of the part I took in it, in opposing legislation on the subject of ritualism.[38]

EPISCOPAL ELECTIONS

Frederic Cook Moorhouse in his work *Some American Churchmen,* commented on DeKoven's stature in 1872:

> Dr. DeKoven was now the central figure in the American Church. No name more frequently appeared in the Church papers; no one received equal attention.[39]

In light of his successful work at Racine College, it seems logical that he would be considered for other positions in the field of academic leadership. Such was the case with his nomination for the deanship at the General Theological Seminary on two occasions, in 1869 and 1878. He did not receive many votes in either instance. However, it wasn't as an educator that DeKoven began to be considered for positions of leadership but rather as a member of the clergy.

In light of his visibility and administrative talents, it only seems natural that James DeKoven would be considered for a leadership role as a bishop in his church. The first time his name was placed in nomination for an Episcopal role came with the election of an assistant bishop to aid

38. DeKoven, *Journal*, Nu2, 103.

39. Morehouse, "James DeKoven, Warden of Racine College," 172.

the aging Bishop Kemper in 1866. This was when William E. Armitage was elected as Assistant Bishop of the Diocese of Wisconsin on June 14, 1866.[40]

DeKoven's name was entered in several Episcopal election lists over the last ten years of his life, the first one being for the position of bishop for the diocese of Central New York in January of 1869.[41] A far closer contest was the election for the bishop of Massachusetts. DeKoven mentions this event in his journal. This was his first entry after a pause of almost eighteen months. It is dated August 30, 1874.

> My year had been saddened by the following ecclesiastical events. In the spring of 1873, an effort was made to elect me Bishop of Massachusetts. Some 40 Clergy voted for me and almost as many Laity. Dr. Paddock had however I think some dozen more votes and was elected. All summer in the *Church Journal,* owing to some unadvised remarks of Dr. Evans and the real want of principle of the editor, there were attacks upon me as being an extreme man, etc., of which I took no notice.[42]

DeKoven's ideas on the Eucharist and the importance of ritual were cited by those who opposed his election. The issue of DeKoven's high churchmanship also was key in the election of a bishop for the newly formed diocese in New Jersey in November of 1874. This was a closer contest during the early stages of the voting, but eventually DeKoven's reputation was used against him.

The second of the "ecclesiastical events" that DeKoven alluded to in his journal was the very unexpected death of his friend, Bishop Armitage, on December 7, 1873. Armitage had served as bishop of Wisconsin for three years since the death of Bishop Kemper in 1870. A close friend and supporter of James DeKoven, Armitage was only forty-three at the time of his death at St. Luke's hospital in New York City. The question of who would succeed Armitage as bishop of Wisconsin produced a veritable whirlwind of discussion in the both the religious and secular press. James DeKoven was undeniably the best-known Episcopal priest in Wisconsin and the upper Midwest. No one doubted that he would be put forward as a candidate by those who supported the ritualist ideas he so ably defended.

40. *Journal of the Proceedings of the Twentieth Annual Convention of the Protestant Episcopal Church in the Diocese of Wisconsin,* Janesville, 1866, 28.

41. "Important Religious Movements–Special Convention for the Diocese of Central New York," *Utica Herald,* Jan. 14, 1869.

42. DeKoven, Journal, O02, 108–9.

A special council to elect a successor for Armitage was scheduled to meet at the cathedral in Milwaukee during the second week of February. Prior to the special council there was much activity in the form of newspaper articles and letters in the daily press not only in Wisconsin but also in Chicago. Church papers had become embroiled in the campaign and discussions of the merits and failings of James DeKoven were the topic of the day. The issue was brought to a new level of intensity when a series of interviews with different clergy from the diocese of Wisconsin, including James DeKoven, were published in the *Chicago Times.*[43]

The controversy that resulted from this interview centered around a reply DeKoven gave to the following question. The reporter asked, "Is the contest one between the moderate or conservative school and the advanced party?" DeKoven replied that he didn't see the issue as one between two different schools of thought because in his opinion "we are all more or less high churchmen." He concluded with the simple statement, "The contest, I take it, will be one of men, rather than measures." Those who objected to this characterization of the issue reframed the statement to read "Principles, not Men." A pamphlet with this title, authored by John E. Egar of Nashotah Seminary, and co-signed by six fellow clergymen of the Diocese of Wisconsin, was published, accusing James DeKoven of extreme practices and views.

In the evening of Wednesday, February 10, at the Cathedral of All Saints in Milwaukee, a memorial service was held in commemoration of Bishop Armitage. James DeKoven preached the sermon in which he reviewed the history of the Episcopate in the United States and the role that Armitage played in establishing the See Principle with a cathedral church in Wisconsin. The next day the special council began meeting in the cathedral to establish procedures for the election. On Thursday, February 12, after the noon recess, James DeKoven spoke in his own defense. He spoke for over an hour and a half. He later published his speech in the pamphlet *A Theological Defense.* In it he dealt with all the issues that had been raised about his beliefs and practices, including real presence in the Eucharist, consubstantiation and transubstantiation, liturgical ritual, and confession. It is a thorough presentation of his ideas in a characteristic, calm, academic style.

43. *Chicago Times,* Jan. 24, 1874.

A

THEOLOGICAL DEFENCE

FOR THE

REV. JAMES DE KOVEN, D.D.

WARDEN OF RACINE COLLEGE,

TO

The Council held at Milwaukee,

FEBRUARY 11th and 12th, 1874.

RACINE, WIS.:
ADVOCATE STEAM PRINTING HOUSE AND BOOK BINDERY,
1874.

DeKoven's speech on his beliefs.

Voting for the bishop took place in the evening of the twelfth. On the first ballot DeKoven and Rev. Eugene Hoffmann of Philadelphia each received thirty-two votes. Thirty-five were necessary for election. Finally, on the fourth ballot, the clergy elected Dr. DeKoven by a vote of thirty-five with thirty-three cast for Hoffman. From the beginning of the roll call, the disposition of the parishes was clear: fifteen voted to approve the choice of the clergy and thirty-one to disapprove. The laity refused to elect James DeKoven as Bishop of Wisconsin. The election of the bishop was thus held over to the regular council meeting in June.[44]

44. The story of the Chicago Times interview, and the pamphlet authored by John J. Egar of Nashotah Seminary, is told in a detailed article entitled "James DeKoven and the Wisconsin Election of 1874" by Gary A. McElroy.

Even though DeKoven was defeated, his critics could not rest without providing some final commentary on the events that had taken place. The *Church Journal* provided this assessment:

> Never before, we believe, had a gentleman proclaimed himself a candidate for the Episcopate in the columns of a "Satanic press" or allowed himself to be "interviewed" in such character, by its correspondents. . . It was a performance which shocked and dispirited the Church and the community. For hitherto it has been decently supposed that the mitre sought the man, and not the man the mitre.[45]

The time between February and the remainder of the year was occupied by a veritable war of pamphlets. DeKoven dated his *Theological Defense* as Lent, 1874, including the document "Principles, Not Men" as an appendix. Professor Egar defended his views in a lengthy document, *The Eucharistic Controversy and the Episcopate of Wisconsin.* Samuel Buel of the General Theological Seminary examined DeKoven's publication in *Eucharistic Presence, Eucharistic Sacrifice, and Eucharistic Adoration.* DeKoven published a final paper, "The Eucharistic Controversy," in the October issue of *The Church and the World.* Other issues were raised in opposition to DeKoven's suitability for a bishopric, including the question of confession.

DeKoven would not allow his renomination for the position of bishop of Wisconsin in June and eventually worked with Lewis Kemper, Bishop Kemper's son, to recommend the election of Edward R. Welles as the successor of Bishop Armitage. Thus were the months of bitter arguments and theological debates resolved with the selection of a noncontroversial pastor from Red Wing, Minnesota.

New York City, October 7–November 3, 1874

The General Convention of October 1874 took place amid concerns of a growing secession movement on the part of more radical low-church clergy and congregations. One of the issues was that of ritualism and the ritualistic practices of men like James DeKoven. There was a general consensus among delegates that something had to be done to prevent more members from leaving the church. Some stressed the need for more regulations.

45. *Church Journal*, Mar. 19, 1874, Vol. XXII, No. 103, 184.

The tension was heightened by a report from the Committee on Canons, which included a proposed canon on ritual. This was obviously a move to stamp out ritualism, and James DeKoven rose to the occasion. His speech entitled "On the Canon on Ritual and the Holy Eucharist" was delivered on October 26, 1874, and is a sterling example of oratory and the power of words.[46] His speech was introduced by the president of the assembly with this caution: "Before Dr. DeKoven commences his speech, I wish to inform the House that I cannot permit any interruption. I will call to order any person who rises to ask a question. If questions are to be asked, let it be done after the speaker has taken his seat or left the stand." True to his word—no interruptions were permitted. DeKoven was eloquent without being pedantic, powerful in the expression of ideas while always being reasonable and accessible:

> We live in troublous times, and around us are all sorts of terrible questions. It does seem to me the day is not now to legislate on nice points of doctrine, or to prescribe exactly the measure of a genuflection, or the angle of inclination which can express an orthodox devotion . . . I see the storm-clouds gathering. I see the lightning's flash. I hear the thunder roll afar. I hear the trumpet call. In my ears the bugle-blast is ringing. And I call you, brethren, in a time like this, not to narrow-hearted legislation, but to broad, Catholic, tolerant charity, and to work, as men never worked before, for the souls of those for whom the Saviour died.[47]

46. Published as a separate pamphlet: DeKoven, "Canon on Ritual."

47. DeKoven, "Canon on Ritual," 42.

THE CANON ON RITUAL,

AND THE

HOLY EUCHARIST;

A SPEECH DELIVERED IN THE GENERAL CONVENTION,
OCTOBER 26TH, 1874,

BY THE

REV. JAMES DE KOVEN, D.D.,
WARDEN OF RACINE COLLEGE.

NEW YORK:
T. WHITTAKER,
2 BIBLE HOUSE.

DeKoven's speech on this subject.

The Canon on Ritual was passed by the General Convention, but the impact on the church was negligible. The high point of public debates about ritual seems to have been reached in this assembly, with this speech, although there were continued efforts to legislate locally.

James DeKoven returned to his life at Racine College, and there had to deal with additional personal and professional challenges. His mother, Margaret Sebor DeKoven, died in Middletown, Connecticut on December 8, 1874, and he returned to the East Coast to officiate at her funeral. Two more Episcopal elections took place during the winter months of 1875. In January he was supported by the clergy of Fond du Lac, but not the laity, for the first bishop of this new diocese in Wisconsin.

A LETTER

FROM

THE REV. JAMES DEKOVEN, D. D.,

WARDEN OF RACINE COLLEGE,

TO THE

CLERGY AND LAITY

OF THE

Diocese of Illinois,

IN CONVENTION ASSEMBLED,

September 14, 15, 16, 17. A. D. 1875.

TOGETHER WITH THE

ACTION OF THE CONVENTION OF THE DIOCESE OF ILLINOIS THEREON.

CHICAGO:
MITCHELL AND HATHEWAY.
1875.

DeKoven's withdraws his name from consideration as bishop of Illinois.

On February 4, at a special convention in Chicago, DeKoven was elected as bishop of Illinois. This vote by the Illinois delegates was seen as a "sublime act of insolence on the part of that diocese."[48] Once again DeKoven was the subject of criticism in letters and pamphlets. Although he had accepted the election, he eventually withdrew his acceptance to avoid additional embarrassment for the diocese of Illinois. The statement of his decision was printed in September, 1875: *A Letter from the Rev. James DeKoven, D.D. to the Clergy and Laity of the Diocese of Illinois.* The essence of his letter is an exposition of how his statements about the Eucharist had been misinterpreted, and how these misinterpretations had led to seriously false accusations. DeKoven also questions his rejection

48. Morehouse, "James DeKoven, Warden of Racine College," 209.

by the standing committees "as an injury to truth and justice."[49] This was the last serious effort to provide a bishopric for DeKoven, but it did not isolate him from other controversies and concerns. His repeated failure to be elected a bishop is symbolized in several images which show him with one or several miters at his feet.

Some thoughtful, straightforward, and stinging comments by James DeKoven on the role of a bishop and those who work with a bishop are found in a sermon he delivered at the Convocation of the Diocese of Milwaukee on April 19, 1876.[50] Although bitterness was never a theme in DeKoven's reactions, it must be recognized that he had repeatedly suffered the criticism and, in his opinion, the unjust accusations of those who opposed him. This sermon provided him the opportunity to express his opinions on the condition of bishops in the Episcopal Church in America, as well as his vision of what it should be.

According to DeKoven, many members of his Church held "a lofty idea of the Episcopal office—sometimes an exaggerated notion of it." He points out that often the wealthy people of a parish are the members of the vestry as well as delegates to the diocesan council. In effect, these lay delegates have veto power in the election of a bishop, whether or not this is a valid use of their position. These same delegates are the ones, or their predecessors were the ones, who create or created the canons or constitutions which describe the responsibilities of a bishop. This is the list of the essential duties of a bishop that DeKoven provides:

> He is to ordain, and confirm, and hold visitations; he is to preside at councils and be the chairman of committees . . . He is to attend to routine duties without end, and, above all, to be in journeyings often.[51]

Other talents, such as preaching well, being a good executive, being tireless and having nerves of steel are pluses for holders of the position. He concludes with this somewhat sarcastic description, "If he concentrates himself upon nothing, and diffuses a mild Episcopal perfume over everything, he meets the common theory which prevails of what a Bishop ought to be." The take-away image from this description is that of a bishop processing into a sanctuary preceded by an atomizer rather than a censor.

49. DeKoven, *Letter from the Rev. James DeKoven*, 14.

50. DeKoven, *Sermons Preached on Various Occasions*, 276–87.

51. DeKoven, *Sermons Preached on Various Occasions*, 282.

At the time DeKoven preached this sermon he was also working on the canon of the cathedral that was eventually published in 1877. Many of the ideas found in this sermon are also present in the canon about the organization of the cathedral and the chapter of clergy assigned to it. He states directly this guiding principle, "The Bishop's Chapter must be a missionary body." He described very clearly the duties and responsibilities of this clerical body:

> The most effective work, orderly services, the teaching of the young, the care of public institutions—all these could be done by such a body; and, in addition, missionary stations within a radius of thirty miles could be served by them far more usefully than if the clergy resided in the smaller community.[52]

What is particularly interesting about this outline of how a cathedral chapter could and should work, is the fact that it is a description of how the chapter of the Collegiate Church of St. John at Racine College was functioning at the time.

Early on in his career at the college, James DeKoven had outlined additional areas of need in the community of Racine. In addition to the school for young men, he hoped to play a role in the creation of a hospital, an orphanage, a home for elderly women, and a school for girls and young women directed by a sisterhood. By 1876, all of these goals were either accomplished or in the final planning stage of development. The eight priests of the chapter of the college church, in addition to their teaching and administrative responsibilities, served as clergy for local parishes and missions. Ever the practical thinker, DeKoven gives a final reason for the organization of the cathedral around a mission-guided chapter: "Such a system as this proposed would meet, I believe, another question which is of the gravest importance to all missionary efforts—the proper way to raise money." And finally, he returns to the essential role the bishop has a priest, teacher, and shepherd:

> He is called to be one upon whose soul the awful burden is laid to convert men to the obedience of the faith. He must offer the Holy Eucharist; he must preach the Word; he must bind and loose; he must organize; he must, above all things be a shepherd, a guide, a Father.[53]

52. DeKoven, *Sermons Preached on Various Occasions*, 285.

53. DeKoven, *Sermons Preached on Various Occasions*, 283.

Boston, October 3–25, 1877

After the tempestuous meetings of the General Convention in 1871 and 1874, that of 1877 in Boston seemed relatively calm and friendly in spirit. There was, however, one idea that came to the fore and with which the Wisconsin delegates were involved. This was the question of the name of the Episcopal Church. James DeKoven had authored a resolution that was passed at the Diocesan Council of 1877:

> Resolved, That the deputies to General Convention from this diocese be requested to ask of the General Convention the appointment of a Constitutional Commission, to which the question of a change in the legal title of the Church, as well as similar questions, may be referred.[54]

At issue was the title "Protestant Episcopal," and the concern that this implied that the church was not catholic in the sense of not universal. On the third day of the Convention, James DeKoven presented the resolutions from Wisconsin calling for a Constitutional Commission and the change of name. There was little support for these ideas and although DeKoven made a lengthy presentation, the resolution presented to the delegates called for a negative vote, "Resolved, That no change be made in the name of this Church, as used in the Constitution." There were only three negative votes; all other delegates voted for the resolution.

What is most interesting about this resolution is how much in advance DeKoven was on this issue. The words "Protestant Episcopal" were removed from the title-page of the prayer book in 1886 and eventually the legal name of the church was changed in 1979.

This was the last time that DeKoven attended a General Convention. He continued to write and speak on issues that were of importance for him. A new church journal was started in 1873: *The Church Eclectic.* This periodical published several of his writings and provided information about him, Racine College, and its activities. DeKoven's speech on the Constitutional Convention, given at the General Convention, appeared in the December 1877 issue. Two of his papers were read at church congresses and printed in issues of the journal. They dealt with freedom of religious thought and the question of absolution.[55]

54. *Journal of the Proceedings of the Thirty-first Annual Convention of the Protestant Episcopal Church in the Diocese of Wisconsin, June 19–20, 1877*, xxv–xxvi.

55. Thomas Gailor in his work *Some Memories* provided this summation of DeKoven's importance in religious thought: "Against the narrow provincialism of mere

During the last year of his life DeKoven was encouraged by family and friends to accept pastoral positions offered him at different churches. He turned them all down, writing the last letter of refusal on the day before he died. Over the years he had been criticized for being more interested in becoming a bishop than in administering the college. An anonymous document found in the Eckels-Pope Papers addresses this question directly:

> It has been said and thought (though the passing years weaken and lessen such words and thoughts more and more) that Dr. de Koven was unduly ambitious of ecclesiastical preferment, so much as to prejudice the interest of the College, and detract from his educational interest. But none who were in contact with that education over which he presided, could harbor such a thought for one moment. Those who were privileged to be with him at a Faculty meeting, when individual cases and incidents were concerned, will ever remember the careful and solicitous interest he manifested; always striving carefully to keep a due proportion between allowance for an individual shortcomings and the general collegiate tone.[56]

Protestant dogmas that were making thought impossible, he worked, he pleaded, he fought for liberty. He did more for the recognition of freedom of opinion in the American church than any man who has ever served in her ministry; and discussion which his speeches evoked, the widespread interest—the very timid alarm of some and the very biter indignation of others—made the church think as it had never thought before." Gailor, *Some Memories*, 22.

56. Probable author is Flavel Luther.

9

Recuperation, Sudden Death, and Funeral

RECUPERATION

On Friday, February 28, 1879, a brief article appeared in the *College Mercury* of Racine College under the rubric "College and Campus":

> We are glad to be able to announce that the Warden is again in a fair way for recovery. He has, for a few days past, suffered much pain in his chest from an attack of rheumatism, but is now nearly over it, and as his ankle is doing nicely will soon be able to be among us again.[1]

The weeks of rest James DeKoven spent recuperating in his home on the Racine College campus were ones he had needed for several years. Although he had traveled to the east on many occasions since the turmoil of 1875, there had been few times of real vacation and respite from his duties and obligations.[2] Even while he slowly reestablished his ability to walk, he worked on the immediate concerns of the college. He loved

1. The *College Mercury* had given the most accurate account of DeKoven's accident on February 12, two weeks after the incident. The information about the exact nature of his injury was the one provided by his attending physician, Dr. John Meachem, Sr. *College Mercury,* Feb. 12, 1879.

2. He did take a four-week vacation to attend the Centennial in Philadelphia in 1876. He stayed with the Stephens Parker family in Elizabeth, New Jersey, on this trip. DeKoven, *Journal,* Si1, 130.

being in the midst of the school activity even while those around him, including his sisters, tried to protect him from the daily stress.

Most of the information about these weeks after the accident comes from the reports of others. The last entry that DeKoven made in his journal was dated January 2, 1879. He mentions the weather, "The thermometer has been 20 below zero today. I should say it would be colder tonight. The wind blows a hurricane almost . . ."[3] He indicates that his sisters are in Chicago, but he is warm and cheerful in his study. We learn of an increase in the number of students ("having this term about 172"), and he has been able to pay off $5,000 of the floating debt. He writes about the Yellow Fever epidemic in Memphis, the deaths of Sister Constance and Father Schuyler, and a conversation he had with Bishop McLaren of Chicago. His final note is about a possible change in the administrative structure of Racine College and Nashotah, which eventually did not take place.

On Sunday, January 26, 1879, DeKoven had traveled to Fond du Lac, where he preached a sermon in the Cathedral Church of St. Paul. His good friend John Henry Hobart Brown was the first bishop of this new diocese and had invited him for this occasion. Upon his return to Racine (January 29), DeKoven wrote to Bishop Brown and provided this information in his letter:

> Give my best regards to your wife and the young ladies. We are in the midst of the thaw and suffering, on the whole from heat, to the destruction of the new rink, for the present at least. I have drawn up a cathedral canon, which if it finds favor in committee, I shall inform you.[4]

On Thursday, January 30, DeKoven traveled to Milwaukee, where he presented the document to the committee. The next day, early in the morning on his way to the train station, he fell on the ice-covered sidewalk. Cold weather had returned during the night and the January thaw was ended.

The confinement prescribed for DeKoven by Dr. Meachem was strictly observed and enforced by the small group of individuals who made up his immediate household. These people included his two sisters, Margaret and Elizabeth; his valet, Charles O. Olson; and the matron who supervised the infirmary, Miss Van Deusen. They valiantly tried to limit visits and make sure that he kept off his ankle; a wheelchair was procured, which DeKoven dubbed his "chariot," and slowly he graduated to walking

3. DeKoven, *Journal*, Tu1, 142.

4. Hobart Brown Letters, Jan. 29, 1879.

with crutches. The confinement was difficult for such a social person as James DeKoven. He concluded many of the notes he wrote during this time with the invitation, "come and see me." He encouraged visits by the college students who lived so closely by in Taylor Hall, and sought information from the teachers and others about the activities and events going on around him. After attending him daily for four weeks, Meachem commented on the fact that DeKoven had gained weight and was the very picture of health. Meachem told him, "Dr., it is not necessary for me to visit you daily as you are so well, I will come twice a week." To this statement, DeKoven replied, "If you stop coming, I shall miss your visits so much, so come every day until I tell you to stop."[5]

During the weeks of recuperation, DeKoven continued his correspondence, although generally writing only short notes in pencil. He also remembered events in the lives of his friends, such as the election of George F. Seymour, as bishop of Springfield, Illinois. DeKoven designed an Episcopal ring for Seymour and had his niece Mary Beach arrange for its creation in New York.

As DeKoven grew stronger, he began to reassume his role in some of the regular events of school life. It had been his practice to begin his weekly lecture, on Friday, with a review of the previous week's discipline report. He returned to this task on Friday, March 14. On this, his first Friday to again deal with the boys in person, he was able to say, "My dear boys, for the first time that I can recall, I have no reports against any one of you. Oh, that I might never be obliged to present such reports to you again!"[6] The students in the school were obviously on their best behavior and this was reflected in their observance of rules and regulations. They had undoubtedly been drilled on the need for quiet and calm for the recuperating warden. Another tradition that was important in DeKoven's institutional life were the weekly receptions. On Sunday, February 22, 1879, at DeKoven's request, Flavel Luther hosted the college students in his residence in the north section of Taylor Hall from 8 to 9 p.m. Although DeKoven did not attend, it was important for him to know that this custom had restarted. DeKoven did hold a reception for the college students on Sunday, March 16, and according to "Student" in the

5. Meachem, "Autobiography," 102–3.

6. Recounted in the letter of Francis J. Hall to William Cox Pope, dated May 12, 1899. Eckels-Pope Collection. Hall adds this commentary about DeKoven's wish of never having to report on their demerits and misbehavior: "He never did."

Scholiast articles, his attitude and behavior were much like the warden they all knew and missed.

One of the issues that had concerned DeKoven during the five years preceding this enforced period of relative calm was the opportunity to accept another position in the Protestant Episcopal Church. In addition to the nominations that he had received to be bishop of various dioceses throughout the United States, different congregations had extended offers of parish leadership to him.[7] He had been encouraged by friends and family, including his sister, Mrs. Casey, to accept such an offer. Those around him, and he himself, realized that the stress of his duties as warden of the college was damaging his health. The last of these offers, which was waiting on his desk during this time, was from St. Mark's Church in Philadelphia. On Tuesday, March 18, he wrote a letter of refusal. In his letter, he expressed gratitude for the confidence shown him by the call "to such an important post." He indicated that he was torn by the seriousness of refusing such a call, as well as the deep responsibility that would come with accepting it. He outlined the reasons behind his turning down the earlier call to Trinity Church in New York City the previous year. Although conditions had changed somewhat, he still felt duty-bound to remain in Wisconsin and had to refuse this important offer.[8]

James DeKoven the administrator, priest, and teacher was ever present and active. He had discovered that his valet Charles Olson had never been confirmed. During his recuperation, DeKoven used the early minutes of each day, before they began their other routines, to catechize Olson in preparation for his confirmation. He had given Charles a prayer book to guide him in his spiritual life.[9]

Another frequent visitor to the warden's quarters during this time was Alexis duPont Parker, son of DeKoven's good friend and colleague, Stephens Parker. Alexis was in his last year at Racine College and had developed a special relationship with DeKoven, who was convinced Alexis should become a clergyman. On the evening of March 18, they had had a serious discussion on this topic, during which Alexis insisted

7. Included in this list were Trinity Parish in New York City, the Church of the Advent in Boston, and a new Episcopal parish in Cincinnati.

8. William C. Pope included a transcript of this letter in his biography of DeKoven. Pope, *Life of James DeKoven*, 94–97.

9. This prayer book was donated many years later to the DeKoven Center Archives by the son of Charles Olson. This son told the story of how his father visited DeKoven's tomb every year on the anniversary of the warden's death.

on his unworthiness, and the warden insisted on Alexis's duty. The next morning, obviously feeling he had been too forceful in his discussion with Alexis the night before, DeKoven sent for him to come to his rooms before the first class. When Alexis arrived, DeKoven assured him of his love and his concern about his future. The warden at this time especially wanted to bring a peaceful conclusion to their discussion.

SUDDEN DEATH

At the end of their conversation, as Olson and Parker were moving DeKoven out of the study, he suddenly called out and lapsed into unconsciousness. The two young men tried to revive him; he came to for a moment, had a second seizure, and then died. There are several different published versions of this scene, with different indications of what was said and what was done.[10] They all contain this essential information as given here.

His sisters heard the call for help from upstairs; they came down and tried to revive him. They sent for Miss Van Deusen from the infirmary and dispatched a worker to fetch Dr. Meachem, who was met at the college gate, as he arrived for his daily visit. There was nothing the doctor could do; it was too late. A horse and rider were sent into the town to begin sending the necessary telegrams. The news spread throughout the school and it was a day of intense sorrow and loss. A special edition of the *College Mercury*, published April 7, recounted:

10. The section in the *College Mercury* under the heading "The Death of Our Warden" is one of the most succinct. *College Mercury*, April 7, 1879:

"Dr. DeKoven had so far recovered from the effects of the fall, with which he met in Milwaukee in January, that he was able to walk a little on his crutches. He had however a wheeled chair, which had been lent to him, in order to be moved around more easily. On the morning of his death, he seemed in good spirits as he was wheeled to breakfast. At quarter to nine, he sent for Mr. A. du P. Parker, '79, to explain more fully a subject about which he had been speaking the evening before. The Dr. had entirely finished his remarks, when he suddenly exclaimed, 'Quick, Pont, help.' Mr. Parker, supposing the Dr. to be fainting, opened his shirt at the neck and also gave him some water, at the same time bathing his head. In a few moments, in response to Mr. Parker's call, came Mrs. Dyer and Mrs. Casey, the Dr.'s two sisters who were living with him, and everything that could be done was done. Miss Van Deusen, the sick room matron was summoned, and Dr. Meachem, his physician was sent for. For a time he seemed to be better, and when told that he was only fainting, he responded, 'It's coming again, and in a few moments he was in the Paradise of God.'"

> It was a touching sight indeed to see how dearly loved he was. Professors, Tutors, College students and Grammar School boys all wept, as if he were their father. Nor was the feeling of sorrow confined to the College, but through the city it was felt the same, and all through the country every city has shown how much he was respected, honored, loved.[11]

A sense of sorrowful calm covered the campus and dominated the daily activities in the classrooms, dining hall, gymnasium, and farm. Slowly as the events began to take on the vague feeling of reality, decisions about the next steps in the drama of DeKoven's life were made.

Dr. Meachem indicated apoplexy as the cause of death. No such certificate has been located. John Meachem had obviously discussed death and dying with DeKoven because he wrote, "He did not fear death, for his life had been so pure and holy that he had no reason to, and his union with the Holy Catholic Church filled him with that faith which knows no fear."[12] Many years later, in 1913, Flavel Luther shared his personal feelings about DeKoven's passing. He and many others, including Bishop Clarkson of Nebraska, believed that he died, in some ways, as a martyr, the result of persecution.

> The physicians were doubtless right in saying that Dr. DeKoven died, physically, of apoplexy. His dearest friends will always believe that he died of a broken heart. Yet, probably, death was merciful. For the saintly head of the college was spared the sorrow of seeing the downfall of his hopes.[13]

Among the visitors of note who began to arrive on the campus during the day was Bishop Welles, coming from Milwaukee. He remained on the campus until Saturday evening. He wrote in his daily calendar, "March 19, Wednesday—Received, this morning, from Racine, a message announcing the sudden death of the Warden of the College. Went directly to Racine, calling in my appointments for the week . . ."[14] One of

11. *College Mercury*, Apr. 7, 1879.

12. Meachem, "Autobiography," 101.

13. Luther, "Racine College," 30.

14. Published in the *Journal of the Thirty-third Annual Council of the Protestant Episcopal Church in the Diocese of Wisconsin*, Milwaukee, November 1879, 9. In a more complete statement on James DeKoven in the same publication Bishop Welles provided this additional information: "The Monday before [17 March] I had been in Racine, and spent the morning with him, and left him in the firm conviction that in a few weeks he would be able to resume active duties at the College."

the first concerns of Bishop Welles was the welfare of the students, and upon his arrival the bishop arranged for a meeting with all of them that evening. He wanted to assure scholars and boys that the school would continue and that their sorrow was shared in the loss of the warden.[15]

An article appearing in the *Chicago Tribune* on the afternoon of the nineteenth indicated that John DeKoven, the warden's brother, and E. K. Hubbard, son of his sister, Elizabeth Dyer, had left for Racine on the 5 p.m. train. Upon their arrival, the family and colleagues began making plans and arrangements for the funeral. It is not known when they learned of the conversation which had taken place the previous Sunday between DeKoven and Rev. John Converse.[16] In this conversation Dr. DeKoven had outlined his wishes for his funeral and burial. Most specifically, he had indicated his wish that there be three services of holy communion on the day of interment and that he be buried on the campus next to Dr. Roswell Park, the first president of the college. These wishes were followed, although the spot chosen for his tomb was not directly adjacent to the burial site of his predecessor Dr. Park. No explanation has ever been given as to why this conversation with Converse took place.

The shock and intensity of the feelings that were experienced by many can be seen in the *In Memoriam* statements written and published by groups associated with the college and James DeKoven. This shock was due in part to the unexpected nature of his death. One of the earliest statements was subscribed to at a meeting of the faculty on the day of his death:

> Resolution—March 19, 1879.
>
> The Faculty of Racine College, who have this day, by God's inscrutable dispensation, been deprived of the Warden, wish to render their united testimony to the faithfulness, zeal and love, to the untiring watchfulness and never-failing courtesy which they have witnessed day by day, and year after year. Even up to the last day and the last moment of his life, the welfare of the College and of every one of its members was his unceasing care.

15. In a more detailed obituary note about James DeKoven, Bishop Welles wrote the following about the impact of DeKoven on the Diocese, "As I have gone about the Diocese since his death, I have been deeply moved by the many and touching tokens of respect and affection cherished for him in all parts of the State. His pupils and students especially, dating back to the school at Delafield, cherish his memory with a reverence and love which only a character and such a life will beget." *Journal of the Thirty-third Annual Council*, 2.

16. John Converse was the professor of Latin and Greek in the college, chaplain of the Taylor Orphanage, and secretary of the faculty.

> He has fallen at his post, faithful until death to the work which God gave him to do.
>
> The Faculty can only mourn with those that mourn, and put on record this poor testimony to what words fail to express.
>
> Jno. H. Converse, Secretary of the Faculty[17]

Similar statements were written and published by the alumni of Racine College studying at the General Theological Seminary in New York City and alumni living in Milwaukee and Chicago, as well as Racine. Meetings of the alumni in these cities were called and decisions made about how to honor James DeKoven. Arrangements were made for special trains from Milwaukee and Chicago for those wishing to attend the funeral. There were also proclamations of condolence and sorrow made by the City Council of Racine, the Senate of the State of Illinois, and the Legislature of the State of Wisconsin.

Obituaries and news articles about James DeKoven's death began appearing in newspapers across the country by the morning of March 20. Two collections of the obituaries and related articles have survived and are valuable sources of information in detailing the importance of DeKoven in the church world of the United States. These two scrapbooks were assembled by James's sister, Mary DeKoven Beach and her daughter, Mary, living in New York City.[18] In the first of the articles that appeared in the *New York Times* on March 20, the information was given that his sister had received a letter from DeKoven the day before "written in the most hopeful spirit and speaking very lightly of the accident." The hopeful nature of his recuperation was thwarted by the news of his sudden death. The information in the numerous articles was not always accurate. The same article that mentioned the letter to his sister indicated that his accident had occurred in Chicago and that there were 400 students at "Racine University."

The family and friends of DeKoven began assembling at the college. Late Friday afternoon, the bishops and trustees of the institution held a meeting at which several individuals spoke about the life and labors of their departed colleague and friend. There were tears as well as smiles as

17. *College Mercury*, Apr. 7, 1879.

18. In their research for a biography of James DeKoven, the Sisters of the Community of St. Mary at the DeKoven center learned of these two scrapbooks housed in the archives of the Rockfall Corporation in the DeKoven House in Middletown, Connecticut. In 1961 one of the scrapbooks was given to the DeKoven Foundation by the Rockfall Corporation.

they remembered his devotion and love of the college and its mission. At the end of this gathering of clerics and laymen, the doctor's brother, John DeKoven, read his last will and testament. It had been written on September 30, 1876. In it he mentions all his family members by name, making his sister Margaret Casey the "residuary legatee." He left to the board of trustees of Racine College the sum of $39,645.50 in cash securities and his library to the college. The will was closed with these words:

> I leave to all of my dear relations, whom I dearly love, my blessing and the assurance of my unceasing gratitude for all the love and kindness they have shown me. To all my old boys and students, and to all my beloved professors and teachers, I leave the assurance of my love and prayers, and ask of them the same.[19]

FUNERAL

There are some trees so great you cannot measure their size until they are down.[20]

The morning of March 22 dawned on a Wisconsin, mid-March vigorous snow fall. The final rites began at 7 a.m. with the first Holy Communion service in the chapel. Rev. Dr. Falk was the celebrant. The second service took place at 8 a.m., with Rev. Mr. Converse officiating. Bishop Welles was the celebrant at the last Eucharist, assisted by Dr. Ashley of Milwaukee at 9 a.m. The body of James DeKoven was in the chapel at these ceremonies and then moved to the ante-chapel for public viewing. According to a newspaper report, there was a continuous line of students, friends, and townspeople for nearly two hours past his open coffin.[21] This

19. *College Mercury*, April 7, 1879.

20. Unknown author, identified only as a "dear friend" who wrote a letter to the editor of the *Church Eclectic*, Rev. William Gibson, congratulating him on the attention paid in this journal to the events surrounding the death of James DeKoven. This powerful image is indeed a fitting one for the impact of DeKoven's life and death. *Church Eclectic*, "Literary Notes," Vol VII, June 1879, No. 3, 151.

21. The number of attendees at the services was large, with the *Racine Advocate* estimating that 1,500 people were present. An article in the *Church Eclectic* on DeKoven's death and burial provided this information: "The evening before, and all the morning trains brought throngs of people from all directions. The day dawned dismally with a driving snow-storm which soon covered the ground to the depth of several inches. "Miscellanea," Vol. VII, No. 2, May 1879, 113–23.

description of James DeKoven's body and funeral procession was given in the *College Mercury*:

> He was clad in priestly robes; on his breast was the gold crucifix which he had received shortly before his death from a friend in England. In his hands was a bunch of violets.
>
> At 11 o'clock a procession of attendees exited Taylor Hall and marched to the chapel in the following order:
>
> Grammar School.
> College students.
> Cross bearer.
> Choir.
> Clergy.
> Bishops.
> Pall Bearers.
> Relatives.
> Members of the Faculty.
> Masters of the Grammar School.
> Trustees.
> Alumni and old students.
> City officers of Racine.

There were eight bishops, with Bishop McLaren of Chicago at the head, and thirty-three clergy members in the procession. The members of the city council attended as a group led by the mayor of Racine, DeKoven's physician, Dr. John G. Meachem. According to a council resolution, all businesses in the city were to be closed during the times of the services and flags in Racine were flown at half-mast on Saturday, March 22. Two sets of pallbearers participated in the burial, the first being composed of employees of the college and the second made up of DeKoven's former classmates from the General Theological Seminary.

Choral music played a significant part in the funeral services. The hymn "Paradise, O Paradise" was sung as the procession moved from Taylor Hall to the Chapel. The thirty-two voices of the robed choir of Racine College, which was well-known in the Episcopal Church, led the singing. The choir intoned the psalm "Lord Let Me Know My End and the Number of My Days" as the procession passed up the aisle of the chapel. Several of the bishops present participated in the service: Bishop Clarkson of Nebraska read the opening words of the burial service; Bishop Talbot of Indiana read the lesson, which was from St. Paul's first Epistle to the Corinthians.

The recessional hymn was "For All the Saints Who from Their Labors Rest,"[22] and the procession moved from the Chapel to the south side of the Chapel, where the open grave awaited the coffin and the assembled people. The grave was located under the window nearest the warden's seat in the Chapel. Upon arriving, the choir sang Psalm 23, "The Lord Is My Shepherd." A special anthem, composed by Professor Elmendorf of the faculty, was sung as the body was lowered into the final resting place. Bishop Robertson of Missouri read concluding prayers, and the crowd began to file past the open grave placing flowers and evergreen sprigs on the coffin. The pallbearers remained through the end; his classmates from General Theological Seminary continued to sing anthems and hymns as the people walked solemnly away.

Interestingly enough, in light of the "ritual controversies so associated with DeKoven," there is no description of the vestments being worn by the officiating clergy or any mention of incense being used in the service. The priestly robes on DeKoven's body were listed as an alb and chasuble with white stole.[23] Altar lights are mentioned as being located on either side of a pure white cross that was framed against a purple reredos:

> The vacant "Warden's chair" was draped in black and purple, and on the prayer desk, where he had so often bowed his noble head in reverential devotion, the early violets of spring were laid to typify the sweet memories of his life.[24]

The floral decorations received special mention in the published accounts of the funeral and were described as "magnificent." The chapel was filled with them. This is especially noteworthy considering the time of year and the weather conditions. Some of the flower arrangements mentioned in the following excerpts can be seen in the accompanying photo taken on the day of the funeral:

> Among the more notable floral offerings was a broken column formed of roses and calla lilies of royal size which came from the old students of Milwaukee, who also sent a superb pastoral staff seven feet in length, composed entirely of white carnations, tea roses and violets . . . The tribute of the old students now resident

22. This version of the hymn is not the one we know today as composed by Ralph Vaughn Williams. However, it was a particularly moving tribute to the warden and from this date forward, in the history of the school, came to be associated with the death of DeKoven and his funeral service.

23. Pope, 98

24. The *Standard*, New York, Apr. 2, 1879.

in Chicago was a cross five feet high of choice white flowers. On the upper arm of the cross was a large crown of tea roses with a bank of purple flowers. At the intersection of the cross were the letters I.H.S., in scarlet blossoms. The base consisted of three broad steps inscribed with purple violets with the prayer "Grant, O Lord, Eternal Rest."[25]

St. John's Chapel the day of DeKoven's funeral.

The centrality of Eucharist in DeKoven's life was honored through the three services said at his funeral. DeKoven's love of music and his dedication to choral music in the religious services of Racine College was reflected in the role of the college choir in the funeral service. The importance of James DeKoven in the Racine community was emphasized by the participation of the city council as well as many ordinary citizens

25. *College Mercury,* Apr. 7, 1879.

in this final tribute. The last two people to leave his grave site on the day of his burial were two sisters of the Community of Saint Mary who were teaching at Kemper Hall in Kenosha. They knelt at his grave site and prayed in the falling snow after all others had left. Their devotion to their spiritual director reflected the solemn dignity of the ceremony that honored James DeKoven.

The next day was mid-Lent Sunday and, in the past, it had been a special day for the college and its students. Bishop McLaren of Chicago was chosen by the board of trustees to remain and speak to the students at the service of morning prayer. This was a sincere effort on the part of the trustees to assure the students and their parents that there would be a continuation of the work of the College in the manner of James DeKoven. Bishop McLaren concluded his remarks with these comments about Father DeKoven:

> He was ever a dear friend, the noble, thoughtful counsellor; the wise, brave theologian; the successful administrator; the thorough educator; the man who had a heart for every woe, a hand for every friend, and was capable of entering into the joys and sorrows of so wide a circle.[26]

In the days and weeks that followed upon the death and burial of James DeKoven, there were numerous memorial services and sermons preached in his honor. Each of the sermonizers provided special insights into the importance and impact of the warden. One of the first sermons was preached at Trinity Church, Chicago, on Sunday Mar. 23, 1879. In his sermon on that day, Rev. Edward Sullivan dealt with the profound sorrow provoked by DeKoven's death and attempted to explain it. He described DeKoven's personal magnetism and his character in these striking images:

> One of the peculiar features of Dr. DeKoven's character, was its completeness. It was as a rounded, full-orbed, perfect sphere. He was learned like St. Paul; practical like St. James; fervid, though not impulsive, like St. Peter; loving like St. John, and gentle and tender as any woman. Firm as an oak, yet sympathetic as a sensitive plant. Wise as a serpent, yet harmless as a dove.[27]

On the same day, Rev. David Swing, a very well-known and popular Presbyterian minister in Chicago, also memorialized DeKoven, emphasizing the extent of his impact through his role as an educator:

26. *College Mercury*, Apr. 7, 1879.

27. *College Mercury*, April 7, 1879.

> Quite an army of men in the prime of life remain in all the walks of manifold duty, who were molded into better mental and moral shape by that hand of Dr. DeKoven, which had a touch of both love and learning. Some teachers impart only scholarship, and send out a learned but not a warm manhood; but this president gave out to his students a force of knowledge and a force of friendship.[28]

One of the best known and most frequently published memorials for James DeKoven was written and delivered by his good friend and colleague Rev. Clinton Locke. The occasion was a citywide memorial service held at Grace Episcopal Church in Chicago on Wednesday, March 26. It was entitled "The Upright Man." Locke unabashedly called it a eulogy and defended his choice of this title because he was going to praise James DeKoven: "For could it be tolerated that I, the friend of his life, should strive to bring out into the light of day any fault of his character? Before God I *know* not any, if it were my place to mention them."[29] Locke chose to study DeKoven in his several roles in life, beginning with his powerful ability as an orator and preacher. He mentions the effect DeKoven had when speaking before the General Convention of the church. He then treated DeKoven as a theologian, a teacher, a "man of the world," and a realist. Locke indicates that with supreme confidence he had sent his own son to be educated in the school in Racine. His final two segments dealt with the warden as a priest and as a Christian. His conclusion is moving in its earnestness:

> And so I finish the picture of this holy man. You may say it has been painted by too partial a pencil, and is too flattering a likeness. It may be so, but it does not seem so to me. It seems merely the truth, to which hundreds can bear witness. I, for one, thank God with all my heart that such a man has lived.[30]

In light of the controversies that surrounded James DeKoven during the last ten years of his life, it should come as no surprise that there were protests associated with the way in which he was memorialized by

28. Sermon by David Swing of Chicago reprinted in *College Mercury*, Apr. 7, 1879.

29. This eulogy was published in the *Chicago Tribune* the following day and later in the *Church Eclectic*. The version here cited here is from the *Church Eclectic*, Vol. VII, No. 2, May 1879, 117–22.

30. The writer of the column in the *Chicago Tribune* on March 26 added this comment about Locke's delivery, "Although not a graceful orator, there was that burning power in all he said that made his preaching wonderfully effective."

different high church congregations. One event in particular attracted the attention of different writers. This was a "Requiem Mass" celebrated at St. Clement's church in Philadelphia "for the repose of the soul of the Rev. Dr."[31] As described in an article in the Washington, D.C. *Evening Star,* "The paraphernalia used was very similar to that used in the Roman Catholic Church."[32] This idea of praying for the dead was seen as particularly "Roman" and definitely not Protestant Episcopal.

A virulent attack was published in pamphlet form in Milwaukee soon after DeKoven's death. It was entitled *In Memoriam, Rev. James DeKoven; Warden of Racine College* and was written by newspaper editor John W. Hinton. Hinton, an Episcopalian, does recognize DeKoven's goodness and intellectual skills, but he also condemns him as "the most dangerous enemy with which Protestantism ever held conflict in Wisconsin or in the Northwest."[33] His main criticism of DeKoven was that he worked for "the elevation of the priesthood and the depression of the laity."[34]

The amount of attention paid to the death, and consequently to the life, of James DeKoven in the press of his day is significant. In many ways, he had become a lightning rod for religious controversies that occupied the minds and spirits of good, faithful Christians in this country. Was the nation particularly interested in contested elections, having experienced the controversy surrounding the presidential elections of Lincoln in 1860 and Hayes in 1876? The election of an Episcopal bishop would not normally seem to raise a great deal of interest today. It was a different time, a different church, a different newspaper-reading public. Articles devoted to DeKoven's death and life were published throughout the United States and in England.[35] What was published ran the gamut from accurate and objective to biased and false. Only in looking through the prism of distance and time can a more healthful analysis of James DeKoven's life and work be made.

31. "St. Clement's Ways. A Requiem Mass for the Repose of the Soul of Rev. Dr. DeKoven." *Augusta Chronicle,* May 21, 1878.

32. The *Evening Star,* May 16, 1879.

33. Hinton, "In Memoriam, Rev. James DeKoven, 6.

34. Hinton, "In Memoriam, Rev. James DeKoven," 4.

35. The list of newspaper clippings included in the two scrapbooks prepared by Mrs. Beach and daughters is impressive. There were approximately fifty articles in each scrapbook; many are duplicates, although some are unique to the particular book. New York, Chicago, and Milwaukee newspapers are the main sources. There are also clippings from newspapers in Boston, Indianapolis, Cincinnati, and Racine.

10

The Legacy of James DeKoven

St. James DeKoven window, Chapel of St. Mary the Virgin, Nashotah, Wisconsin.

In a letter dated November 8, 1935, Mother Mary Ambrose, Superior of the Western Province of the Community of Saint Mary, wrote to the Rt. Rev. Benjamin P. Ivins, Bishop of Milwaukee, regarding the purchase of the property of Racine College by her community:

> The question of the name has to be settled right away. After some discussion we decided on "DeKoven Foundation for Church Work," thinking that it was better to avoid a title which was in any way restrictive. Will you let me know by return mail just what you think of this? It seems to me that Dr. DeKoven's name is the one to be perpetuated.[1]

This action by the sisters to dedicate this new undertaking to the memory of James DeKoven was the most notable effort to honor the warden of Racine College in the fifty-six years following his death. The sisters of the Community of Saint Mary continued their work at the DeKoven Foundation until 1986. The foundation continues to function today and is one of the most visible legacies of James DeKoven. It has evolved in its service to the city of Racine, the Episcopal Church in Wisconsin, and the Episcopal Church of the United States almost one hundred years after its creation in 1935.

This was not, however, the first time that efforts were made to memorialize the life and work of James DeKoven. Soon after his death, as published in the *College Mercury* of April 24, 1879, a DeKoven Memorial Endowment was announced: "The Board of Trustees of Racine College have resolved to appeal to the friends of the Rev. Dr. DeKoven, their late Warden, for not less than $150,000 toward the partial endowment of the institution which he loved so dearly and to which he gave all the energies of his life."[2] In the circular announcing this fundraising effort, the amounts already raised are listed. It is noted that the students at Racine bad already subscribed $1,000 to the endowment. In addition, the DeKoven Memorial Endowment Fund was seeking "a sum sufficient to endow six College Professorships." Along with this endowment effort was the creation of another committee to work for the construction of a DeKoven Memorial Hall.

Different efforts to honor his memory continued throughout the months that followed his death. One of the most unusual was announced in a short article that appeared in the *Racine Weekly Journal* that appeared on Sunday, Apr. 9, 1879:

> Peterson, the well-known Chicago artist, has painted a striking likeness of the late Dr. DeKoven. He has sent the picture in a

1. Mother Mary Ambrose to the Rt. Rev. Benjamin P. Ivins, Bishop of Milwaukee, dated November 8, 1935. Document File, Correspondence, DeKoven Foundation Archives.

2. *College Mercury*, Apr. 24, 1879.

> magnificent frame, to Mrs. H. S. Durand and she invites a call at her residence from all who would like to see the picture.[3]

The portrait was based on a photo of DeKoven taken at the Thomas Photographic Studio in Racine sometime before 1875. Eventually the portrait was purchased by the board of trustees and today hangs in the library of Taylor Hall which was DeKoven's private study during his lifetime.

RACINE COLLEGE AS LEGACY

It is safe to assume that many of those associated with James DeKoven looked upon the continuation of Racine College as a physical memorial to his legacy. He spent twenty years of his active life dedicated to this institution, and the city of Racine had become home for him. His role in the community had been recognized in his lifetime when the street on the northern edge of the college campus was named DeKoven Avenue in his honor.

As to be expected, life and work at the school continued in the established pattern. There were 169 students in the school, and their education was of prime importance to the administration. The efforts to continue the work of the school is reflected in a note written on April 4 to a concerned parent:

> Dr. DeKoven's death was indeed a great blow to us all but he had so impressed his method upon the institution that it will move along as he would have directed it. The Trustees are using great precaution in finding another man, and we all feel that whoever is Dr. DeKoven's successor will be well fitted for the place. Yours, most truly, S. E. Smith[4]

The issue of a finding a candidate to become warden of Racine College was of prime importance for the board.[5] During the last few years

3. Henry Eric Christopher Peterson (1841–1918) was a Chicago portrait artist born in Stockholm, Sweden, and educated at the Royal Academy in that city. He immigrated to Chicago and served in the American Navy during the Civil War.

4. This was in reply to a request from Mrs. E. F. Wynkoop, of Rock Island, Illinois, to allow her son, George, to leave early for the Easter break. Seth E. Smith, a master in the grammar school, stressed the fact that they were continuing to operate according to the guidelines of James DeKoven. Letter from the James Mercier private collection of related Racine College documents.

5. According to the revised Statutes of the College, the warden had to be an ordained Episcopal priest.

of his life, DeKoven had worried about the school being too closely associated with his leadership.[6] He doubtless had thought about who might replace him, and on one occasion had indicated to the board that he had in mind someone who would be an effective college president.[7] The speed with which his successor was named seems to indicate that such discussions had gone on before his death.

The board chose Rev. Stephens Parker, a close friend of James DeKoven and a fellow graduate of the General Theological Seminary in 1854. During the last years of his life, whenever DeKoven traveled to the East Coast he regularly visited with the Parker family in Elizabeth, New Jersey. Parker's acceptance of the presidency was announced on May 24, 1879. At the same time notice was given that Parker had begun efforts to raise an endowment for the institution as a memorial to James DeKoven.[8]

The board of trustees had moved with amazing swiftness in naming Parker, and his installation was scheduled to take place at the same time as the commencement ceremony on the June 25, 1879. The installation was held at noon on that day in the College Chapel following the actual graduation ceremony. There was a general feeling of optimism surrounding the arrival of the new warden. As part of the celebrations there was a student performance of the Gilbert and Sullivan comic opera *A Trial by Jury*. It is interesting to note that the new warden's son, Alexis, sang the leading role of the judge in this production which took place in the gymnasium.

One subject that DeKoven repeated frequently in letters and speeches during his administration was the difficulty of managing a school without an endowment. Relying solely on income from tuition to finance the institution was almost an impossibility. It was a reality that the new warden was forced to face as soon as he arrived at the college. He learned how intently James DeKoven had overseen the budget of the school and how he had worked consistently with the curator to cut expenses when possible. Under the new warden additional advertising efforts were made to increase enrollment. The cost of the tuition for the college course was

6. He worried that it was becoming known as DeKoven's School for Boys. Pope commented on this concern in his biography, "During the later years of his life, there was ever present to his mind the problem of making the College independent of himself." Pope, *Life of The Rev. James DeKoven, D.D.*, 32.

7. Racine Board of Trustees Minutes, May 25, 1878, 182.

8. *Churchman*, May 24, 1879.

reduced and several of the employees were terminated.[9] Although a slight increase in enrollment helped with the income, the trustees were not satisfied with the efforts undertaken by Parker.

At the annual meeting of the board of trustees on June 28, 1881, Rev. Stevens Parker made a powerful statement that was included in the record. He pointed out why he accepted the position and what he found when he arrived: "I was staggered at the very beginning to find Dr. DeKoven's ways criticized, and suggestions of changes made by some of the members of this Board . . ."[10] Among other concerns, he accused the curator of mismanaging the affairs of the school and suggested that the board of trustees was too removed from its daily operation. Stevens Parker submitted his resignation effective January 1, 1882, although he continued to function as head of the institution until September of that year.

As a replacement for Rev. Parker, the board of trustees eventually settled on Rev. Albert Zabriskie Gray, rector of the Church of St. Phillip in the Highlands, Garrison, New York. Gray did not assume his duties until the spring of 1883, and by that time the trustees had thoroughly rewritten the statutes of the college. When Gray arrived, there were only 108 students in the institution and he undertook the task of rebuilding enrollment and creating an endowment. He had some initial success but could not maintain long-term interest in supporting this church school. One effort that was doomed from the start was the creation of a law school section in the college. It lasted only two years and was closed along with the college course in 1888. Gray resigned his position on December 4, 1888.[11]

It is not an exaggeration to say that the impact of closing Racine College was felt throughout the United States. The alumni of this institution were active not only in the Episcopal Church but were also successful in the worlds of business, science, law, education, and politics. Four bishops of the church, as well as a governor of the state of Minnesota and the chief justice of the Wisconsin Supreme Court, were graduates of the college. Walter Prehn, in his thoroughly researched lecture entitled "James DeKoven, Educator," wrote about the education students received: "Racine College was a serious place. By the time of the Rector's untimely death in

9. Some poor decisions were made: all the matrons were fired, including those who had been employed since the early days of DeKoven's arrival. The servant girls and farm employees were reduced in number from 41 to 27.

10. "Warden's Report," Annual Meeting of the Board of Trustees, Jun. 28, 1881.

11. Gray died of pneumonia in Chicago on February 16, 1889.

1879, it was one of a handful of truly outstanding schools in the United States."[12] The quality of education provided, the spirit of family created by the overarching influence of James DeKoven, and the dedication of the teachers and staff to their work, instilled a love of the place and its memories in those who experienced it during its prime days.

In an attempt to explain the magic of the school and its failure to be a lasting legacy to DeKoven, two prominent individuals wrote their thoughts about the place and the man who led it to success. In an article entitled "Racine College—A Chapter from its History," Flavel S. Luther, who taught at the school from 1872 through 1882, and who went on to be the president of Trinity College, expressed his admiration for DeKoven:

> No one who came within the reach of his personality can ever forget his splendid eloquence, his complete self-consecration, the singular sweetness of his character, and his wonderful power over other men old and young.[13]

A follow-up to this article was printed in the November issue of the *Church Times*. It was written by Thomas F. Gailor, the Bishop of Tennessee, a graduate of Racine College in 1876, and when he wrote his comments he was Chancellor of the University of the South, in Sewanee, Tennessee. He, too, acknowledges the solid education provided and profound influence of Dr. DeKoven and Racine College on many men "occupying high and responsible positions in the learned professions and in political and commercial life"[14] He is also very straightforward in his assessment of why the college failed to continue in its educational mission:

> Racine College failed because, first of all, it was an autocracy—a noble and beautiful autocracy indeed—but after all, it was dominated and pervaded by the gracious and noble personality of one man, and when his presence was withdrawn, the life died. The attempt to widen the scope of the institution by putting nine Episcopal "counsellors" or "visitors" on the Board of Trustees

12. Prehn, "James DeKoven, Educator." Prehn studied the Church School Movement in his doctoral dissertation in history at the University of Virginia, entitled "Evangelical, Catholic, Republican: William Augustus Muhlenberg and American Education, 1828–1877."

13. Luther, "Racine College—A Chapter from its History," *Church Times*, Vol. XXIV, No. 2, Oct. 1913, 26–30.

14. Gailor, "Racine College—A Reply." *Church Times*, Vol. XXIV, No. 3, Nov. 1913, 42.

> came too late. A little more Church control at the beginning might have saved it.
>
> Then, secondly, it was a troublous time and unfortunately Dr. DeKoven was at the center of the storm and for at least ten years before his death he was compelled to give more time to theological controversy than to upbuilding his college.[15]

After the decision to eliminate the college courses in 1888, numbers in the grammar school declined until there were fewer than twenty students enrolled. Eventually, with the infusion of new ideas and new administrators the grammar school regrouped and continued, under different names, until 1933 when the impact of the stock market crash of 1929 forced its permanent closure.

ST. JOHN'S HALL—DELAFIELD, WISCONSIN

There were other ways in which the legacy of James DeKoven lived on. In 1884, at the same time that the future of Racine College was under discussion, a former student of that school was involved in reviving an earlier educational venture of James DeKoven, St. John's Hall in Delafield, Wisconsin. The following notice in the *Nashotah Scholiast* announced the "rebirth" of this institution:

> St. John's Hall, Delafield, is daily developing new marks of strength and reality. In our next [issue] we hope to give our readers some account of this school, its past work, and workers. Suffice to say that, at a recent vestry meeting, the school property was leased to Mr. S. T. Smythe. The Hall will be formally opened by the Bishop of the Diocese and the Rev. Professor Adams, Sept 11, 1884. Mr. Smythe, Head Master, will issue a circular in a few days.[16]

Sydney Thomas Smythe had been a student at Racine College in the years 1877–79. These two years were obviously of special importance in Smythe's life. He wrote about James DeKoven later on in his life: "Outside of my family, no one has ever had a greater influence on my life and thinking that had Dr. DeKoven. I loved him as I loved my father."[17] Smythe did not return to Racine after the death of DeKoven but continued

15. Gailor, "Racine College—A Reply," 42.
16. "St. John's Hall," *Nashotah Scholiast*, Jun. 1884, Vol. I, No. 7, 8.
17. Quoted by Harris H. Holt in *Story of the Church of St. John Chrysostom*, 13.

his education at St. Stephen's College in Annandale-on-Hudson, New York, where he graduated at the head of his class in 1883. In that same year he returned to Wisconsin and enrolled at Nashotah Seminary.

During his first year at the seminary, he became involved with the youth in the area, creating what he called the "Delafield Guild." His ideas soon led him to think about reviving the school that James DeKoven had created when he was rector of the Church of St. John Chrysostom. In May of 1884, Smithe leased the old schoolhouse and reopened St. John's Hall. The school was successful, and by 1885 he was able to ask for a ninety-nine year lease on the property with the promise that he would build a new dormitory.

The name of the institution was later changed to St. John's Military Academy and continued in the tradition established by DeKoven with the motto, "Work hard, play hard, pray hard." Smythe guided this institution until his death in 1923 and saw it become one of the outstanding military academies in the country.

THE VISIT OF THE GENERAL CONVENTION OF 1886 TO RACINE COLLEGE (OCTOBER 16, 1886)

The single event that affirmed the legacy of James DeKoven in the annals of the Protestant Episcopal Church was the visit of the General Convention to Racine College on Saturday, October 16, 1886. For the first time in its history, the triennial convention took place in what was considered the western United States. The General Convention began its meeting in Chicago on October 6 and then on October 12: "The Presiding Bishop presented to the House an Invitation from the Warden and Trustees of Racine College to visit the College by special train on Saturday."[18] The purpose of this trip seemed to be threefold: acquaint the members of the convention with the current status of the college, validate the work of the current warden, Albert Z. Gray, and honor the memory of James DeKoven seven years after his death. Dr. Gray, working with the Merchants' Association of Racine and supported by Alexander Mitchell, President of the Chicago, Milwaukee & St. Paul Railroad,[19] had arranged a well-planned and informative trip.

18. *Journal of the General Convention*, "Sixth Days' Proceedings," 20. *Journal of the Proceedings of the Bishops, Clergy, and Laity, 1886.*

19. Mitchell was a trustee of the College and a very well-known Episcopalian in Milwaukee. His grandson, General Billy Mitchell, is one of the more famous graduates

The General Convention adjourned an hour early so that delegates could reach the special train at the Milwaukee & St. Paul depot by one o'clock. There a train with four brand new coaches and a parlor car, for the bishops, awaited them. At the Racine depot the approximately three hundred guests were met by all the private carriages and buggies in the town and were taken directly to the college. A series of events followed, including a visit to the tomb of James DeKoven and a dinner in the Refectory where the student choir sang. Numerous speeches and welcomes were given by Warden Gray, Bishop McLaren of Chicago, Senator Doolittle of Racine among others. Gray concluded his welcome:

> And lastly, there is another welcome—let me speak it with bowed head and reverent breath –I welcome you in the name of him beneath whose portrait I stand, in the name of one who loved you all and the dear Church which you represent, in the name of one who labored with you, as he labored for us, and died in the holy cause of Catholic Education, in the name of one whose remains sleep in peace beneath the shadow of our Chancel, in the sainted name of James DeKoven I welcome you to his loved Racine.[20]

The most frequently cited speech given during this visit was that of the Rt. Rev. John Scarborough, bishop of New Jersey. In his remarks, Scarborough spoke of the important place that DeKoven holds in the history of the church:

> There are two Shrines, one on this side, one on the other side of the water, which always appeal to the hearts of Churchmen; one is the shrine of John Keble,[21] in England, and the other is the shrine of James DeKoven, in America.[22]

The day's visit concluded with a choral Evensong in the college Chapel of Saint John. The guests were conveyed back to the train and returned to Chicago by 10 p.m. that evening.[23]

---

of Racine College.

20. "The Visit of the General Convention of 1886 to Racine College," Souvenir booklet distributed to the participants in the event. DeKoven Center Archives, RC History, Box 10, Folder 21.

21. John Kebel (1792–1866) English Anglican priest and poet. One of the leaders of the Oxford Movement. Kebel College, Oxford, was named after him.

22. This speech appeared in several newspapers. This quotation was from the *New York Evening Post*, Oct. 30, 1886, 7.

23. "Visit of the General Convention of 1886 to Racine College," Racine College

THE BIOGRAPHY OF JAMES DEKOVEN AS LEGACY

It is logical to assume that part of a person's legacy is the story, either biography or autobiography, of that individual's life. However, in the case of James DeKoven, such a legacy did not exist. His death at the young age of forty-eight was unexpected. His short, busy life did not provide him the time or situation for an extended looking back or writing of a thorough memoir.

Fortunately, he did keep one journal that still exists and recorded in it special events as well as his thoughts about these events. On one occasion, in his notebook, he indicated that he had gone back and looked over what he had written.[24] Yet he does not elaborate on any plans to write about these remembrances.

There was, however, interest in preparing such a life study. There were two series of biographical-type articles published in the *Nashotah Scholiast* in 1885–86 and 1886–87. These articles provide valuable information about James DeKoven and his life from two different viewpoints. Although neither resulted in a complete biographical study, they represent the interest that existed in DeKoven and the attempts that were being made to provide information for readers.

Soon after DeKoven's death, John Henry Hopkins Jr. (1820–91) began collecting materials to help in producing such a biography. Hopkins was a friend and colleague and had at least on one occasion traveled to Racine when he preached at a college commencement. Hopkins' research efforts resulted in a series of seven articles entitled "A Few Recollections of James DeKoven," published in the *Nashotah Scholiast* in 1885.[25]

A revelatory reference to Hopkins' biographical efforts is found in the first article of another series in the same publication from the following year of 1886. The "Student" author wrote:

> It is probably not a matter of general knowledge that it is reported that shortly after the Doctor's death, the Rev. J. H. Hopkins, D. D., stood ready to write a life of Dr. deKoven, but unexpected obstacles prevented the accomplishment of such an undertaking. This unlooked-for termination of the plan was

---

Collection, DeKoven Center Archives.

24. DeKoven, *Journal*, S01, 132.

25. These articles appeared consecutively in the issues of the *Scholiast* from May through October of 1885, Vol. 2, No. 4 through Vol. 3, No. 1. With the publication of Vol. 3 the name of the journal was changed to the *Church Scholiast*.

> most unfortunate, for there is probably no one better fitted for such a task, or one whose work would be received with more respect and favor by the Church than Dr. deKoven's fast friend, Dr. Hopkins. The lack of such an account of James deKoven's life is a great loss.[26]

The "Student" author does not give any details about what these "unexpected obstacles" were, although later information indicates that others knew of the efforts to prevent this biographical enterprise.

The author of the eight articles entitled "Racine and Dr. DeKoven," although identified only as "Student," was most probably Alexis duPont Parker.[27] Alexis came to Racine College as a student in 1875 and was the son of Stevens Parker. He became a trusted student and was with DeKoven when he died. His father succeeded DeKoven as warden of Racine College, so Alexis was well placed to learn the details of the administration and challenges of the school. Although he did go on to study at the General Theological Seminary, he was never ordained and became a successful businessman in Colorado.

The "Student" presents a very personal and intimate view of life at Racine College under the leadership of James DeKoven. He discusses the daily life of the institution, deals with the issue of "ritualism" which was a "hot" topic during the years he spent at Racine, describes the regular receptions hosted by the warden, and dismisses the issue of "confession" as essentially a non-topic. He gives insight into the manner in which DeKoven dealt with criticism as well as day-to-day issues at the school. He describes his preaching and public speaking as well as his regular interactions with the students. He describes special holidays and ceremonies and some of the goals that DeKoven had for the future of Racine College. "Student" provides this explanation of why he had written this series of articles:

> In the hope that some who knew the Doctor most intimately may be led to give their recollections of him and of the college under his care, I have been moved to offer these inadequate sketches of Dr. deKoven, as I was privileged to know him and his work in my daily life.[28]

26. "Student," *Church Scholiast,* Vol. 3, No. 12, Sep. 1886, 202.

27. There are different clues throughout the articles that can be used to identify the author: the date of his enrollment at Racine College (1875); the initial letter of his first name as spoken by DeKoven ("A"); his responsibility in the life of the institution (head of his dormitory in the Fifth Form). These all point to one person.

28. Student, "Racine and Dr. DeKoven I," *Church Scholiast,* Vol. III, No. 12, Sep.

In 1892, five years after the publication of these articles, Frederick Cook Morehouse included a lengthy, final chapter on James DeKoven in his work *Some American Churchmen*.[29] Morehouse dealt primarily with the controversies surrounding DeKoven and his ideas concerning the topics of ritualism and the Eucharist. He also provided information about the role DeKoven played in several general conventions and in defending the "cathedral question" for Milwaukee, as advocated by bishops Armitage and Welles.

The search for a qualified author to undertake the biographical task continued for many years. In 1896, the board of trustees of Racine College, realizing the lack of a suitable biography, voted to authorize Rev. Clinton Locke of Chicago to write this important work. The minutes of the Trustees' meeting of June 9, 1896, include this entry:

> The Bishop of Nebraska moved that Dr. Clinton Locke, the DeKoven family concurring, write for publication, the life of the Rev. Dr. DeKoven and that the profits from its sale go to the DeKoven Endowment Association to aid them in their work for the College.[30]

There is no record of Rev. Locke ever working on this biography. He and DeKoven had been students at the General Theological Seminary and worked closely together in Illinois and Wisconsin. An explanation for why he never undertook this project is found in Locke's personal reminiscences written at the end of the nineteenth century and published posthumously eighty years later in 1976:

> The Church very much needs a good life of Dr. DeKoven, for the existing one is a small work, not even touching the fringe of his garment. The Trustees of Racine College wished me to undertake this task, and I would gladly have done it, but John

1886, 202.

29. Morehouse, "James DeKoven, Warden of Racine College." In *Some American Churchmen,* Morehouse included this statement in the preface to the volume: "No apology, the author believes, is necessary for the proportionately great amount of space devoted to the life of DeKoven, since his brilliant career has never before been sketched, and the material might not be accessible to most persons. Yet his peer can hardly be found, even in the galaxy of brilliant names which make up the roll of the Church's saints." Morehouse, *Some American Churchmen*, 7–8.

30. Racine College Board of Trustees Minutes, Mar. 10, 1852–Jun. 9, 1896, 475. DeKoven Center Archives.

DeKoven, the Doctor's brother, disliked me and objected to it. John DeKoven disliked most things and most people.[31]

Another reference to interference with the writing of the DeKoven biography is found in an address given by Thomas F. Gailor, bishop of Tennessee, which was published in the *Church Times*, in 1902. This is Gailor's summation of why a biography had not appeared:

> By the mistaken zeal of a few people, one of our most brilliant men was denied the privilege which he sought, of writing Dr. DeKoven's biography; but some day that life will be written and Churchmen everywhere will come to know how truly and nobly he loved and wrought for Christ's Kingdom, and how great a saint he was in his generation.[32]

This statement raises more questions than it answers. Who were the few people? Was DeKoven's brother John in this group of "the few"? If so, why? Who was "one of our most brilliant men"? Was it John Henry Hopkins? Or Clinton Locke? Both were writers who were well-known in the Episcopal world, and both were primed to write a biography

The fact remains that the only more or less complete biography of James DeKoven that was written and published during the seventy-plus years following his death was the work by William Cox Pope.[33] Pope was a student of James DeKoven both in Delafield, Wisconsin, and at Racine College. He was the first graduate of the college under DeKoven's leadership and the valedictorian of his class.

Pope was a devoted student of the rector/warden and they were close friends throughout their lives. When Pope began to work on his biography of James DeKoven, he wrote to former friends, students, and family members asking for their reminiscences and suggestions about the life story. Some of the letters Pope received in response are found in his collected papers in the National Episcopal Archives. Most of these inquiries were written in 1898; some answers did not arrive before the Pope biography was published in 1899. Why did Pope undertake the biography twenty years after the death of his mentor and friend? What was his sudden rush to complete a biography? It does not seem to be a matter

31. Locke, *Personal Reminiscences of the Diocese of Illinois, 1856–1892*, 60.

32. "Rev. James DeKoven, D.D.–Bishop Gailor's Address," *Church Times*, Vol. XII, No. 12, 593.

33. Pope, *Life of the Reverend James DeKoven.*

of coincidence that John DeKoven, younger brother of James, died on April 30, 1898.[34]

The biography Pope published in 1899 is a relatively modest publication. It is a small book of 102 pages. There are eight chapters of varying length in the biography. The first chapter, entitled "Birth to Ordination," is only four pages long and contains very little information about the DeKoven family, James' upbringing, or relevant historical information. The use of long quotations dominates the biography; they easily account for at least 30 percent of the text.

Although there are some interesting insights given into DeKoven's personality, these are relatively few and leave the reader essentially unsatisfied about the nature of the man and his motivations. The facts about DeKoven's life and the life of those around him are minimal. There are as many omissions of important events as there are inclusions. Pope doesn't provide details of his own relationship with DeKoven and its origins. Pope was devoted to Father DeKoven and named his son, to whom he dedicated this work, James DeKoven Pope. Because this was the only book length source of information about James DeKoven, it is easy to understand the interest of the Community of Saint Mary in promoting a more complete biography of the man for whom they created a non-profit foundation and religious education center. Although a good effort, it is not a great contribution to the legacy of the man it seeks to honor.

Over the years, different writers and different groups of individuals have attempted to do research and launch the project of a biography. Several faculty members from Nashotah House and the General Theological Seminary have investigated this task. In the early 1920s, Arthur Whipple Jenks of General started searching for resource materials.

Prior to his position at General, he taught at Racine College and then was professor of Church History at Nashotah. He died in 1922 before he could work on the DeKoven biography. This statement is found in the *Living Church* obituary: "The Late Professor Jenks. He had in hand

34. This explanation is not a particularly pleasant one. John DeKoven was definitely convinced of his responsibility to control his family and the image of its members. His daughter, Louise DeKoven Bowen, tells how her father forbade her participation in activities he thought inappropriate for a woman of her social standing. On two separate occasions John attempted to manage the news relating to James. He offered money to news reporters at the time of the Illinois Episcopal Election to report the story as he thought it should be told. On James DeKoven's death, he threatened the local papers in Racine with a lawsuit if they published information that Racine College was in debt. It was; they did; he didn't.

a brief history of the General Theological Seminary and was actively engaged in writing a much-needed life of James deKoven, for which he had collected a large amount of material.[35]

In the late 1950s and early 1960s the sisters of the community began a serious campaign to sponsor the writing and publication of what they referred to as an "up-to-date" and "full scale" biography. Mother Mary Ambrose, long-time mother superior of the Western Province of the Community, spoke of the need for such a study to provide information to the many retreatants and conference participants who visited the center and asked questions about their patron.[36] During this same period, Sister Mary Bianca, sister-superior of the DeKoven Center, contacted several potential authors. The correspondence undertaken by Sister Bianca is remarkable for the diligence she demonstrated in pursuing this goal of an adequate biography.

Unfortunately, the efforts of Sister Mary Bianca as well as other interested individuals were not successful. One of the reasons for this consistent failure to produce a modem biography has been the lack of available resources. The number of primary sources is limited, although efforts to uncover more information have been aided greatly by the organization of more complete archives and the availability of web data bases.

THE DEKOVEN FOUNDATION FOR CHURCH WORK, INC.

As seen in the letter written by Mother Mary Ambrose and cited at the beginning of this chapter, this foundation was created to honor the name and work of James DeKoven. It continues to function today. Like many other vibrant organizations, it has undergone developments and revisions in its mission as it has adapted to new and different clientele. The first purpose for the purchase of the Racine College campus by the Community of Saint Mary was to continue a summer camp for orphan children from Chicago who were under the care of the sisters at St. Mary's Home for Children.

In November 1935, the sisters purchased the property for $85,000 and launched a new focus in their ministry on retreat and conference

35. "Late Professor Jenks," 13.

36. Letter to Longmans Green and Company, Publishers, dated July 2, 1959. DeKoven Center Archives.

work. Bishop Ivins was a strong supporter of this effort and saw the new foundation as a vital element in the work of the church in the Midwest. In a letter dated February 26, 1936, he wrote:

> A major consideration of the Sisters in this attempt is the hope of establishing at the College a House of Retreat and Conference. The Church needs such an House. The Conferences throughout the Church are well-established as valuable factors in knitting the Church together, and for their educational values. And we do need an House of Retreat in the Middle-West.[37]

Two sisters, Sister Eanswith and Sister Valerie began the long and difficult process of restoring and preserving the large buildings that made up the campus. A major financial campaign was begun and in 1938 a group of sisters established year-round occupancy in Taylor Hall where a chapel had been created in the space previously used for the college library. Between 1934 and 1987, twenty-five sisters of the community worked at DeKoven. Although the sisters undertook a new vision for educational and spiritual formation, the camp work that first brought them to DeKoven was not forgotten. For nearly forty years St. Mary's Camp retained its own life, under the guidance of the sisters and a staff of counselors.

Over the years the scope of the sisters' work broadened greatly. They offered a wide variety of retreats and conferences for youth, clergy, university students, altar guilds, and seminarians. Other activities included numerous weddings celebrated in St. John's Chapel as well as retreats for married couples. All along the sisters continued to improve the buildings and maintain the extensive grounds with the help of Associates and friends of the Community. Sister Eanswith continued in her role as Sister-in-Charge until 1957.[38] She was succeeded by Sister Mary Bianca, who wrote of the wide range of activities that were sponsored by the foundation:

> It is fitting that here where James DeKoven labored for the cause of Christian education an institution bearing his name

37. Letter of Bishop Ivins, dated February 26, 1936.

38. The *Milwaukee Churchman* published the following commentary about Sister Eanswith on her death in May, 1964: "By her determined and utter dedication, her own hard labor, shrewd business sense, and above all her unsurpassed faith and vision of possibilities, Sr. Eanswith provided the leadership and direction for developing the flourishing retreat and conference center and summer camp for girls that have brought the Foundation to the service and affection of the Church throughout the nation."

> should be carrying on a work that is so at one with his own aims and ideals.[39]

Although the DeKoven Foundation did not engage directly in sponsoring an educational institution, it did offer space for different organizations to serve the Racine community. For many years beginning in 1948, the Cove School, a residential program for brain-injured children, was housed in the East building. The Racine Montessori School opened in 1976 and continued its classes in the same building until it moved to its own facility. Arts studios and galleries have also been housed on the DeKoven campus.

The DeKoven Foundation continued to be a source of spiritual stability throughout the turbulent 1960s. Change was coming to the lives of those who provided the primary work force of the organization. The number of sisters was decreasing, and those who were still involved in the day-to-day activities were growing older. The years of the 1970s and 1980s were years of transition and change. In 1985, Western Province of the Community of Saint Mary made the decision to sell the property and in June 1986, under the guidance of Bishop Roger White, the Diocese of Milwaukee purchased the DeKoven Foundation. A new beginning brought with it a new executive director and a revised board of directors, with local Racine members as well as representatives of the diocese. This resulted in an unbroken line of the retreat and conference ministry of the foundation which had begun with the Community of Saint Mary.

There were good days as well as challenging days ahead for the DeKoven Center. An ill-advised housing project for seniors resulted in a major default on the entire history property. As in the beginning of its history, the citizens of Racine and friends of the organization raised substantial funds to repurchase the property, and the DeKoven Foundation was able to begin its life anew in 1998. Since that date there have been positive developments in the continued growth of the organization that honors the memory and work of James DeKoven.

TO HEAR CELESTIAL HARMONIES

In 2002, on the occasion of the sesquicentennial of the founding of Racine College, the DeKoven Center published a book of essays dedicated

39. Sister Mary Bianca, address to the Priests' Institute, cited in Clark, "DeKoven Foundation for Church Work," 70.

to the story of this place and the people associated with it. These essays present the rich history of what is colloquially called "DeKoven" and the role that this place continues to play in the history of Racine and the Episcopal Church.[40]

The first three chapters of this book deal directly with the life and the ideas of James DeKoven. The first chapter, a biography of DeKoven, was written by Rev. Lawrence N. Crumb and represents the first serious attempt to situate him in relationship to his family and his time. In the second essay Robert Boak Slocum studied the idea of romantic religion as it is evident in the work and life of James DeKoven. Slocum emphasized DeKoven's belief in the limits of reason and "his discernment of the interpenetration of the natural and supernatural orders." The title of this collection expresses the longing to be free from our limiting senses. James DeKoven as novelist is discussed in chapter 3, a review of *Dorchester Polytechnic Academy,* the only published example of his storytelling talent. Mabel DuPriest provided an analysis of the literary techniques and themes found in this work.

The next three chapters are devoted to the history and impact of the place that is today called the DeKoven Center. Chapter 4 is entitled "A Brief History of Racine College" and takes the story through 1933 and the closing of Racine Military Academy.[41] The fifth and sixth chapters are devoted to the work of the sisters of the Community of Saint Mary as they developed the concept of the DeKoven Foundation for Church Work and undertook the preservation of this historic campus. The seventh and final essay, by Travis DuPriest, summarizes the struggles that this institution has faced, the triumphs it has witnessed, and the promises that it holds for the future. This collection of essays began the task of enlarging knowledge and understanding about James DeKoven. It is hoped that the publication of this new biography will add to this knowledge and appreciation.

THE TANGIBLE LEGACY

There were sincere efforts over several years to create a named structure in honor of James DeKoven on the Racine College campus. It was to be called DeKoven Memorial Hall and was mentioned in several newspaper

40. *To Hear Celestial Harmonies.*

41. In 1930, Racine College became known as Racine Military Academy, after being closed for a year and then reorganized.

articles as well as the records of college committee meetings. At one point it was scheduled to house the law school proposed for the college.

There were, however, and continue to be, efforts to memorialize the life and work of James DeKoven in tangible and visible ways. The administration building at St. John's Northwestern Academies is called DeKoven Hall. It was given this name by Sydney Smythe when the building was constructed in 1906. On the nearby campus of the Nashotah House Seminary a more modem structure, built in 2013, is called DeKoven Commons and includes four named facilities that honor early religious figures in the history of the Episcopal Church in Wisconsin: Adams Hall, Grafton Room (Lobby), Breck Refectory, and DeKoven Classrooms.

James DeKoven has been celebrated with a variety of liturgical items, including memorial panels and windows. In December 1879, in the reconstructed church of Saints Peter and Paul in Chicago, a specially designed reredos was installed to honor deceased clergymen. The central panel was *in memoriam* of the "Rev. Dr. James DeKoven, late warden of Racine College."[42] There are other artistic memorials that were dedicated to his memory. In the Church of St. Luke in Racine, a panel above the rear exit is dedicated to DeKoven, who was a frequent preacher at this church where many ceremonies for Racine College were held. This panel contains the motto of Racine College, *Vigeat Radix*, as well as three bishop's miters used to symbolize the failure of DeKoven to obtain this Episcopal rank.

A stained-glass window with his image was created for the Church of the Holy Innocents in Racine. This window was removed when the church building was sold and now hangs in the administrative office of the DeKoven Center. A similar commemorative window is located in the Chapel of Saint Mary the Virgin on the Nashotah House seminary campus. This window repeats the theme of the DeKoven's failure to win the bishop's miter and associates the title of saint with him. A series of four windows in the Church of Saint Matthias in Waukesha honors pioneer clergymen in Wisconsin. One of these windows depicts DeKoven.

In 1963, the Standing Liturgical Commission of the Episcopal Church did place his name in the Church calendar, and he is acknowledged as "Blessed James DeKoven." His Feast Day is celebrated on March 22, the anniversary of his burial at St. John's Chapel. In the nomination document the Commission stated that DeKoven "has left a permanent

42. At the time the Church of St. Peter and St. Paul in Chicago was the diocesan cathedral. The building burned in 1921 and was not rebuilt.

stamp upon the learning and piety of the Episcopal Church, through his reasoned and compelling defense of its Catholic heritage."[43]

CONCLUSION

It seems contradictory, if not disingenuous, to conclude a chapter on the legacy of James DeKoven with a discussion of how he is a forgotten man. The title given to this biography was chosen to emphasize the fact that although his name is remembered, his importance as an individual of historical consequence is essentially unknown. Almost totally ignored in the summary biographies that have been written is the human side of the man, the nature of his dedication and devotion to his responsibilities and to those around him. Even the very thorough biographical summary in the *Episcopal Dictionary of the Church*[44] fails to mention some of the important reasons why he should be remembered. It has been the goal of this biography to correct this omission and to add some of these qualities to the list.

Most of these attributes fall into the category of "who he was" rather than "what he did." They include his dedication to the importance of Christian education; his direct influence on more than eleven hundred young men from throughout the United States who attended Racine College during his twenty years of leadership; his role in the creation of a diocesan structure and a cathedral church in Wisconsin; his saint-like patience despite frequent and intense personal attacks; his great love for his real as well as his adopted family; the historical importance of his family; his keen and refreshing sense of humor; and most importantly his consistent calls for tolerance and acceptance.

Several of the issues that brought DeKoven to prominence in the Episcopal Church faded from importance as the nineteenth century came to its end. The intense feeling once generated by discussions of ritualism, for example, gave way to other concerns. In 1893, Bishop Thomas Gailor wrote:

> "The Champion of Ritualism," as he was called, has been at rest himself for fourteen years, and in many quarters his name

43. 1962, Standing Liturgical Commission, Nomination document.

44. Armentrout, *Episcopal Dictionary of the Church.*

> already has become a distant memory, and the meaning of his life and labor misunderstood or quite forgotten.[45]

Bishop John Henry Hopkins, when he published his landmark book entitled the *Law of Ritualism,* predicted the change that would happen in the Episcopal Church. The role that DeKoven played in fostering this change should not be forgotten. It seems safe to assume that his leadership and ability to present ideas clearly facilitated a quicker and wider acceptance of this movement.

The importance of James DeKoven in the life of the Episcopal Church was acknowledged by Frederic Cook Morehouse in his work *Some American Churchmen* with this opening statement for chapter 10: "If one should ask who was the greatest product of the American Church during the century and more of its existence, the answer of one informed would almost certainly be, James DeKoven."[46] Fifty-five years later, Rev. Harold E. Wagner would echo this idea in his centennial history of the Episcopal Church in Wisconsin. In writing about DeKoven he made the following statement: "He has been nominated by some as the only 'saint' the American Church has produced to date."[47]

Why then was the role that DeKoven played in the history of his church so easily forgotten? There are several possible explanations, and they are all intertwined. In the fading of DeKoven's stature, first and foremost is the troubled history of Racine College in the decade following his death. He was accurate in his assessment that the institution was too closely identified with himself. His role was dominant, and it was difficult for anyone to assume this particular burdensome mantle of leadership. DeKoven was definite in his ideas about the way things should operate. He was firm in his convictions and strong-willed in their pursuit. His good friend and colleague Clinton Locke in his memorial sermon shared a characterization of DeKoven as an "iron pillar cased in velvet."[48] This strength of will allowed him to succeed where failure seemed to be certain. Unfortunately, this strength of will did not result in financial or leadership security for the school he created and nurtured.

Another contributor was the lack of a direct or designated heir to the responsibility of preserving the college he had created and honoring his

45. Gailor, "Reverend James DeKoven," 340.

46. Morehouse, "James DeKoven, Warden of Racine College," 157.

47. Wagner, *Episcopal Church in Wisconsin,* 67.

48. Locke, "Upright Man," 120.

memory. Rev. Stephens Parker apparently was the person that DeKoven saw as assuming this role. However, Parker's struggles with the trustees of the college, in what amounted to a battle for control, weakened the structure needed for survival of the school. The resulting administrative struggles led to the closing of the college program in 1888.

Since James DeKoven had never married and had no children of his own, there was no heir to assume this responsibility. His friends, who could have played a role in the preservation of his memory and continuation of his work, were involved in their own careers. His family members led busy lives, and most had returned to live on the East Coast. His brother John continued to serve on the board of trustees of Racine College for several years after DeKoven's death. He was dedicated to his brother's memory but seemed determined to prevent the publication of a biography.

This lack of a thorough biography published in a timely fashion was a third problem that contributed to the lack of a vigorous promotion of his memory and legacy. The twenty years that elapsed between his death and the publication of the work by William C. Pope allowed for the natural calming of the strong emotions that resulted from his sudden and unexpected death.

At the time of his funeral in 1879, a priest wrote of DeKoven's celebrity as being based solely on his failure to become a bishop: "Remember, we did not know him, never should have known him, except for his defeat, and defeat, and defeat." This line is cited by Sister Hilary, CSM, in an article she published in 1959, entitled "James DeKoven: Magnificent Failure."[49] She talks about the failure of what he did, not who he was. It is this idea of a lack of "success" that Bishop Jeffrey Lee rephrased very positively during his sermon at the 2023 observance of DeKoven Day in Saint John's Chapel:

> He gave himself completely to the worship of God and the service of God's people as pastor and teacher. Not unlike the Apostle Paul, by the standards of his day, DeKoven was never a great success. Projects failed to flourish, struggles were the order of his day, the seeds he scattered right here were indeed small ones. But those seeds he planted in hearts across the church and in this very place, those mustard seeds have sprouted and

49. Hilary, "James DeKoven: Magnificent Failure."

> grown and borne so much fruit. Much more than he could ever have imagined.[50]

Just as it was once difficult to separate the life story of James DeKoven from the story of Racine College, so today it is difficult to separate the legacy of James DeKoven from the reality of the DeKoven Center. It is a reality that celebrates many of the values he so deeply cherished.

Present day panoramic view of the East Building, DeKoven Center, Racine, WI. Photography by Denise Zingg.

50. Homily preached by Bishop Jeffrey D. Lee on March 22, 2023. Copy provided the author by Bishop Lee. Quotation used with permission.

Appendix

TIMELINE—THE LIFE OF JAMES DEKOVEN

1831—September 19—Birth of James DeKoven in Middletown, Connecticut. Ninth of the ten children of Henry Louis DeKoven and Margaret Yates Sebor DeKoven.

1832—June 24—Baptism of James, son of Captain DeKoven.

1840—August 7—Death of father, Henry Louis DeKoven, burial on August 9 (b. June 16, 1784, m. February 24, 1813).

Circa 1842—Catechized by Rev. Samuel Jarvis, Rector of Christ Church, Middletown, Connecticut.

1842—February—June—Attended Middletown Male High School.

1843—At age 12 wrote an epiphany hymn. (This story from the preface written by Rev. Morgan Dix for the collection of DeKoven's sermons).

1846—At age 15 published a small book of poems. (Another story from the preface by Rev. Morgan Dix).

1846—March 1—Confirmed by Samuel Allen McCoskry, bishop of Michigan, at Christ Church, Anthony Street, New York City.

1846—May 23—Received first communion, Christ Church, Anthony Street, New York City.

1847—1851—Student at Columbia College, N.Y. City; absent junior year (1849–50) due to illness.

1851—May 31—Death of brother William Sebor DeKoven in San Francisco, California (b. May 9, 1814).

1851—July 30—James DeKoven graduated from Columbia College with highest honors.

1851—1854—Student at the General Theological Seminary, New York City. Valedictorian of graduating class; absent last three months of senior year due to illness.

1854—May 18—James DeKoven visited Chicago and Nashotah, Wisconsin (Letter to Hobart Brown describing his time at Nashotah House).

1854—August 6—Ordination to the Diaconate by Bishop John Williams (1817–99) in Middletown, Connecticut. Declined call to a parish in Brooklyn and one at Lower Red Hook on the Hudson.

1854—September 15—Arrived at Nashotah, Wisconsin. Tutor in ecclesiastical history at Nashotah House Seminary.

1854—Younger brother John DeKoven moves to Chicago.

1854—November 15—James DeKoven appointed rector of the Church of St. John Chrysostom, Delafield, Wisconsin. Began teaching in the day school associated with the church.

1855—September 23—Ordination to the priesthood by Bishop Jackson Kemper (1789–1870) at the Church of St. John Chrysostom, Delafield.

1857—Published *A Catechism on Confirmation*. New York: E & JB Young & Co. with Rev. Morgan Dix.

1857—May 6—Agreement of James DeKoven and Trustees of Nashotah House to establish a Training School, "St. John's Hall," Delafield. Effective January 1858.

1858—June 8—Parish School at Delafield was chartered as St. John's Hall.

1858—July—October—Traveled to Europe with good friend, Rev. George B. Seymour (Departed New York on July 7, ship *Persia*, returned October 15, ship *Africa*.)

1858—September 30—St. John's Hall opened.

1859—August—Named rector of Racine College, Racine, Wisconsin.

1859—September 30—Moved to Racine with twenty-eight students of St. John's Hall.

1859—November 30—Formal opening of Kemper Hall, Racine College.

1863—June—Granted the honorary Doctorate of Sacred Theology degree by Hobart College, New York.

1863—July—First set of statutes passed by Trustees of Racine College.

1864—January 15—Park Hall destroyed by fire. Rebuilding begun immediately.

1864—August 17—Cornerstone of St. John's Chapel laid. Eighty acres added to campus.

1866—June—Nominated to the position of coadjutor bishop of Wisconsin; does not win. William E. Armitage chosen to assist Bishop Kemper.

1867—December—Construction of Taylor Hall completed. Dedication of the new building took place on January 29, 1868.

1868—February 7—August 6—Second trip to Europe; visited Radley Hall in England. Traveled to France and Italy. Excursion to the Holy Land cancelled because of his poor health.

1868—October—Participated as a deputy to the General Convention of the Protestant Episcopal Church, held in New York City, October 7–29. Ritualism an important issue at this convention. DeKoven spoke on behalf of the Oneida Indians and their protection from the injustice of the Federal government.

1871—October—Deputy to the General Convention held in Baltimore, Maryland, October 4–25. Controversy concerning the Eucharist and Ritual.

1871—Refectory (Dining Hall) built on the Racine College campus. Today called the Great Hall.

1872—School Room built (today called the Assembly Hall). The East Building complete.

1872—The Holy Eucharist: a correspondence between Rev. Dr. (James) Craik of Louisville and Rev. Dr. (James) DeKoven of Racine College. Milwaukee, Riverside Print House.

1873—June—Nominated as Bishop of Massachusetts; Rev. Dr. Benjamin Paddock of Brooklyn elected.

1874—January 31—Publication of *Principles—Not Men*, by Dr. Egar and colleagues. Campaign against ritualism and James DeKoven.

1874—February 10—A Sermon preached in all Saints' Cathedral, Milwaukee, in Memory of Rt. Rev. William Edmond Armitage, STD.

1874—February 12—Nominated as Bishop of Wisconsin, received a large clerical vote, rejected by the laity. Edward Welles elected third bishop of the diocese in June.

1874—February 12—A Theological Defense. Racine, Advocate Steam Printing.

1874—October—The Eucharistic Controversy, published in The Church and the World.

1874—October—Deputy to the General Convention in New York City, October 7–November 30.

1874—October 26—The Canon on Ritual and the Holy Eucharist; a speech delivered in the General Convention, October 26, 1874. New York, T. Whittaker.

1874—December 8—Death of mother, Margaret Yates Sebor DeKoven (1790–874) in Middletown, Connecticut.

1875—January—Elected Bishop of Fond du Lac, Wisconsin, by the clergy; rejected by the laity.

1875—Racine College adopted by nine mid-west bishops as the collegiate institution of the respective dioceses.

1875—February 4—Elected bishop of the Diocese of Illinois. Controversy about the validity of the election. DeKoven accepts and then withdraws his name from consideration

1875—February 4–5—Taylor Hall destroyed by fire. No injuries; building gutted.

1875—September—Margaret DeKoven Casey, DeKoven's sister, moves to Racine College.

1875—September—A Letter from Rev. James DeKoven, D.D., Warden of Racine College, to the Clergy and Laity of the Diocese of Illinois, September 14–17, Chicago, 1875.

1875—Taylor Hall rebuilt. Gymnasium and science laboratory built.

1876—April—Elizabeth DeKoven Dyer joins brother and sister in Racine.

1877—October—Deputy to the General Convention in Boston, Massachusetts, October 3–25. Proposed removing the word "Protestant" from the name of the Episcopal Church.

1877—March—"Review of Canon Trevor on the Holy Eucharist," The *Church Eclectic*.

1878—The Community of Saint Mary assumes responsibility for Kemper Hall in Kenosha.

1878—June 7—DeKoven announced his decision to remain at Racine College and turn down the appointment at Trinity Church, New York City.

1879—January 31—Early morning fall on an icy sidewalk in Milwaukee; broken right ankle.

1879—March 19—Death at Taylor Hall, Racine College.

1879—March 22—Funeral and Burial, St. John's Chapel, Racine College.

1879—Posthumous publication of Dorchester Polytechnic Academy, Dr. Neverasole, Principal. Published by L. H. Morehouse, Milwaukee.

1880—Posthumous publication of Sermons Preached on Various Occasions. Preface by the Rev. Dr. Morgan Dix. New York, D. Appleton & Co.

1886—October 16—Pilgrimage to Racine College and the tomb of James DeKoven by members of the General Convention meeting in Chicago.

Bibliography

"Accident to Dr. DeKoven." *Racine Journal*, Feb. 5, 1879.

Adams, William, D.D. *Three Letters upon the Confessional to James DeKoven, D.D. with the Resolutions of the Faculty of Nashotah*. Milwaukee: Burdick & Armitage, 1874.

Agreement of James DeKoven and Trustees of Nashotah House. May 6, 1857.

Ancestry.com. *Illinois, U.S., Wills and Probate Records, 1772–1999*. Original data: Illinois County, District and Probate Courts.

Ancestry.com. *New York, U.S., Arriving Passenger and Immigration Lists, 1820–1850*. Original data: *Registers of Vessels Arriving at the Port of New York from Foreign Ports, 1789–1919*. Microfilm publication M237, rolls 1–95; NAID: 6256867; Records of the U.S. Customs Service, 1745–1997, Record Group 36; National Archives at New York, NY.

Ancestry.com. *U.S. School Catalogs, 1765–1935*.

Ayres, Anne. "Chapter X, 1839–1843." In *The Life and Work of William Augustus Muhlenberg, Doctor of Divinity*. New York: T. Whittaker, 1889. Project Canterbury.

Baker, Sister Dorcas, CSM. "The DeKoven Center, 1958–1986." In *To Hear Celestial Harmonies: Essays on the Witness of James DeKoven and the DeKoven Center*, edited by Robert Boak Slocum and Travis Talmadge Du Priest, 71–92. Cincinnati: Forward Movement, 2002.

Beach, Helen, compiler. *The Descendants of Jacob Sebor of Middletown, Connecticut, 1709–1793*. N.p., 1923.

Biographical Memoranda of Yale College for 1831. New Haven, CT: Yale University Press.

Black, Vicki K. "A History of Racine College and the DeKoven Foundation." Dec. 1986. Research paper written for American Church History course, taught by Father Charles Henery, Nashotah House Theological Seminary.

Bowen, Louise de Koven. *Growing Up with a City*. Urbana, IL: University of Illinois Press, 2002.

———. *Open Windows: Stories of People and Places*. Chicago: Ralph Fletcher Seymour, 1946.

Breck, Charles, D.D., compiler. *The Life of the Reverend James Lloyd Breck, D.D.* 2nd ed. New York: E & J. B. Young, 1883.

Bryans, Ernest. *A History of St. Peters College, Radley (1847–1924)*. 2nd ed. Oxford: Basil Blackwell, 1925.

Buel, Rev. Samuel, D.D. *Eucharistic Presence, Eucharistic Sacrifice and Eucharistic Adoration, Being an Examination of a Theological Defense for the Rev. James DeKoven, D.D., Warden of Racine College, February 12, 1874*. New York: Thomas Whittaker, 1874.

Carroon, Robert G. "The Early Years of Racine College." Unpublished manuscript for Frederick Olson, PhD seminar in Urban and Wisconsin History. University of Wisconsin-Milwaukee, Jul. 20, 1966.

Case, James R. "American Masonic Roots in British Military Lodges." Canadian Masonic Research Association, 41st Meeting, 1965.

Catalogues and Registers, Racine College. Beginning with first annual in 1853. Published in November of each year; different publishers. The Racine College Collection, DeKoven Center Archives. Racine, WI.

Chicago District. Land Title Certificate 4884, May 20, 1841.

Chicago Tribune. Chicago, IL. Nov. 8, 1859. 2. Newspapers.com.

Chicago Daily Tribune. Chicago, IL. Feb. 15, 1874. 14. NewsBank.

Chorley, E. Clowes. "The Anglo-Catholic Movement." In *Men and Movements in the American Episcopal Church*, 315–55. New York: Charles Scribner's Sons, 1948.

Church Journal, Vol. VII, No. 47, Sep. 21, 1859.

Church Journal, Vol. XII, No. 88, May 4, 1864.

Church Journal, Vol. XXII, No. 103, Mar. 19, 1874.

The Churchman, Nov. 3, 1894. 548.

Clark, Katherine Greer. "The DeKoven Foundation for Church Work: The Middle Watch." In *To Hear Celestial Harmonies: Essays on the Witness of James DeKoven and the DeKoven Center*, 63–70. Cincinnati: Forward Movement, 2002.

Coggeshall, George. *Voyages to Various Parts of the World: Made Between the Years 1800 and 1831. Selected from His MS Journal of Eighty Voyages*. New York: D. Appleton, 1851.

The College Mercury, Vol. II, No. 1, December 1, 1867.

The College Mercury, Vol. II, No, 3, January 4, 1868.

The College Mercury, Vol. XIX, No. 5, May 30, 1876.

The College Mercury, Vol. XIX, No. 6 June 12, 1876.

"Columbia College Commencement." *Evening Post* (New York), Jul. 30, 1851.

The Constitution, Act of Incorporation, and Statutes of the General Theological Seminary. New York: General Theological Seminary, 1822.

Craik, James. "Sermon." *Church Journal*, Vol. XIX, No. 984, Nov. 29, 1871.

Crist, Richard A. "James De Koven." 1956. Unpublished research paper, General Theological Seminary, New York City.

Croft, Sidney Hugh. "A Hundred Years of Racine College and DeKoven Foundation." *Wisconsin Magazine of History* 35.4 (Summer 1952) 250–56, 262.

———. "The Life of James De Koven and a Historical Sketch of Racine College." Circa 1939. Unpublished thesis, Nashotah House.

Crumb, Lawrence N. "Biography of James DeKoven." In *To Hear Celestial Harmonies: Essays on the Witness of James DeKoven and the DeKoven Center*. Cincinnati: Forward Movement, 2002. 1–13.

———. "Blessed James De Koven." *The Anglican* 31.4 (Oct. 2002) 14–18.

———. "Religion." In *Racine: Growth and Changes in a Wisconsin County*, edited by Nicholas C. Buckle, 487–542, 599–613 (523–24 for DeKoven). Racine, WI: Racine County of Supervisors, 1977.

Dean's Annual Report. General Theological Seminary, 1854.

Daley, Bill, "Descendants of DeKoven Visit Middletown," *Hartford Courant*, Oct. 19, 1996.

Dawley, Powel Mills. *The Story of the General Theological Seminary: A Sesquicentennial History, 1817–1967*. New York: Oxford University Press, 1969.

"The Death of Our Warden." *College Mercury*, Racine College, Vol. XXV, No. 2, Apr. 7, 1879.

Debates of the House of Deputies in the General Convention of the Protestant Episcopal Church in the United States of America, Held in Baltimore, Maryland, October, A. D. 1871, as Reported for "The Churchman." Hartford, CT: D. F. Murphy, 1871.

Debates of the House of Deputies in the General Convention of the Protestant Episcopal Church in the United States of American, Held in New York City, N.Y. October A.D. 1874, As Reported for "The Churchman." Hartford, CT: D.F. Murphy, 1874.

"The DeKoven Family of Middletown." Unpublished, anonymous document located in the Middlesex County Archives, Middletown, CT.

DeKoven, James. *The Canon on Ritual and the Holy Eucharist, a Speech Delivered in the General Assembly, Oct. 26, 1874*. New York: T. Whittaker 1874.

———. *Dorchester Polytechnic Academy*. Serial publication of the novel, in monthly issues of *The Church Register*, Aug. 31, 1869 to Nov. 1870. A chapter appeared each month, except for the May 1870 issue.

———. *Dorchester Polytechnic Academy, Dr. Neverasole, Principal*. Milwaukee: L. H. Morehouse, 1879.

———. "The Eucharistic Controversy." *Church and the World*, 1874.

———. *A Letter from the Rev. James DeKoven, D.D., Warden of Racine College, to the Clergy and Laity of the Diocese of Illinois in Convention Assembled, Sep. 14, 15, 16, 17, A.D. 1875, Together with the Action of the Convention of the Diocese of Illinois Thereon*. Chicago: Mitchell and Hatheway, 1875.

———. "Letter to the Patrons and Friends of Racine College," Jun. 19, 1875. Racine College Object File, Racine Heritage Museum Archives.

———. "The New Testament Doctrine of Absolution, a Paper Read at the Cincinnati Church Congress." *Church Eclectic*, Vol. VII, No. 1 (Apr. 1879) 1–12.

———. "The Relation of the Protestant Episcopal Church to Freedom of Religious Thought." In *Authorized Report of the Third Church Congress in the United States*, 84–95. New York: T. Whittaker, 1876.

———. *A Sermon Preached in All Saints' Cathedral, Milwaukee, in Memory of the Rt. Rev. William Edmond Armitage, S. T. D., Bishop of Wisconsin, Feb. 10, 1874*. Racine, WI: Advocate Steam, 1874.

———. *A Sermon on the Sacred Order of the Priesthood, Presented on the Occasion of an Ordination in Milwaukee, in 1863*. Chandler, AZ: Rev'd Dr. Glenn Colyer Smith of Chandler.

———. An unpublished sermon, document no. 12 from the Street Papers, National Episcopal Archives, Austin, Texas. Copy of the original handwritten document. Transcription prepared by John E. Magerus, May 10, 2016.

———. *Sermons Preached on Various Occasions*. New York: D. Appleton, 1880.

———. "The Story of a College." Manuscript memoir covering the dates Jul. 31, 1862, through Jan. 1879. Original manuscript housed in the Nashotah House Archives. Typed transcription, DeKoven Center Archives.

———. *A Theological Defense for the Rev. James DeKoven, Warden of Racine College.* Racine, WI: Advocate Steam, 1874.

———. *Twenty-Five Years of the Work of Racine College, A Sermon Preached in the Collegiate Church of St. John, by the Warden.* Racine, WI: Advocate Steam, 1877.

———., and Rev. James Craik. *The Holy Eucharist: A Correspondence Between the Rev. Dr. Craik of Louisville and the Rev. Dr. DeKoven of Racine College.* Milwaukee: Riverside, 1872.

"The DeKoven Letters, V." *Nashotah Scholiast* 2.5 (Oct., Dec. 1834) 78–79.

DeKoven Letters & Accounts, Walter Steding Material, Wadsworth Archive, Middlesex County Historical Society. Middletown, CT.

"DeKoven Memorial Endowment," *College Mercury,* Racine College, Vol. XXV, No. 3 (Apr. 24, 1879) 6.

DeKoven, Mrs. Reginald (Anna Farwell). *A Musician and His Wife.* New York: Harper & Brothers, 1926.

DeMille, George E. *The Catholic Movement in the American Episcopal Church.* Philadelphia: Church Historical Society, 1950.

Dix, Morgan. "Preface." In *Sermons Preached on Various Occasions,* iii–xviii. New York: D. Appleton, 1880.

DuPriest, Mabel Benson. "James DeKoven, Novelist, A Review." In *To Hear Celestial Harmonies, Essays on the Witness of James DeKoven and the DeKoven Center,* 33–46. Cincinnati: Forward Movement, 2002.

DuPriest, Travis Talmadge. "DeKoven: Holy Man, Holy Place." In *To Hear Celestial Harmonies, Essays on the Witness of James DeKoven and the DeKoven Center,* 93–103. Cincinnati: Forward Movement, 2002.

The Eckels-Cox-Pope Collection, RG 137-1-9. The Archives of the Episcopal Church, Austin, TX.

Egar, John H., D. D. *The Eucharistic Controversy and the Episcopate of Wisconsin. A Review of the Pamphlet Entitled, Principles Not Men, By the Light of Dr. DeKoven's Theological Defense with a Special Examination of His Eucharistic Doctrine.* Milwaukee: Burdick & Armitage, 1874.

———. *The Story of Nashotah.* Wokingham, UK: Dodo, 2009.

The Evening Post (New York). May 23, 1835.

"Extracts from Bishop Kemper's Diary in Regard to Beginnings of Nashotah." *Nashotah Scholiast,* Vol. I, No. 1 (Nov. 1883) 1–3.

Fout, Jason. "A Brief History of Racine College." In *To Hear Celestial Harmonies, Essays on the Witness of James DeKoven and the DeKoven Center,* 47–61. Cincinnati: Forward Movement, 2002.

Gailor, Thomas Frank. "The Reverend James DeKoven, D. D." *Sewanee Review,* Vol. I, No. 3 (May 1, 1893) 340–54.

———. "Racine College—A Reply. *Church Times,* Vol. XXIV, No. 3 (Nov. 1913) 42.

———. *Some Memories.* Kingsport, TN: Southern, 1937.

Gallagher, Katherine Jeanne. "DeKoven, James." *Dictionary of American Biography,* 205. Vol. 3. New York: Charles Scribner's Sons, 1928–50.

General Theological Seminary Annual Meeting, 1854. 878.

General Theological Seminary of the Protestant Episcopal Church in the United States: The Proceedings of the Board at the Stated Annual Meeting. New York: Daniel Dana, Jr., 1854.

General Record of Middletown Male High School, Mar. 2, 1842. C352, M58h, gr. Main Reading Room, Connecticut State Library.

Gospel Messenger and Church Record of Western New York. Utica, NY. Oct. 14, 1859.

Gospel Messenger and Church Record of Western New York. Utica, NY. May 26, 1870.

Hartford Courant (Hartford, CT), Nov. 5, 1900. 2.

Hibbert, Christopher. *No Ordinary Place: Radley College and the Public School System, 1847–1997*. London: John Murray, 1997.

Hilary, Sister Mary, CSM. "James DeKoven: Magnificent Failure." *American Church News*, Sep. 1959.

———. *Ten Decades of Praise: The Story of the Community of Saint Mary During Its First Century, 1865–1965*. Racine, WI: DeKoven Foundation, 1965.

———. "Was James DeKoven A Saint?" *Living Church* (Oct. 11, 1959) 12–13, 18.

Hinton, John W. "In Memoriam, Rev. James DeKoven, Warden of Racine College." Milwaukee, 1879.

History of Racine and Kenosha Counties, Wisconsin. Chicago: Western Historical, 1879.

Holt, Harris H. *The Story of the Church of St. John Chrysostom, Delafield, Wisconsin, 1851–1956*. Delafield, WI: 1956.

Hopkins, Rev. John Henry. "The Baccalaureate Sermon." *College Mercury*, Racine College, Vol. XXV, No. 5 (Jun. 30, 1879) 8.

———. "A Few Recollections of James de Koven." A series of seven articles published in *Nashotah Scholiast*, Vol. 2, No. 4 (Feb. 1885) through Vol. 3, No. 1 (Oct. 1885).

The Inter Ocean. Chicago, IL. May 11, 1898.

"Interview." *The Chicago Times*. Chicago, IL. January 24, 1874.

"James DeKoven." In *An Episcopal Dictionary of the Church*, edited by Don S. Armentrout and Robert Boak Slocum. Online glossary definitions, Church Publishing.

"James DeKoven," Introductory Biography for the Archives of Wisconsin, Aug. 13, 1941.

The James DeKoven Collection. DeKoven Center Archives, Racine, WI.

"John DeKoven." *Encyclopedia of Biography of Illinois*, Vol. 3, 39. Chicago: Century Publishing and Engraaving Company, 1892–1902.

Johnson, Samuel. *The Rambler*, Oct. 13, 1750. 60. Cited by Nigel Hamilton in *How To Do Biography*, Harvard University Press, 2008, 12.

Journal of the Proceedings of the Bishops, Clergy, and Laity of the Protestant Episcopal Church in the United States of America, Assembled in a General Convention, Held in the City of New York, Oct. 12–29, in the Year of Our Lord, 1868. Hartford, CT, 1869.

Journal of the Proceedings of the Bishops, Clergy, and Laity of the Protestant Episcopal Church in the United States of America, Assembled in a General Convention, Held in the City of Baltimore, Md., Oct. 4–26, Inclusive, in the Year of Our Lord, 1871. Hartford, CT, 1872.

Journal of the Proceedings of the Bishops, Clergy, and Laity of the Protestant Episcopal Church in the United States of America, Assembled in a General Convention, Held in the City of New York, Oct. 7–3, Inclusive, in the Year of Our Lord, 1874. Hartford, CT. 1875.

Journal of the Proceedings of the Bishops, Clergy, and Laity of the Protestant Episcopal Church in the United States of America, Assembles in a General Convention, Held in the City of Boston, Oct. 3–25, inclusive in the Year of Our Lord, 1877. Hartford, CT. 1878.

Journal of the Proceedings of the Nineteenth Annual Convention of the Protestant Episcopal Church in the Diocese of Wisconsin, Held in St. Paul's Church, Milwaukee: On the 14th and 15th of June, 1865. Milwaukee, WI. 1865.

Keating, Ann Durkin. *The World of Juliette Kenzie: Chicago Before the Fire*. Chicago: University of Chicago Press, 2019.

"The Late Professor Jenks." *Living Church* 67.1 (May 1922) 13.

"Lazarus." *Church Journal,* Vol. XIX, No. 980 (Nov. 8, 1871) 356.

Leach, Eugene Walter. "History of Racine County, James DeKoven." Unpublished manuscript, Leech Documents, Area Research Center, University of Wisconsin-Parkside. Somers, WI.

———. "Marshall Mason Strong, Racine Pioneer." *Wisconsin Magazine of History* 5.4 (Jun. 1922) 335.

"Letter to Samuel Eliot from James DeKoven." Oct. 19, 1866. Boston Athenaeum Collections, Boston, MA.

"Local News." *Racine (WI) Advocate*. Jan. 20, 1864.

Locke, Rev. Clinton. "The Upright Man—Memorial Sermon for James DeKoven." *Church Eclectic* (1879) 117–22.

Lowell (MA) Daily Citizen and News. Oct. 30, 1873.

Luther, Flavel S., LLD. "James de Koven, Teacher," *Living Church*, Vol. III (Jun. 11, 1921) 172–174.

———. "Racine College—A Chapter from its History," *Church Times*, Vol. XXIV, No. 2 (Oct. 1913) 26–30.

Mammana, Richard J. "James DeKoven on the Internet." *Anglican*, Vol 31, No. 4 (Oct. 2002) 21.

———. "The Journal of James DeKoven, Excerpts Selected with an Introduction." *Anglican Life*, Vol. 32. No. 3 (Jul. 2003) 18–21.

Manross, William Wilson. *A History of the American Episcopal Church*. New York: Morehouse, 1935.

McCain, Diana Ross. "A Colonial Women Rises Above Scandal." *Courant* (Middletown, CT). Dec. 3, 1997.

McCaughey, Robert A. *Stand Columbia: A History of Columbia University in the City of New York, 1754–2005*. New York: Columbia University Press, 2005.

McElroy, Gary A. "James DeKoven and the Wisconsin Election of 1874." Unpublished research paper, General Theological Seminar, Dec. 1963.

———. "James DeKoven and the Wisconsin Election of 1874." *American Church Quarterly,* Vol. IV No. 3. (1964) 182–96.

Meachem, John G., Sr. "Autobiography of Dr. John Goldesborough Meachem, Sr. 1823–1896." Typed transcription, 1975.

Minutes of the Board of Trustees of Nashotah House. Jul. 13, 1857.

Morehouse, Frederic Cook. "James DeKoven, Warden of Racine College." In *Some American Churchmen*. Milwaukee: Young Churchman (1892) 157–234.

Nashotah House Early Records, Archives in the Frances Donaldson Library, Nashotah House Theological Seminary. Nashotah, WI.

News (Chicago). Apr. 15, 1984.

Newton, William Wilberforce, D. D. *Dr. Muhlenberg*. Boston: Houghton Mifflin, 1899.

"Obituary." *Racine (WI) Advocate*. Mar. 22, 1879.

"Of Admission." *Statutes of Columbia College, Revised and Passed by the Board of Trustees, July 1843*, 16–17. New York: Columbia College, 1843.

Osborne, Dorothy. "A History of Racine College." Preservation Racine, Inc. Newsletter. Summer 2002.

Osborne, Frank O. "Letter to Claudia Winslow, 1924." Reeves Collection, Archives in the Frances Donaldson Library, Nashotah House Theological Seminary. Nashotah, WI.

Perry, William Stevens. *The History of the American Episcopal Church, 1587–1883*. Vol. II, *1783–1883*. Boston: James R. Osgood, 1885.

Philadelphia Inquirer. Philadelphia, PA. July 21, 1852.

Pittinger, W. Norman. "Jackson Kemper in the Northwest." New York: National Council, 1957.

Pope, William Cox. "Diaries." In the Eckles-Cox-Pope Collection, Archives of the Episcopal Church, RG 137 1–9.

———. *Life of the Reverend James DeKoven, D. D., Sometime Warden of Racine College*. New York: James Pott, 1899.

———. "S. John's Hall, Delafield, Wis." *Church Scholiast*, Vol. V, No. 12 (Sep. 1888) 189–93.

"Population of Wisconsin." Wisconsin Historical Society. https://www.wisconsinhistory.org/records/article/CS1816.

Prehn, W. L. "James DeKoven, Educator—The 2004 DeKoven Center Cushman Lecture." Unpublished manuscript.

"Prices and Wages by Decade: 1860–1869." University of Missouri. https://libraryguides.missouri.edu/pricesandwages/1860-1869.

The Racine College Collection. DeKoven Center Archives, Racine, WI.

"Racine College Mourns Her Beloved Warden." *Racine Advocate*, Mar. 22, 1879.

Reeves, Thomas C. "The Anglo-Catholic Movement in Wisconsin." *Wisconsin Magazine of History*, Vol. 68, No. 3 (Spring 1985) 188–98.

———. "James DeKoven." *American National Biography. Vol. 6*. New York: Oxford University Press (1999) 358–59.

———. "James DeKoven, Anglican Saint." Racine, WI: DeKoven Foundation for Church Work, 1978.

"Report of the Faculty." In *Proceedings of the Board at their Annual Meeting*. General Theological Seminary, June, 1852.

Richter, Alice Bridge. *History of the Church of the Holy Trinity, Middletown, Connecticut*. 1963.

Schultz, Rima Lunin. "The Businessman's Role in Western Settlement: The Entrepreneurial Frontier, Chicago, 1833–1872." Boston University Graduate School, 1985.

Seymour, Rev. George Franklin. "James DeKoven." *Nashotah Scholiast*, Vol. I, No. 8 (Jul. 1884) 16.

Simpson, James B. "James DeKoven's Enduring Influence." *Living Church* (Sep. 15, 1991) 8–9.

Slocum, Robert B. "Romantic Religion and the Witness of James DeKoven." In *To Hear Celestial Harmonies: Essays on the Witness of James DeKoven and the DeKoven Center*, 15–32. Cincinnati: Forward Movement, 2002.

———. "Romantic Religion in Wisconsin: James DeKoven and Charles C. Grafton." *Anglican and Episcopal History*, Vol. LXV, No. 1 (Mar. 1996) 82–111.

———., and Travis Talmage DuPriest, eds. *To Hear Celestial Harmonies: Essays on the Witness of James DeKoven and the DeKoven Center*. Cincinnati: Forward Movement, 2002.

Statutes of Columbia College, Revised and Passed by the Board of Trustees, July 1843. New York: Columbia College, 1843.

Statutes of the General Theological Seminary of the Protestant Episcopal Church of the United States. Chapter VII, "Of the Students," 21. Appendix C in *Proceedings of the Board at their Annual Meeting*, June, 1852. New York: Pudney and Russell.

"Statutes of Racine College, 1869." Racine College Collection. DeKoven Center Archives, Racine, Wisconsin.

"The Story of Kemper College, St. Louis." *Nashotah Scholiast*, Vol. II, No. 3 (Dec. 1884) 41.

The Street Collection. MS:Col, 70.82, UP024, Street. Archives of the Episcopal Church, Austin, TX.

Stone, Fanny S., ed. *Racine, Belle City of the Lakes and Racine County, Wisconsin*. Vols. I and II. Chicago: S. J. Clarke, 1916.

Student (Anonymous). "Racine and Dr. De Koven," Parts I–VIII. *Nashotah Scholiast*, Vol. III, No. 12 (Sep. 1886) through Vol IV, No. 8 (May 1887).

Sweet, Rev. Charles F. *A Champion of the Cross, Being the Life of John Henry Hopkins, STD., Including Extracts and Selections from His Writings*. New York: James Pott, 1894.

Tiffany, Charles C., D. D. *A History of the Protestant Episcopal Church of the United States of America*. New York: Christian Literature, 1895.

Turner, Justin G., and Linda Levitt Turner. *Mary Todd Lincoln: Her Life and Letters*. New York: Random House, 1972.

"The Visit of the General Convention of 1886 to Racine College." Racine, WI: Racine College, 1886.

Wagner, Rev. Harold Ezra. *The Episcopal Church in Wisconsin, 1847–1947: A History of the Diocese of Milwaukee*. Milwaukee: Diocese of Milwaukee, 1947.

Walsh, Walter. *The Secret History of the Oxford Movement*. London: Swan Sonnenschein, 1898.

Welles, Rt. Rev. Edward Randolph, STD. The Rev. Edward Sprague Welles, ed. *Sermons and Addresses by the Late Third Bishop of Milwaukee, with Portraits and Memoirs*. Milwaukee: Young Churchman, 1889.

Wesleyan University. "The Charter of Wesleyan University." https://www.wesleyan.edu/acaf/faculty/faculty-handbook/2_university-governance/charter.html.

Wheeler, Rev. Homer. *Historical Sketch of Racine College, Founded at Racine, Wisconsin, AD 1852*. Madison: Atwood and Culver, 1876.

White, Greenough. *An Apostle of the Western Church: Memoire of the Right Rev. Jackson Kemper*. New York: Thomas Whittaker, 1900.

Whittemore, Henry. *History of Middlesex County, Connecticut, with Biographical Sketches of Its Prominent Men*. New York: J. B. Beers & Co., 1884.

———. "Town and City of Middletown." *The History of Middlesex County, 1635–1885*. New York: J. B. Beers, 1884.

www.ingramcontent.com/pod-product-compliance
Lightning Source LLC
Chambersburg PA
CBHW062005220426
43662CB00010B/1231

9798385229086